# Sheffield
# Troublemakers

*Rebels and Radicals in Sheffield History*

# Sheffield and Environs

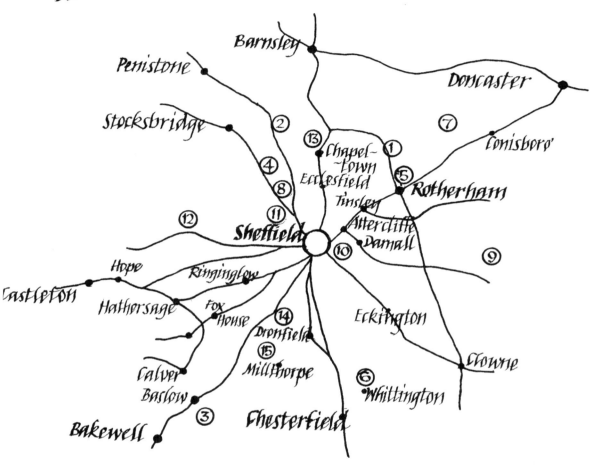

Barnsley

Penistone

Doncaster

Stocksbridge

②

⑦

Conisboro'

⑬
Chapel-
town
Eccesfield
Tinsley

①

⑤ Rotherham

④

⑧

⑫

⑪

Sheffield

Attercliffe
Darnall

⑩

⑨

Hope

Ringinglow

Castleton

Hathersage

Fox
House

Eckington

⑭
Dronfield

⑮
Millthorpe

Crowne

Calver

Baslow

⑥
Whittington

Bakewell

③

Chesterfield

——— Turnpike Roads (1759–1815)
① Wentworth Woodhouse
② Wortley Hall
③ Chatsworth
④ Wharncliffe Lodge
⑤ Masborough
⑥ Revolution House
⑦ Newhill Grange/
     Wath upon Dearne
⑧ Greno Woods
⑨ Dinnington Hall
⑩ Skye Edge
⑪ Hillsborough Barracks
⑫ Hollow Meadows
⑬ Hood Hill
⑭ St. George's Farm
⑮ Carpenter's House

Sheffield and environs in the early 19th century by David Bradley, drawing in part on material published in *Sheffield and its Region*, ed. David L. Linton, 1956.

# Sheffield Troublemakers

*Rebels and Radicals in Sheffield History*

David Price

Phillimore

First Published in 2008 by Phillimore & Co. Ltd

Reprinted 2011, 2012


Phillimore & Co. Ltd
The Mill, Brimscombe Port,
Stroud, Gloucestershire, GL5 2QG
www.thehistorypress.co.uk

ISBN 978 1 86077 660-1



Printed and bound in England.

# Contents

# List of Illustrations

*Frontispiece*: Sheffield and environs in the early 19th century

# Acknowledgements

In writing this book and collecting illustrations, I have received a tremendous amount of help from a wide variety of people – some academic and some drawing on their own memories of personalities and events. I should like to thank them all and apologise to any whose names do not appear below.

Two libraries have been critical in my work – Sheffield Local Studies Library and the Western Bank Library of the University of Sheffield. I should like to thank the staff of both libraries for their unfailing helpfulness. In the former, I must mention especially Mike Spick's help in accessing that magnificent collection, Picture Sheffield. In the university library, I would like to pay tribute to a succession of fine theses and dissertations that have shed light on the events described in this book.

I owe special thanks to David Bradley for his skill in drawing three maps.

Among many individual helpers, I must mention Michael Atkinson, Keith Baker, John Baxter, Derek and Valerie Bayliss, J.P. Bean, Stuart Bennett, Alan Billings, Clyde Binfield, Suzanne Bingham, David Blunkett, Robert Chamberlain, Alice Collins, John Cornwell, Joan Flett, Pam Gould, Michael Jarratt, Howard Knight, Keith Lemm, Julie Macdonald, Peter Machan, David Martin, Helen Mathers, John Roach, Tanya Schmoller, Dorothy Sellars, Father Simon, David Sissons, Noreen and Peter Smith, David Sutton-Jones, Andy Tickle, Joan Unwin, Geoff Usher, Mike West, Peter Whittingham and Jenny Wickham.

I would particularly thank my wife Judith for her support and patience during this exercise and her help in checking numerous drafts.

The author and publisher are most grateful to the following owners, trustees of copyright and holders of collections for their permission to publish these images: National Portrait Gallery, London, for illustrations 1, 13 and 53; the National Gallery of Ireland: 6; University of Sheffield: 38 and 39; Upper Chapel: 8; Cutlers' Company of Hallamshire: 9, 15 and 22; Sheffield Galleries Trust: 42; Eve McQuater: 51; Sheffield Cathedral: 55; Robert Chamberlain and Merlin Theatre: 60 and 61; the Undenominational Chapel, Wincobank: 62; the Women's Library: 63; the People's Museum, Manchester: 66 and 74; The *Sheffield Star*: 76; CPRE Peak and South Yorkshire: 79, 81 and 82; David Sissons: 85; the Bishop of Sheffield: 86; Noreen and Peter Smith: 87; Jenny Wickham: 89, 90 and 91; John Baxter: 93, 95, 96; Derek Bayliss: 94 and the Sheffield Local Studies Library: 10, 12, 16, 17, 19, 20, 21, 23, 25, 26, 28, 29, 32, 33, 34, 35, 37, 40, 41, 43, 45, 46, 47, 49, 54, 57, 58, 59, 64, 65, 67, 68, 70, 71, 72, 73, 75, 77, 80, 92 and 97.

Every effort to trace copyright holders of material has been made, but the author and publishers would be grateful to be informed of any omissions.

# Foreword

To begin with a cliché: this is a timely book. Quite how timely is for its readers to discover. It is about rebels, radicals, troublemakers in general and Sheffielders in particular. Radicalism is a political dimension of economic, social, religious and cultural factors; British history is not to be understood without some awareness of it. It has been found both in the countryside and market towns as well as in the industrial cities. It is usually, but not invariably, a reaction to established ways of doing things. But there are radical establishments, often fostering a distinctive yet decided conservatism, and natural (and avowed) conservatives have been influential radicals. The relationship of radicalism to human and civil rights, to liberalism as well as to libertarianism, has never been straightforward although the debates in which radicals have shared have shaped our attitudes to all those matters.

All this can be seen in Sheffield's history as outlined here from the rise of the French Revolution to the fall of South Yorkshire's Socialist Republic. Sheffield's radicals have been neither isolated nor unique. They can be linked to radicals in Norwich, Newcastle and Edinburgh, Bristol and Bath, Birmingham, Nottingham and Leicester, Leeds, Liverpool, Manchester and Bradford. The radical accent of each city, however, was defined by the local economy, the balance of its class structure, the balance between its Church establishment and religious dissent (and, within dissent, between the old dissent of Unitarians, Congregationalists, Baptists and Quakers and the new dissent of Methodism, in all its shadings: each was changing and each had a different take on authority), and the opportunity for secularism. The last was the most problematic factor of all, but all depended on personalities, how they saw and seized their openings, their organisational abilities. Were they prophets, strategists or opportunists? What links Joseph Gales and James Montgomery, the Shores, the Leaders and the Wilsons, Ebenezer Elliott, Isaac Ironside, and John Arthur Roebuck, Mary Anne Rawson and Ethel Haythornthwaite, Alan Ecclestone and Ted Wickham, Ernest Rowlinson and David Blunkett, beyond an appearance in this book?

And what about its timeliness? Have the factors that determined Sheffield's radicalism for 200 years, from the 1780s to the 1980s, and which were perhaps forming for 200 years before that, now vanished beyond recall – the metal industries, religion (an influential old dissent overtaken by a Methodist preponderance, always accompanied by a resilient Anglicanism) and homogeneity (ethnic immigration was markedly less than in comparable cities; it is surprising how many names in this narrative are peculiar to South Yorkshire or long settled in it). Was the culminating success of Sheffield's radical tradition the point in the 1970s when its municipal leadership became nationally known for its ability and its determination also the point at which all the factors that had consolidated that success ceased to hold the stage – the steel magnates, the town hall and trade union bosses, the Methodists, the Industrial Missionaries, Old Labour and New Labour painfully replacing it? Was that radical outsider Margaret Thatcher too much for these experienced municipal insiders? Yet what survives is what they made, and what might still be made of that remains a task best suited to instinctive radicals, however much they are shaped by quite new circumstances.

David Price captures the idiosyncrasies, complexities and contradictions of this Sheffield. He does not ignore its violent undercurrents. Might a twist of circumstances, a touch of organisational genius on a troublemaker's part, or a loss of nerve on authority's part, have changed national history? Or was it merely an unusually coloured thread, a metallic gleam, in an otherwise close woven, almost seamless, national robe? *Sheffield Troublemakers* presents the evidence.

CLYDE BINFIELD
Professor Emeritus in History,
The University of Sheffield

*To*
*Jo, Philip and Becky*

# Introduction

George III, taking the air on the beach at Weymouth, saw some children playing in charge of a nurse. 'And whose children are these?', asked the King good-naturedly. The nurse curtseyed and replied, 'May it please your Majesty, they are Mr Shore's of Norton, near Sheffield.' 'Ah, Sheffield! Sheffield!' exclaimed his Majesty, as he continued his promenade. 'Damned bad place, Sheffield!'[1]

This incident occurred around 1800. It raises an interesting question. Why did the King suddenly switch from avuncular enquiries about children to passionate denunciation of one of the towns in his realm? The explanation is that in the 1790s the people of Sheffield had built up a reputation for radical, even revolutionary, behaviour.

George III's reactions were not entirely inappropriate. The charming children he had encountered were the grandchildren of Samuel Shore, then aged 62, about the same age as the King, a wealthy unitarian ironmaster, who for the previous 20 years had been

one of Sheffield's leading advocates of parliamentary reform. Shore, while deeply patriotic, sympathised with the radical working class movement of the town and in 1819 at the age of 81 he would chair one of the biggest demonstrations ever held in Sheffield to protest about the massacre of Peterloo in Manchester. His great niece was Florence Nightingale. Therefore, the children on the beach did in a sense represent the 'radical Sheffield' that this book is about.

In 1926, the 80-year-old local historian Canon William Odom, stalwart defender of Protestantism, produced a book called 'Hallamshire Worthies',[2] containing 200 biographical sketches of men and women 'whose names lend honour to the city of their birth or adoption'. Despite some overlap between Odom's list and mine, this book is about 'Hallamshire Not So Worthies' – men and women who were prepared to be troublesome and unpopular and to challenge the establishment of their day.

This radical tradition has been influential in recent times. In 1976, South Yorkshire County Council – the short-lived institution most identified with the 'Socialist Republic' – produced a most unusual local authority publication – *Essays in the Economic and Social History of South Yorkshire*, recounting radical episodes in

1  King George III. He called Sheffield 'a damned bad place' because it was a centre of radical agitation.

South Yorkshire's past. One of the editors was Sidney Pollard, Professor of Economic History at the University of Sheffield. Pollard, who had escaped from Vienna in 1938 on the *Kindertransporte* and had a feeling of 'not belonging anywhere', felt a deep sympathy with the struggles of Sheffield artisans.[3] He wrote in the introduction:

> South Yorkshire … stands out in one respect, again and again taking the national lead and setting the tone for national movements. This was its independence of spirit, its rebelliousness … There is a consistency in the defence of the weak against the strong, the poor against the rich, the under-privileged against those who have usurped power, pelf and privilege, and these represent some of the finest expressions of the human spirit. But there is a consistency here also of opposition to central authority as against the region.[4]

The radical tradition has not been ignored in the city's recent regeneration. The cascades in Sheffield's remodelled Peace Gardens are dedicated to Samuel Holberry, seen as a left-wing martyr, who died of consumption in 1842 after two years' imprisonment. Up to 50,000 people are said to have lined the route of his funeral procession to the General Cemetery. Today, he would probably be labelled a 'terrorist', for he planned to seize the town hall and the *Tontine Inn* in a military insurrection. Readers of this book may reflect that there are many other impressive radicals whom civic leaders could celebrate in the city centre.

I have drawn my title – 'Sheffield Troublemakers' – from A.J.P. Taylor's fascinating Ford Lectures of 1956, entitled 'The Trouble Makers'. Taylor's lectures were about 'dissenters' in foreign policy, whom he described as 'the Englishmen I most revere'. He defined a 'dissenter' as follows:

2  The cascades in the Peace Gardens, Sheffield, dedicated to the memory of Samuel Holberry, the Chartist revolutionary.

> A conforming member of the Church of England can disagree with the Bishops and, I understand, often does. A Dissenter believes that Bishops should not exist ... Dissent is a quality peculiar to the English-speaking peoples. A man can disagree with a particular line of British foreign policy, while accepting its general assumptions. The Dissenter repudiates its aims, its methods, its principles.[5]

Many, but not all, of the troublemakers described in this book met Taylor's criteria. Middle-class 'rational dissent' is one of the great streams of Sheffield radicalism. But there is another no less important stream – the radicalism of the cutlery artisans.

Having embarked on this study, I have found the subject so vast that I cannot hope to be comprehensive. Many worthy radicals have been omitted. Sheffield is fortunate to have fascinating accounts of its trade union history by Sidney Pollard[6] and its religious history by Ted Wickham.[7] I have drawn on these works but avoided duplicating them.

**3** Tablet dedicating cascades to Holberry.

The purpose of this book is to trace Sheffield's radical tradition by looking at the lives and opinions of some local radicals over the last 200 years. It looks at radicalism both in politics and religion and the interaction between the two. I have tried to place these radicals in their historical context and to describe the part they played in the history of Sheffield.

# SHEFFIELD 1789-1801

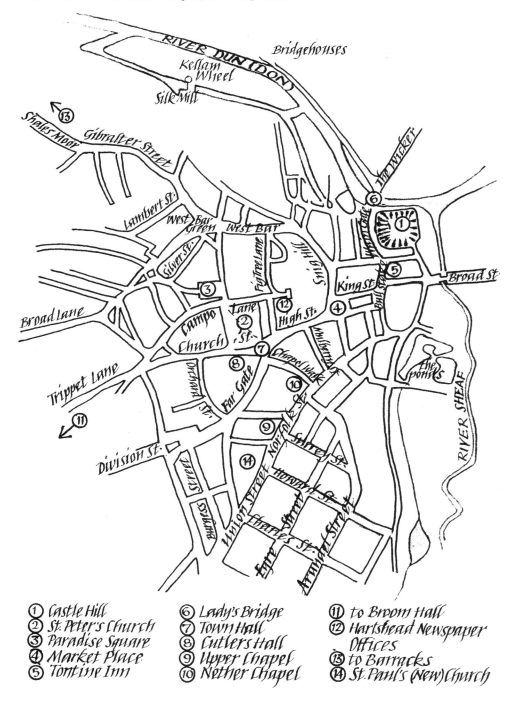

RIVER DUN (DON)

Bridgehouses

Kellam Wheel

Silk Mill

Shales Moor

⑬

Gibralter Street

The Wicket

⑥

⑤

① Castle Hill

Lambert St.

West Bar Green

West Bar

Pig Tree Lane

Snig Hill

Water Lane

King St.

Broad St.

Bull St.

Silver St.

③

Campo Lane

Church St.

⑫

High St.

④

Broad Lane

② St. Peter's

⑦

Chapel Walk

Mulberry St.

The Ponds

RIVER SHEAF

Trippet Lane

Orchard St.

⑧

Far Gate

⑩

⑨

Norfolk St.

Surrey St.

⑪

Division St.

Burgess Street

Union Street

⑭

Howard St.

Charles St.

Eyre St.

Arundel Street

① Castle Hill
② St. Peter's Church
③ Paradise Square
④ Market Place
⑤ Tontine Inn
⑥ Lady's Bridge
⑦ Town Hall
⑧ Cutlers Hall
⑨ Upper Chapel
⑩ Nether Chapel
⑪ to Broom Hall
⑫ Hartshead Newspaper Offices
⑬ to Barracks
⑭ St. Paul's (New) Church

4    Map of Sheffield 1789–1801. This draws on maps of 1771 and 1797 by William Fairbank.

*Chapter 1*

# Sheffield at the Time
# of the French Revolution

If any place was to be a Faubourg St Antoine to an English Revolution, it was surely Sheffield.
Professor Gwyn Williams[1]

This chapter considers what Sheffield was like in 1789 when the French Revolution burst upon the world. What factors made Sheffield such a centre of political agitation that one historian called it the 'storm centre' of the North[2] and another compared it with the most celebrated *sans culotte* neighbourhood of revolutionary Paris?

*What Sheffield was like in 1789*

Sheffield had grown up around the castle (destroyed by order of Parliament after the Civil War) and St Peter's Church on the hill above. At this time, the town extended to the Wicker in the north-east, to Gibraltar Street in the north, to Division Street in the west, to just beyond Burgess Street in the south and to the River Sheaf (near where the station now is) in the east. It still felt like a small town.

In 1801, the town had 31,000 inhabitants and the Parish of Sheffield as a whole had 46,000.[3] Most of the notable citizens lived in the town itself, along with shopkeepers, artisans and the poorer citizens who lived in increasingly crowded and squalid conditions, as the population expanded.

Sheffield was the centre of Hallamshire, a district of 72,000 acres, roughly coterminous with the then Parishes of Sheffield and Ecclesfield and the Chapelry of Bradfield and the territory of the present city council.[4] It was a highly distinctive area because of the predominance of the cutlery trade and related iron and steel trades. Much of the grinding took place in the steep river valleys around Sheffield. There were villages around Sheffield that specialised in particular products, such as scythes or scissors.

The cutlery trades in Hallamshire were controlled by the Cutlers' Company, set up in 1624. Although artisans had to be freemen of the company in order to work independently in these trades, the company's officers were not selected by the freemen but were in effect a self-perpetuating oligarchy. This had become a major source of grievance.

Sheffield was in some ways improving. An elegant new area, Paradise Square, had been created, new water supplies had been introduced, the markets had been greatly improved and Assembly Rooms had been created where the small smart set could dance the minuet and enjoy subscription concerts. A theatre was attached to the Assembly Rooms. Moreover,

1

significantly for our story, newspapers had been founded. But the town remained dirty, undistinguished and poorly built with narrow streets and little architecture of merit.

Sheffield had always been handicapped by poor communications but by 1789 its links with the outside world had improved. A canal and river route had been opened up from Tinsley (three miles east of Sheffield) all the way to Hull and the North Sea. This offered trade routes by sea to London, Europe and the United States. Moreover, turnpike roads had been created. There were five great coach roads[5] and three subordinate ones – many starting from the famous *Tontine Inn*. In 1787, it took just 26 hours to go by coach to London – starting at 5 a.m. from Sheffield one morning and reaching London at 7 a.m. the next morning.[6]

**5** *Tontine Inn*, near the old castle site. From here, several coaches a day set off in all directions. Picture by T.P. Willcox, *c*.1830.

Sheffield was not just the foremost centre of cutlery production in Britain. Its traditional industries were developing and diversifying, making it a boom town. In 1742, Thomas Bolsover had invented silver plate, which Joseph Hancock and others developed into a substantial new industry. This stimulated increased production not only of silver plate but also of solid silver goods. In 1773, Sheffield was granted permission to open an Assay Office. In the 1740s, Benjamin Huntsman, a clockmaker from Doncaster, moved to Sheffield and invented the crucible method of making steel – an ideal steel for cutlery and edge-tool making. After some hesitation, the conservative Hallamshire cutlers accepted the steel produced by the new method and it developed on a large scale. Around 1769, Britannia Metal was invented by James Vickers. In 1774, a 'railway' or tramway with wooden rails had been introduced by the Duke of Norfolk's manager to convey coal to the town, provoking serious riots since local people wrongly believed that the intention was to charge higher prices.[7]

In the 1790s Sheffield became known nationally as a centre of radical and revolutionary politics. Revolutionary ideas spread rapidly in Sheffield because of its happy-go-lucky administration, its radical nonconformists and its militant artisans.

### 'Happy-go-lucky' Administration

One of Sheffield's historians, R.E. Leader, wrote that in this period: 'The affairs of the town continued to be administered in an informal happy-go-lucky fashion.'[8] The town was freer – or more anarchic – than many others because it was not tightly controlled by an aristocrat or town corporation. It was surrounded by estates belonging to leading aristocrats, the Earl Fitzwilliam at Wentworth Woodhouse, the Duke of Devonshire at Chatsworth and the Duke of Norfolk, who, as hereditary Lord of the Manor of Sheffield, owned the park and much else besides. There were also the Wortley Montague estates in the North, soon to be inherited by the Stuart-Wortleys of Wortley Hall (see frontispiece). As these families owned land in and around the town, Sheffield's expansion enhanced their wealth. But none of them, not even the Duke of Norfolk, controlled town affairs. The Duke of Norfolk's family seat was far away at Arundel Castle, but he had an agent, Vincent Eyre, and a house in Sheffield – the Lord's House on the corner of Fargate and Norfolk Row. In this period, Eyre helped Sheffield to develop by releasing Alsop's Fields (beyond Norfolk Street) for sale to entrepreneurs and by reforming the markets.[9]

6   William Wentworth, 2nd Earl Fitzwilliam (1748–1833), later Lord-Lieutenant of Ireland. He kept a close eye on Sheffield and was disturbed by its radicalism. In 1794, he issued a warning to Gales.

*Portrait by Joseph Grozer after an oil of 1786 by Joshua Reynolds © National Gallery of Ireland.*

Of these aristocrats, the Earl Fitzwilliam kept the closest eye on Sheffield. His magnificent home, Wentworth Woodhouse, was a few miles to the north. It presented a striking contrast to the humble dwellings of most Sheffield citizens, having an east front of 600 feet, the longest of any English country house. Fitzwilliam was a Whig grandee, nephew and heir to the former Prime Minister Lord Rockingham. In September 1789, Fitzwilliam was host to the Prince of Wales at Wentworth Woodhouse, with 40,000 people assembled and entertained outside.

Sheffield lacked a town corporation. Instead, there were three historic bodies each with a stake in town governance – the Church Burgesses, the Cutlers' Company and the Town Trustees. The burgesses supported the parish church and educational ventures. The Cutlers' Company regulated local industry. This left the Town Trustees to look after other aspects of town affairs, such as roads and bridges, and to their credit they had helped to secure the water route to Hull. But they were not a town corporation and their powers and resources were limited.

Day-to-day law and order was in the hands of the Justices of the Peace, one of whom was the Rev. James Wilkinson, Vicar of Sheffield (see below). In 1792, the War Office sent Colonel de Lancey to inspect the instruments of law and order in Sheffield. He commented: 'the magistracy of the place scarcely deserved the name' and 'in the town itself there is no civil power'. He was particularly critical of the fact that, apart from Wilkinson, the magistrates lived miles away.[10]

Under the Justices were a few old constables and decrepit nightwatchmen who were far more afraid of evil-doers than evil-doers were of them. There were a few cells for miscreants in the town hall, which was then at the church gates, and a debtors' prison in King Street. More serious cases were referred to the Assizes. But law and order also ultimately depended on the Lord Lieutenant of the West Riding of Yorkshire, the Duke of Norfolk, who was an absentee and was succeeded by the Earl Fitzwilliam in 1798. All in all, Sheffield was not organised to repress large-scale civil disturbances.

### Radical Nonconformists

A second reason why Sheffield was fertile ground for revolutionary politics was its religious diversity and the strong influence of dissenters.

Sheffield had supported Parliament in the Civil War. At the Restoration, its puritan vicar, James Fisher, was ejected and suffered imprisonment. His followers ceased to worship at the parish church and instead formed a substantial body of presbyterians and independents. In 1700, they built Upper Chapel and by 1715 its congregation comprised one-sixth of the local population.[11] By the 1780s, nonconformity had diversified. As well as Upper Chapel, now increasingly unitarian, there was Nether Chapel, also in Norfolk Street, and five other independent chapels elsewhere. There were many Methodists and there was a Quaker meeting house in Angel Street.

The dissenters included many highly educated and prominent citizens but the Test and Corporation Acts denied them access to public office and votes in elections, though they could hold office in the Town Trust and the Cutlers' Company. Dissenters resented the restrictions placed upon them and leaned towards radical politics.

Nonconformist ministers were influential voices for radicalism – none more so than Rev. Joseph Evans (1728-1803), who was Minister at Upper Chapel from 1758-97. In Upper Chapel there is still a painting of Evans holding a book, which is not the Bible, but is inscribed 'LOCKE'. In other words, Evans drew inspiration from the great radical philosopher who had justified the Glorious Revolution of 1688. Evans also respected advanced unitarian thinkers like Joseph Priestley and Theophilus Lindsey and edged his congregation towards unitarian theology. Evans and his wife adopted Joseph

7   Upper Chapel today. In the 1790s it was increasingly unitarian and had an influential and radical middle-class congregation.

Hunter, a boy whose mother had died and who grew up to become Sheffield's most famous antiquarian and historian. Hunter left us a fascinating account of his adoptive father's politics:

> his opinions were extreme on the side of 'Freedom'. He had been a zealous friend of the Americans … He was a hearty well-wisher to the French in their Revolution. He gloried in the destruction of the Bastille and he certainly did not turn with much abhorrence from the acts of cruelty perpetrated on the French (royal) family and court. Even the atrocities of the Robespierre period scarcely changed his feeling. In the war he most heartily wished them success. Corresponding with this, he had the most cordial hatred of the Ministry of Mr Pitt. This dislike was extended to the Crown and he would gladly have seen a Revolution at home. Nothing was too violent, no expression of sedition however seditious which he would not repeat. In these political sentiments he was by no means peculiar. He was but one of a large class including nearly all the Rational Dissenting Ministry and a great part of the Dissenting laity. This was from 1792 to 1803.[12]

8   The Rev. Joseph Evans, Minister at Upper Chapel, 1758-97. He was 'extreme on the side of freedom' and the book he is holding is inscribed 'LOCKE'. Painting by Nathaniel Tucker *c*.1777.

'Rational dissent' was a powerful force in the influential middle class of Sheffield and was about politics as well as religion. An outstanding lay rational dissenter was Samuel Shore (1738-1828). He was a unitarian and a leading member (and trustee) in Evans' congregation. He belonged to an important family of Sheffield ironmasters and bankers and owned substantial estates. He was a member of the Town Trust and, despite his nonconformity, High Sheriff of the County of Derby in 1761. He gave financial help to pioneering unitarians like Theophilus Lindsey and Joseph Priestley.[13] In the early 1780s, he was a prominent member of the Rev. Christopher Wyvill's Yorkshire Association, campaigning for moderate Parliamentary reform. In 1782, he and the Rev. James Wilkinson (see below) obtained 471 signatures for a reform petition from freeholders in and around Sheffield.[14]

Shore was much more radical than Wyvill or Wilkinson. In 1788, he became a vice-president of the London-based Society for Constitutional Information.[15] He probably met Tom Paine in that Society. He may also have met him when Paine was working in Rotherham on an iron bridge with Shore's relations, the Walkers of Masborough. After his second marriage in 1788, Shore retired to his family seat at Meersbrook but he stuck to his radicalism and in 1819, when he was 81, he chaired Sheffield's demonstration against the Peterloo massacre. Though he lived 90 years, it was not quite long enough for him to see Parliamentary reform come to fruition.

The Anglican Vicar was the Rev. James Wilkinson (1731-1805) whose ministry in Sheffield lasted for more than 50 years – from 1754 to 1805 – even longer than Evans at Upper Chapel. He was a Whig and, by most accounts, had a real sympathy with local people. An active member of the Yorkshire Association, he campaigned with the unitarian Samuel Shore for parliamentary reform. But, as he was also the leading representative of law and order in the town, his support for reform quickly ended in 1791 when it became identified with rioting and civil disorder.

**9** The Rev. James Wilkinson, Vicar of Sheffield from 1754–1805 – 'King and priest of the place'.

In many ways, he was the leading figure in the town. He was rich, having inherited Broom Hall and other estates from the Jessop family on his mother's side. He was magistrate as well as vicar – 'king and priest of the place'.

Earlier historians – Hunter and Gatty – sing his praises. He was 'Father of the town of Sheffield and its neighbourhood,'[16] with a 'commanding personal presence, dignified manner, unspotted character and with a benevolent disposition proportionate to his fine income'.[17] He was a boxer who, when challenged by visitors to display his prowess, did so in no uncertain terms. Later in his life he was known in the town as 'Old Niddlety Nod' because of a peculiar shaking of the head caused by a slight paralysis. As a magistrate, he was not universally popular. Joseph Mather, the alehouse poet, called him 'the old serpent' and 'that black diabolical fiend'.[18] Bishop David Lunn said that the clue to understanding Wilkinson is that he was 'an 18th century gentleman with the toughness that goes with that'. He had 'bottom' – a nautical metaphor.[19] In the coming time of troubles, he was at the centre of the storm.

During his long spell in Sheffield, Wilkinson neglected the parish church for it became 'ruinous and in decay in the walls, arches, pews, roofs'.[20] The nave was entirely replaced in 1805 – the year of his death. The Church of England, with only three churches in the town, was falling behind the dissenters. Its pew rents made it unwelcoming to the poorer members of the community, most of whom attended no church at all. 'The Church of England has not lost the manufacturing districts, because she never included them within her pale.'[21]

By contrast, Methodism had a growing presence in Sheffield and included some of the poorer people. John Wesley came to Sheffield on at least 32 occasions between 1742 and 1788 and attracted huge crowds. The early Methodists' meeting houses were destroyed by angry mobs. Charles Wesley experienced an anti-Methodist riot in the town and said that 'it exceeded in outrage all I have seen before'.[22] After 1760, rioting against Methodism ceased and instead Methodists became a recognised and significant element in the town. On 15 July 1779, Wesley preached in Paradise Square 'to the largest congregation I ever saw on a weekday'.[23] Wesley's use of Paradise Square may have inspired its later use for political meetings. Not all Methodists followed John Wesley's insistence on political quietism. Radical Methodists were emerging who would join in agitation against the authorities (chapter 2).

Finally, there were a few hundred Roman Catholics in the town. The Lord of the Manor was the Duke of Norfolk, who came from the most eminent Roman Catholic family in England, though the current Duke had himself become Anglican at the time of the Gordon Riots in 1780. A Catholic priest had a small room in the Lord's House, used as a chapel.[24]

**10**   The parish church looking towards St James Row, 1793. At this time, the church was in a 'ruinous' state. The old Cutlers' Hall is just visible on the extreme left. The old town hall was on the corner of the churchyard.

Within this remarkable religious diversity, the most potent elements were the dissenters' demands for political emancipation and their openness to radical political ideas.

### Militant Artisans

The third factor making Sheffield receptive to revolutionary politics was its industrial structure and the growing tensions between the artisans and the master manufacturers in the Cutlers' Company. Sheffield's artisans were mostly semi-independent and many, particularly the little mesters, were literate and numerate.[25] A little mester might have 10 or 12 journeymen and some apprentices working together in a workshop.[26] These businesses were vulnerable to adverse trading conditions and to sharp practice by the factors who bought their goods for sale elsewhere and by the master manufacturers who increasingly dominated their trades. But they could control their working hours and many of their working practices. They were highly independent in spirit – important in turbulent times. The grinders in particular were notorious for recklessness and pugnacity attributed to the hazards of their occupation and their isolation in river valleys.

The military inspector, Col de Lancey, described the situation like this:

> the manufactures of this town are of a nature to require so little capital to carry them on that a man with a very small sum of money can employ two, three or four men; and this being generally the case there are not in this, as in other great towns, any number of persons of sufficient weight who could by their influence, or the number of their dependents, act with

any effect in the case of a disturbance. As the wages given to the journeymen are very high, it is pretty generally the practice for them to work for three days, in which they can earn sufficient to enable them to drink and riot for the rest of the week, consequently there can be no place more fit for seditious purposes.[27]

De Lancey was contrasting Sheffield with other industrial towns where large factories operated under tight discipline imposed by dominant entrepreneurs. In Sheffield, there were a few fairly large factories – a silk mill near Kelham Island (converted to a cotton mill) and the new silver plate works developing near Norfolk Street. There was also Walker's ironworks in Masbrough in nearby Rotherham. But most industry was in small workshops.

Even in the silver plate works, the journeymen platers were not a disciplined group. They had been imported into Sheffield from Birmingham, London, York and Newcastle, probably bringing with them radical ideas. They were described as 'the most unsteady, depraved and idle of all the other workmen ... in many respects a pest to the town'.[28]

**11**   Picture of a cutler from George Walker's *Costumes of Yorkshire*, 1814. In the 1780s and 1790s there were acute tensions between the ordinary cutlers and the Cutlers' Company about the company's failure to enforce its own rules.

But the most important factor radicalising the Sheffield artisans was the crisis in the relations between the Cutlers' Company and its freemen.[29] As trade had grown and developed, the company had not enforced strictly its own rules about such things as apprenticeships and the employment of people from outside Hallamshire (known as 'foreigners'). In 1784, a group of freemen protested that this made them vulnerable and insecure. They rediscovered the Act of Incorporation of the Company of 1624 and, with remarkable boldness, appealed to the Court of King's Bench. They also petitioned Parliament, calling for the right of freemen to elect the officers of the company. They impudently held their own election, choosing Enoch Trickett, a sympathetic master manufacturer, as their own 'Master Cutler'. The company, with the support of 'principal inhabitants', argued that democratic elections would 'produce disorder and confusion.' William Wilberforce, as a Yorkshire MP, attempted to resolve the dispute by arbitration.

Eventually, in 1790–1, a new committee of master manufacturers mediated between the company and the freemen. All parties agreed on new legislation, which was enacted in June 1791. This broadened the electorate for the company's officers to include master manufacturers, but ordinary freemen remained excluded. The new Act 'merely prolonged the slow and inevitable decline of the Cutlers' Company as a regulatory body' and left many freemen trapped in a cycle of debt and dependency.[30] In 1814, Parliament would strip the company of its regulatory powers altogether.

This conflict dominated Sheffield's industrial and political life for several years. The freemen fought a losing battle but in the process they learned a great deal about political agitation, which would be fed into the wider political struggles of the 1790s.

We can get some idea of the character of the Sheffield artisans at this time from the poems of Joseph Mather,[31] a file cutter and alehouse poet. He was court jester to the cutlers. His popular ballads provide an acerbic commentary on Sheffield life, politics and power in this period. Here is the chorus of his famous song 'Watkinson and his thirteens' – an attack on a Master Cutler who required workers to produce 13 for a dozen:

> And may the odd knife his great carcase dissect
> Lay open his vitals for men to inspect
> A heart full as black as the infernal gulph,
> In that greedy blood-sucking bone-scraping wolf.

In the 1790s, Mather supported the Jacobin cause and attacked with biting wit those on the other side, such as the local magistrates, the Master Cutler and the Mayor of Doncaster. Mather's lack of deference, sharp observation, sense of humour and general cussedness reflect characteristics of Sheffield artisans in those days.

Traditionally in Sheffield, masters and artisans came from the same background and there was 'an absence of social cleavage compared with the factory system'.[32] This was changing. As master manufacturers built up their businesses, they began to distance themselves from the artisans. But masters resented the domination of Parliament by rich landowning aristocrats and by MPs unrepresentative of Sheffield and of dissenters. For electoral purposes, Sheffield was part of the County of Yorkshire and those freeholders who had the vote had to go to York to exercise it. The centenary of the Glorious Revolution of 1688 was an opportunity to call for reform. It was marked by a procession, a banquet and a ball and by pilgrimages to Revolution House in Whittington, near Chesterfield.[33] Superficially at least, the middle classes and the artisans had a common interest in reform and would be receptive to new libertarian ideas coming from Paris or from Thomas Paine.

To sum up, Sheffield at this time was experiencing rapid growth unaccompanied by efficient or representative administration. Its middle classes were dissenting and reformist and its artisans independent-minded and radicalised. There were grave weaknesses in the instruments of law and order. There was plenty of combustible material and the events of the French Revolution would ignite it.

## Chapter 2

# The Newspaper Editors
# and the French Revolution

To many, even professed ministers of the Gospel, it (Tom Paine's *Rights of Man*) appeared to become dearer than their Bible, and their visits to their flocks were made with the *Rights of Man* in their pockets, to induce them to read it.

Samuel Roberts, Sheffield silversmith and social reformer [1]

At Sheffield … I found that the seditious machinations of Paine and the factious people who are endeavouring to disturb the peace of the country had extended to a degree very much beyond my conception; and indeed they seem with great judgement to have chosen this as the centre of all their seditious machinations.[2]

Colonel de Lancey, Deputy Adjutant to the Secretary of State for War, 13 June 1792

The French Revolution had an extraordinary impact in Sheffield. It fostered a huge wave of optimism, turning to agitation and conflict and eventually to revolutionary activity and harsh repression. Sheffield caused intense anxiety to the authorities, as Colonel de Lancey's comments above indicate.

This can be seen in the story of two newspaper editors, Joseph Gales of the *Sheffield Register* and James Montgomery of the successor newspaper, the *Sheffield Iris*. They became communicators of radical ideas and victims of the reaction against these.

## Joseph Gales and James Montgomery

Both editors were men of outstanding ability. Joseph Gales (1761–1841) was the son of the schoolmaster and parish clerk of Eckington, a few miles South of Sheffield. His early experiences as an apprentice in a printing establishment in Manchester had a Dickensian flavour. His master's wife, 'a notorious vixen', persuaded her husband to whip the young Joseph. She even attacked him with a knife. With the help of an uncle, he got his indenture cancelled and walked home across the Pennines with half a crown in his pocket. His second apprenticeship in Newark-on-Trent was more successful. In a circulating library there, he met his future wife, Winifred Marshall, daughter of a Newark innkeeper who was a cousin of Lord Melbourne. Winifred was a woman of considerable learning who contributed political analysis to her husband's newspaper and wrote a novel. At the time of their marriage, they moved to Sheffield where Gales set up his own printing and publishing establishment in the Hartshead. In 1787, when he was only 26, he founded the weekly *Sheffield Register*.[3]

**12** Newspaper office and the Gales's home at Hartshead. Montgomery continued to live here with Gales's sisters and edit the *Iris* from here long after Gales had fled.

The *Sheffield Register* claimed to serve Yorkshire, Derbyshire and Nottinghamshire. Copies went to manufacturing shops (where workmen clubbed together to pay subscriptions) as well as to respectable homes.[4] It included advertisements for quack remedies and runaway apprentices, announcements of auctions (Gales became a successful auctioneer and estate agent), reports on crime and court cases, together with balls and concerts at the Assembly Rooms and so on. But it also included the latest national and international news, serious commentary and an editorial section on Sheffield, which covered economic and political developments as well as social gossip. Gales promoted good causes like the abolition of the slave trade and subscriptions for poor relief. Gales aimed at 'an impartial and truly independent newspaper' to cater for a wide audience. The *Register*'s political comment was often indirect rather than propagandist. But, as the political battle intensified, the paper became more explicitly partisan.

What influences made Gales a radical? His master in Newark seems to have been a radical. Then there was Gales's unitarianism. Though brought up as an Anglican, he was persuaded by reading a unitarian sermon to become Unitarian. He and Winifred later joined the congregation of Upper Chapel, where they had five children baptised. At Upper Chapel, they would have encountered the radical views of the Minister, Joseph Evans (chapter 1) and of prominent laymen like Samuel Shore, who were closely in touch with distinguished radicals elsewhere. In her recollections, Winifred describes a circle of reformist business people as their 'particular friends', including the Shores, the Paynes of Newhill (Quakers who would help the Gales through their worst crisis), the Moults of Wickersley and the Walkers of Masbrough in Rotherham.[5] The Walkers probably introduced Gales to Thomas

Paine when he came to Rotherham to build an iron bridge at the Walker ironworks in 1789 and 1790.[6]

From 1792, Gales had as his assistant the precocious young writer and poet, James Montgomery (1771-1854). Gales had advertised for a clerk. James Montgomery, a 'mild-mannered youth of twenty',[7] applied for the job. His parents were Moravian missionaries who died out in the West Indies at around this time. Montgomery had literary and poetic aspirations and was frustrated with grocery work in Wath. He got the job and moved into Gales' home in Hartshead. Mrs Gales later called him 'a faithful assistant, a sensible adviser, a devoted friend and a delightful companion'.[8] The Gales household made a huge impression on the young Montgomery. He quickly adopted their radical politics and, sharing Gales's sense of humour, wrote lampoons on self-important dignitaries like the Mayor of Doncaster.

## The Early Impact of the French Revolution

In the early period of the French Revolution, there was no serious cleavage of opinion in Sheffield about developments in Paris. After all, industrial leaders, Vicar Wilkinson and the Whig aristocrats all advocated parliamentary reform. There was satisfaction that the French seemed to be following a British path. This consensus was fragile and would later fall apart, but initially Gales's pro-French stance in the Register was probably uncontroversial. Thus, shortly after the fall of the Bastille, the Register declared: 'To do the French justice on this occasion, they have struggled most nobly for liberty and their actions have been dictated by moderation and firmness … We cannot but admire the regularity with which things were conducted and the small number of lives lost.'[9]

A few months later, Gales linked developments in France with the need for reform in Britain:

> French hearts are warmed with the sacred flame of liberty … so that their new statute book is in no danger of being disgraced with Test Acts and penal laws for religious opinions … We have long imitated the French in dress and dissipation; surely we shall not neglect to imitate them in what is laudable and manly. Many defects remain in our own constitution; to enquire into them and remove them is now absolutely necessary.[10]

But already opinion in Britain was beginning to polarise. A battle of the books began. Dr Richard Price, a leading Unitarian divine and economist with similar views to Gales, delivered a sermon welcoming the advent of democracy in France. This provoked Edmund Burke's *Reflections on the Revolution in France*, which referred dismissively to the 'swinish multitude' (a phrase later much resented by Sheffield artisans) and took a deeply pessimistic view of events in France. This in turn provoked Paine to produce *The Rights of Man* in 1791-2. Paine's book was a runaway publishing success, apparently selling 200,000 copies by 1793.[11] Gales promoted Paine's work in his columns, describing *The Rights of Man* as 'one of the most curious, original and interesting publications which the singular vicissitudes of modern politics have produced'.[12]

13   Thomas Paine, famous radical writer, was at Samuel Walker's ironworks in Masbrough, Rotherham, in 1789 and 1790, designing an iron bridge. Probably Samuel Shore and Gales met him at this time. Gales promoted his *Rights of Man* in the North.

There was a violent reaction to the new radicalism in Birmingham where, unlike Sheffield, the 'Church and King' party was influential. In July 1791, a major riot occurred in protest against a radical dinner to celebrate Bastille Day. The home of Dr Joseph Priestley, outstanding scientist and radical hero, was attacked. The riot raged for two days until the dragoons arrived from Nottingham.

## The Enclosure Crisis

Later in July 1791, a major crisis suddenly broke out in Sheffield over the enclosure of 6,000 acres of common land in Upper Hallam, Nether Hallam, Fulwood, Morewood, Stannington, Storrs and part of Dungworth. There had been previous enclosures in Ecclesall (incidentally eliminating horse races on Crooks Moor) and Brightside. But this enclosure was far larger, including the Rivelin Valley and the Hallam moors, and the village greens of Brookhouse, Newfield, Owlerton and Rivelin.

Parliament were informed that 98.3 per cent of the landowners in the area to be enclosed had given their consent – but they alone stood to gain. No one opposed the Act, which went smoothly through Parliament. The Sheffield public became aware of it when Gales put a notice in the Register and the vicar put a notice on the church door to say that commissioners would be meeting to implement the enclosure. This caused such a reaction among the populace that on 23 July the three 'Inclosure Commissioners' – Vicar Wilkinson, Vincent Eyre and Joseph Ward, the Master Cutler – wrote to the Home Office in great distress. They feared that Birmingham rioters had 'worked on Sheffield passions'. They continued:

> Considerable bodies of disorderly people in this neighbourhood have lately assembled in considerable force with the rioters having the intention of preventing the Commissioners … from doing their duty and not only drove them from the commons near this town intended to be enclosed but also menaced them with the greatest personal danger.[13]

They asked for military aid to suppress the rioting of 'many profligate people'. On 28 July, the mob broke into the debtors' prison and released the prisoners. There then were calls 'To Broom Hall' – the grand house where the vicar lived. They were burning his library and setting fire to his ricks when the Light Dragoons arrived from Nottingham and dispersed them, though some went off to attack Vincent Eyre's house. The arrival of the troops was evidently seen as a momentous event by the populace, as a 'vast concourse of people' greeted the troops.

The enclosure went ahead unchanged, though somewhat later than intended. The Duke of Norfolk received over 1,300 acres. Eighty-one acres went to Vicar Wilkinson and Philip Gell as tithe holders. The remainder was divided between property owners and freeholders in the area, apart from just two acres for the landless poor, who lost their historic rights to pasture for geese and animals, access to footpaths and wild fruit and much else besides.[14]

Many more enclosure acts would be passed in the next 40 years, mostly without protest. Not until the early 20th century would the public fully appreciate the implications of this redistribution of wealth to the rich at the expense of the poor (chapter 11).

This enclosure and the riot it provoked polarised opinion in Sheffield. The authorities were shocked at the sudden breakdown of law and order. Five of the supposed instigators, all under 19, were hauled off to trial in York, where one of them, a half-witted youth called Bennett, was hanged. Vicar Wilkinson, shaken by his experience, kept clear of the 'more profligate' elements in the town for the next year and lost his enthusiasm for parliamentary reform. An anecdote indicates his new mood. A little girl was incited by a mischief-maker to recite to him Mather's lines:

**14**    Broom Hall, home of Vicar Wilkinson. In 1792, the house
was attacked by the mob protesting about the enclosure of
common land.

*They burnt his books,*
*And scared his rooks,*
*And set his stacks on fire.*

He said: 'Yes, my dear, come along with
me' and led the girl to the stocks.[15] Later
in the 1790s, he accepted the leadership
of a loyalist association in Sheffield to
counter seditious ideas.[16]

Gales in the Register trod a cautious
line. He could not condone mob
violence. As an estate agent, he avoided
comment on the enclosure, though his
later denunciation of the game laws as
'feudal tyranny' indicates his lack of
sympathy with the landowners. He
praised the magistrates for their 'spirited
vigilance' and said that the execution of
Bennett should lead 'unthinking youths
and wicked men to conclude that the
vengeance of the law is sure to overtake
the crime'. Gales would become much
bolder in the coming months.

### The Sheffield Society for Constitutional Information (SSCI)

What happened next was surprising and
significant. The Sheffield artisans began
to assert themselves on broad political issues. In the dispute between the freemen and the
Cutlers' Company, they had built up experience of petitioning parliament and perceived
the weakness of their position (chapter 1). The enclosure had illustrated how the propertied
classes used Parliament to their own advantage. The artisans, most of whom were literate,
read Paine's Rights of Man.

In the autumn of 1791, a group of 'five or six mechanics' founded the Sheffield Society
for Constitutional Information (SSCI). The SSCI was artisan dominated, though it had
some middle-class supporters. Gales was probably not a member at this stage, though he
joined later. He had a business to run. But it is likely that he wrote material both for the
freemen in their dispute with the Cutlers' Company and for the SSCI.[17] The artisans took
the title of their society from the London-based Society of Constitutional Information, of
which Samuel Shore had become a vice-president in 1788.

The SSCI's Address of 19 December 1791 was printed not by Gales but by John Crome,
another Sheffield printer and publisher, who took great risks for the radical cause. In
January 1792 Crome also acted as printer when Paine gave permission for SSCI to publish
15,000 copies of a pamphlet edition of volume one of *The Rights of Man* at a price of 3d. a
copy.[18] The speed with which SSCI got into its stride owed much to the previous agitation
against the Cutlers' Company.

E.P. Thompson's famous book *The Making of the English Working Class* argued that 'the
outstanding fact of the period 1790 to 1830 is the formation of "the working class", as seen

both in "the growth of class consciousness" and "the growth of corresponding forms of political and industrial organisation".'[19] SSCI exemplified Thompson's thesis. Indeed, SSCI has been described as 'the first working class reform association of any consequence'.[20] Early on, SSCI sought co-operation with the Whig 'Friends of the People' in London but got nowhere and avoided any further contact.[21]

The SSCI expanded quickly so that by March 1792 it was 2,000 strong. It was organised in cells or 'tythings' of 10 people with each cell represented at the next level up, drawing perhaps on the model of the Methodist class system. With fervour like that of the Methodists, they proselytised in the surrounding towns and villages. Their influence also extended to other big towns. The London Corresponding Society imitated the Sheffield cellular organisation. Leeds appealed to Sheffield for help. John Harrison from Sheffield helped set up the Birmingham organisation. An historian comments: 'there was a power in Sheffield, an intransigence, a sense of identification with the local community, which were rare'.[22] Another argues that Sheffield's importance was partly due to its geographical position midway between London and Scotland, making it 'a crucial centre for the dissemination of popular radicalism over much of the Northern half of England'.[23] There was surely no precedent for the spreading of 'subversive' literature on this scale. In this process, Gales played a crucial role. He stepped up his propaganda efforts by founding a new publication, *The Patriot*.

Among middle-class Parliamentary reformers there were mixed views about SSCI, as illustrated in correspondence between Samuel Shore and Christopher Wyvill, Anglican clergyman and leader of Yorkshire's Association for Parliamentary Reform. Shore welcomed SSCI and tried to reassure Wyvill that several of the SSCI leaders, such as Enoch Trickett, and Edward Smith, had been involved in the freemen's campaign and were considered of good character.[24] But Wyvill was not convinced. He was

> not surprised that many persons are very apprehensive of tumults at that place (Sheffield) and I think fears will increase rather than diminish as the association extends itself more into the neighbouring country. It is unfortunate that Mr Paine took such unconstitutional ground and has formed a party for a Republic among the lower classes of people, by holding out to them the prospect of plundering the rich.[25]

Wyvill's remarks indicated the critical fault line in the parliamentary reform movement with huge consequences in the years to come.

## Conflict and War

There was a wave of popular agitation across the country in 1791–2. Government Ministers were alarmed at the rapid spread of Paine's ideas. In May 1792, they sought to arrest this by means of a Royal Proclamation that condemned the spread of 'divers [sic] wicked and seditious writings'. Ministers condemned local associations that promoted 'subversive' doctrines. Gales commented: 'This is a serious charge! What say the associations?'[26] The SSCI announced that they stood for the right of every commoner to have a vote, but they 'abhorred every idea of attempting a Revolution'.[27]

There were demonstrations and counter-demonstrations. The 'Church and King' party in Sheffield was at last flexing its muscles. In June, they organised a meeting at the Cutlers' Hall at which citizens were invited to support an Address to the King, thanking him for his recent Proclamation against seditious writings. It was voted down by a large majority. A few days later, a second closed meeting was held at the Cutlers' Hall at which 100 people supported the Address. But many opponents of the Address gathered in the town

**15** The second Cutlers' Hall in Church Street in 1831, shortly before its replacement by the present hall. It would have looked much the same in 1792, when an angry mob assembled outside and were eventually calmed by Gales.

hall opposite and were 'threatening to pull down the Cutlers' Hall.' At the time, Gales was conferring with the Earl of Effingham's land agent. Hearing the noise, they ran out immediately 'without their hats' to see what was happening. Someone called out 'Mr Gales take the chair' and it was repeated by a thousand voices. Gales took the chair. He advised the crowd to disperse and they did so. He had calmed a threatening situation but nonetheless he was criticised as a 'dangerous influence'. This may be the point at which he became a leader in the SSCI. He was certainly becoming a marked man in the eyes of the authorities.[28]

In the increasingly tense atmosphere, troops were now regularly quartered in Sheffield. In June 1792, Colonel de Lancey of the War Office visited the town to investigate security risks, concluding that Sheffield was a hotbed of subversion and that the forces of law and order were pitifully weak.[29] In July, the erection of new barracks for the troops began beyond Shalesmoor.

People in Sheffield took a keen interest in developments on the continent – the Austrian and Prussian armies' invasion of France, the arrest of the royal family, the declaration of the French Republic, the September massacres of aristocrats and the republican victories against the invaders. For the British ruling class, these events confirmed Burke's view that the French Revolution would lead to anarchy and that any concessions to liberal opinion would push Britain down the same path as France. Sheffield took a different view. At the *Tontine Inn*, gentlemen commemorated 1688 by toasting the dethronement of a monarch as 'a lesson to all oppressors'.[30] The French victories were greeted with extraordinary celebrations – the firing of guns, the lighting of bonfires and the roasting of sheep after the first victory and an ox after the second.[31] Gales shared these 'joyous sentiments'.

The growing chasm between the SSCI and the supporters of law and order presented great problems for a moderate radical like Samuel Shore, who wanted reform but was not ready for manhood suffrage. On 31 December 1792, he and Vicar Wilkinson called a public meeting in the Cutlers' Hall. Shore wanted a resolution that combined a declaration of loyalty to the Crown with a demand for reform in representation and continued liberty of the press. But Wyvill persuaded him to withdraw this. So the meeting only considered Wilkinson's loyalty resolution, which was overwhelmingly defeated.[32]

By now, the nation was rallying to 'Church and King' and Sheffield was completely out of line with the national mood. Paine had fled and was tried in his absence for publishing the *Rights of Man*. Gales called this a 'new martyrdom' and denied allegations that radicals were levellers or republicans.[33] An American friend who had recently been in London warned Mrs Gales to remove all copies of Paine's works from their premises.[34]

In February 1793, Britain entered the war and quickly moved onto a war footing. There were 'nearly 30 Recruiting Parties' in the town, with drums beating and colours flying. Gales commented sardonically: 'Our Sheffield heroes, routed by the glorious pomp and circumstances of war, enlist very fast, resolved to fight, to conquer or perchance to die.'[35] The authorities decided to double the capacity of the barracks. Gales regretted that party was poisoning friendship.[36]

Gales's pro-French sentiments had become treasonable. Prudence would suggest calling a halt to radical activity. But, with courage or recklessness, he stepped up the propaganda war in the Register and played a leading public role in the radical campaign. In April, he chaired a public meeting on Castle Hill to promote a petition for parliamentary reform. The petition could be signed in Gales's office at Hartshead and 5,000 copies were distributed. Eight thousand signatures were obtained, but the petition was rejected by the House of Commons for 'disrespectful language'.

The *Register*'s radicalism, far from alienating readers, attracted them. Sales rose to over 2,000 copies – perhaps read by four times as many people. Its local rival, the *Sheffield Advertiser*, folded. In its place appeared the *Sheffield Courant*, which superficially looked like the *Register*, but promoted the 'Church and King' cause and was full of anti-Gales invective.[37] The atmosphere was becoming poisonous.

The war damaged trade. The SSCI wrote: 'we have many thousands of members, but the vast majority of them being working men, the war … has deprived many of them of all employment, and almost everyone of half his earnings'.[38]

Across the country, radicals like Gales faced prosecution. Even in Sheffield there was a risk of mob violence. In September 1793, Sheffield's 'Church and King' party celebrated Lord Howe's victory at Toulon by marching with a recruiting party and their drum and fife to demonstrate outside Gales's house, threatening to break all the windows. A hundred 'stout democrats' (later there were 500) assembled in front of the house, singing provocatively Mather's version of the National Anthem:

> *God save great Thomas Paine,*
> *His* Rights of Man *to explain,*
> *To every soul,*
> *He makes the blind to see,*
> *What dupes and slaves they be,*
> *And points out Liberty,*
> *From Pole to Pole.*

## *The Edinburgh Convention, the Arrests and Gales's Flight*

The conflict between the Government and the radicals approached its denouement. The radicals organised a 'convention' in Edinburgh. The SSCI sent Matthew C. Brown, editor of *The Patriot*, to represent them. The convention was broken up by the authorities but the delegates from London, Scotland and Sheffield managed to reconvene. After 17 days, this meeting was forcibly dissolved and Brown, who was in the chair, was dragged away. Following the convention, one of the delegates, Henry Redhead Yorke, a flamboyant young orator with curly red hair and a way with women, came to stay in Sheffield. According to Mrs Gales, 'His manners were so gentlemanly, his conversation so highly interesting ... that every one was fascinated with him'.[39] Yorke and Gales collaborated in producing radical literature.

After the suppression of the convention, radicals elsewhere were lying low, but not in Sheffield. In December 1793, there was a public meeting in the park to call for parliamentary reform. On 28 February 1794 – which the Government had made a public fast day – the SSCI organised a monster meeting at Backfields, near West Street. It opened with a prayer and a hymn specially written by Montgomery, followed by a series of resolutions against the war.

Local radicals feared that ruffians hired by the 'Church and King' party might attack them. One of Gales's compositors, an activist from Leeds called Richard Davison, was in touch with a local cutler about the making of pikes and wrote to Hardy of the London Corresponding Society offering pikes for sale. It is possible that these pikes were intended not just for defence purposes.

Gales and his wife both later said they knew nothing of this correspondence. But by now Gales's whole family circle was alarmed at the risks that he was running. His parents urged him to separate from the societies and stop printing their material, but he said it was his duty to promote parliamentary reform. His wife recalled later that 'Ann Gales, Montgomery and myself held frequent debates upon the posture of affairs and we added to each other's uneasiness by communicating our fears.'[40]

On 7 April 1794 the SSCI held yet another mass meeting, this time on Castle Hill. The crowd supported an Address to the King concerning those imprisoned in Edinburgh. Henry Yorke spoke for two hours in inflammatory terms, saying they should petition Parliament no more and referring to a 'grand political explosion'. Afterwards, the people drew Yorke and Gales through the streets in a coach. Gales published Yorke's speech, providing material that would later cost Yorke his liberty.

In May, one of Fitzwilliam's spies wrote to Gales referring to Fitzwilliam's 'concern at the inflammatory tendency of your paper and he said it was a paper ill calculated for a large manufacturing town ... and thousands are of the same opinion'.[41] With characteristic bravado, Gales published this in the *Register*, but it was a warning that the net was tightening around him.

On 12 May, Hardy and the other leading London radicals were arrested and their papers seized. The authorities discovered in Hardy's papers the apparently incriminating letter from Davison offering pikes. Then five SSCI leaders were arrested in Sheffield and moved to London, where some of them were interrogated by the Privy Council. Yorke was later arrested in Hull. During May, *habeas corpus* was suspended.

In June, a Government messenger and constable came to Gales's Hartshead office to arrest him but he was away in Derby.[42] When Gales learned that he was being pursued, he disappeared to Newhill Grange, the house of the Quaker John Payne[43] in Wath-upon-Dearne about twelve miles from Sheffield, where he continued to write vigorously for his newspaper. One day Montgomery rode for four hours to Wath with Mrs Gales behind him on pillion to enable her to see her husband before he escaped abroad.[44] 'How can I describe the misery of that day?' wrote Winifred Gales many years later.

Before he departed, Gales sent a moving farewell address, which appeared in the *Register* on 26 June 1794. He said that, after 10 years in Sheffield, he had to leave, 'unless I would expose myself to the malice, enmity and power of an unjust Aristocracy'. He asked whether his imprisonment or death would serve the cause and went on: 'Convinced that ruining my family and distressing my friends by risking either would only gratify the ignorant and malignant, I shall seek that livelihood in another state that I cannot peaceably obtain in this.' He would never regret having been a member of the SSCI. He denied having any knowledge of Davison's letter to Hardy about pikes.[45]

Gales made his way to Germany, leaving his wife in a very difficult situation. She had four children and was expecting a fifth. She had 18 employees in the printing office and a weekly newspaper to bring out. The printing company was in danger of being declared bankrupt. But she was a brave and resourceful woman and Sheffield friends stood by her. Samuel Shore's brother, William, offered her financial support, which at first she tearfully refused, but she eventually accepted a loan of £500.[46] With the help of a barrister, the company was temporarily handed over to assignees. She declined a lucrative offer from a Government agent to buy the newspaper and instead sold it to Montgomery and the Rev. Benjamin Naylor, Evans's assistant (and later successor) at Upper Chapel, who gave £500 for the goodwill.

One day Winifred Gales was hauled before Wilkinson, Athorpe and other magistrates at the *Tontine Inn* and interrogated about Gales's printed version of Yorke's impassioned address at Castle Hill. She said she knew nothing of this. She was then locked in a room at the inn for the rest of the day, while the magistrates interviewed all her printers, who likewise disclaimed all knowledge. After this, a deputation of working men came and pledged themselves to protect her.

Winifred was determined to join her husband. She and her children set off in a ship from Hull and, after a terrible storm, eventually met up with her husband in Hamburg. When her baby had been born, they embarked for the United States and settled in Raleigh, North Carolina.[47]

## James Montgomery as Editor

Meanwhile, in Sheffield, James Montgomery and Benjamin Naylor[48] had inherited the newspaper. Montgomery set up a household at Hartshead with Gales's sisters, two of whom ran the booksellers and stationers shop.

In July 1794, the first issue of the *Sheffield Iris* appeared under Montgomery's editorship. The first editorial announced that the *Iris* would avoid party spirit and support the cause of peace and reform, but it was 'attached to the Constitution'. Montgomery, a young man of 23, later said that it was with 'trembling reluctance' that he 'stepped into the post of danger which my abler predecessor had been compelled to relinquish'. 'No young man ever embarked in life with fewer hopes or greater fears.'[49]

To the authorities the *Iris* looked like the subversive *Register* reborn, particularly as an early edition included a message from the SSCI to Joseph Gales, who was hailed as a martyr. They wished him 'Health! Peace! Happiness!' and, in Jacobin language, commended him to the 'guardian care of the Supreme Being'. [50]

**16** James Montgomery succeeded Gales as editor and renamed the paper the *Iris*. After two imprisonments in York Castle, he was careful not to upset the authorities. He became a well-known poet and hymn writer.

Montgomery acknowledged the perils of producing a newspaper at this time, writing in the *Iris*: 'if a man be in love with hanging or transportation, he may speak or write the truth with unimaginable boldness.'[51] In London, treason trials were in progress and were reported in detail in the *Iris*. In December, all five SSCI leaders were released, having agreed to turn King's evidence against Henry Yorke.[52] They received a hero's welcome in Sheffield. Henry Yorke was tried in July 1795 for conspiracy with Gales and Davison and sentenced to two years' imprisonment in Dorchester Gaol.

The authorities resented Gales's escape and wanted to punish Montgomery in a show trial that would 'put a stop to the Associated Clubs in Sheffield'. The Attorney General commissioned a Sheffield Attorney called John Brookfield who achieved this by devious means. In August 1794, Montgomery was asked by a street ballad singer to print some copies of a 'Patriotic Song by a Clergyman of Belfast'. He did so as an act of charity for 18d. Samuel Hall, a local constable, got hold of a copy. Montgomery was charged with a seditious libel because this pre-war ballad contained the line: 'Should France be subdued, England's liberty ends.' In January 1795 at Doncaster, he was sentenced to three months in York Castle.[53]

**17**   Colonel Athorpe of Dinnington Hall, magistrate. He accused James Montgomery of libel for his report on Athorpe's brutal suppression of a riot, leading to Montgomery's second jail sentence.

Montgomery endured this experience with dignity and emerged from York Castle in April. Sadly, he soon faced yet further tribulations. This was because of his account in the *Iris* of incidents in Norfolk Street on 4 August 1795. He reported that a newly raised regiment, which was on parade, refused to disperse because of the withholding of bounty money and arrears of pay. A crowd gathered. The local volunteers were ordered to hold themselves in readiness. Colonel Athorpe of Dinnington Hall, choleric magistrate and Colonel of the volunteers, had been dining with Earl Fitzwilliam at Wentworth. He rode to Sheffield so fast that his horse died the next day. He ordered the crowd to disperse instantaneously but they hung around to view the spectacle. Then, according to Montgomery, 'a person who shall be nameless plunged with his horse into unarmed defenceless people and wounded men, women and children promiscuously'. The people fell back in confusion. The Riot Act was read and one hour later the volunteers fired at the townsmen, killing two and wounding several.

The *Courant* challenged Montgomery's account and Colonel Athorpe accused Montgomery of libel. Tried in Doncaster in January 1796, Montgomery was sentenced to six months in York Castle. Montgomery was indignant, since he had drawn on facts attested by 'creditable and intelligent persons'. The only contrary evidence was Athorpe's 'solemn and repeated asseverations'. In fact, there probably was more to this incident than

Montgomery reported. A radical called Eyre in the crowd behaved provocatively, urging the troops 'not to forsake them' and pointed at their commander, shouting 'knock him off.' When Athorpe tried to arrest Eyre, the crowd blocked his path. The crowd also threw stones and rubbish at the volunteers.[54] Here is Mather's account of the incident:

> *I saw this tragic scene commence;*
> *A madman drunk, without offence*
> *Drew out his sword in false pretence,*
>     *And wounded some more wise;*
> *Defenceless boys he chased about,*
> *The timid cried, the bold did shout,*
> *Which brought the curious no doubt*
>     *To see what meant the noise.*
>
> *The arm'd banditti, filled with spleen,*
> *At his command, like bloodhounds keen,*
> *In fine, to crown the horrid scene,*
>     *A shower of bullets fired.*
> *The consequence was deep distress*
> *More widows and more fatherless,*
> *The devil blushed and did confess*
>     *'Twas more than he required.*

Montgomery was badly affected by his second longer spell in York Castle. His health broke down and he was moved to a single room. He advised the *Iris* to be 'quiet'. For the rest of his editorship, Montgomery was more cautious and managed to avoid clashes with the law.

*Aftermath*

After these events, what happened to the main players?

Gales prospered in North Carolina. He was soon back to printing and publishing, became Mayor of Raleigh for 19 years and a magistrate and later in life published a work by Thomas Paine and an edition of the Bible. Ironically, Gales became an Abolitionist who owned slaves.[55]

Montgomery spent the rest of his life with Gales's sisters.[56] There were early hints of romance but 'the relations of Montgomery to the Miss Gales remained to the end those of brother and sisters.'[57] His early radicalism was cast aside and, anxious for respectability after his youthful indiscretions, he rewrote the history of the 1790s:

> Had all the reformers of that era been generous, upright and disinterested like the noble-minded proprietor of the Sheffield Register the cause which they espoused would never have been disgraced and might have prevailed, since there could have been nothing to fear and all to hope from patriotic measures supported by patriotic men.[58]

This account completely ignores the incompatibility between Gales's radicalism and the policies of Pitt's administration. In 1803, Montgomery attacked trade unionism as a threat to Britain's industrial supremacy.[59] In 1840, news of Holberry's plot led him to call Chartism 'a scheme of murder, conflagration and pillage'.[60] Montgomery became the most revered figure in Sheffield – a renowned hymn writer (author of *Angels from the Realms of Glory*), prolific poet, public benefactor, Chair of the Board of the Infirmary and much else besides. When he died in 1854, there was a grand public funeral and industry and commerce were stilled.

Henry Redhead Yorke, after his incarceration in Dorchester Gaol, married his gaoler's daughter and became a Tory and a Lieutenant Colonel.[61]

What about the radical artisans for whom Gales and Montgomery sacrificed so much? During 1795, they were still publicly active, holding mass meetings on Crookes Moor in August and November. But after this they could not hold large meetings without magistrates present and the SSCI ceased to exist as a public organised force.[62] Some withdrew from political activity but others engaged in underground and illegal activity (chapter 3).

Gales's dissemination of radical ideas in Sheffield and across the Midlands and North of England was of major importance. He helped to establish Sheffield's reputation – or notoriety – as a centre of radical politics – a reputation that has survived to this day. He and Montgomery were far ahead of their time in advocating democracy – the platform of the Chartists half a century later and only achieved much later still. The editors underestimated the obstacles in the way of manhood suffrage but their criticisms of the current system were largely valid. Gales blamed an 'unjust aristocracy' for forcing his exile. Above all, Gales and Montgomery gave self-sacrificing support to the artisans of Sheffield and helped to build a truly pioneering working-class movement.

*Chapter 3*

# The Struggle for
# Parliamentary Reform 1801-32

We were in Sheffield today ourselves and in all my life I never was in so stinking, dirty and savage a place. We did not meet a single carriage of any sort or kind in that great town, so that we were an object of no small admiration and wonder to the inhabitants and collected a perfect mob around us at every shop we stopped at of creatures principally children without the least degree of colour in their cheeks, all ragged and looking like blacksmiths. Altogether I never witnessed a scene of more idleness and filth in my life.

Lady Caroline Stuart-Wortley in 1801[1]

Our opponents ... think we are quite visionary and Utopian and disordered in our intellects but let me tell these gentlemen that our disorder is becoming very infectious. It is travelling all over the kingdom with a rail road speed and, if they do not get on, or get out of our way, we shall be obliged to run them over.

Benjamin Sayle, ironmaster of Brightside, at the inaugural meeting of Sheffield Political Union in January 1831[2]

Lady Caroline was the young wife of James Archibald Stuart-Wortley, who belonged to an important South Yorkshire political dynasty. His grandfather was the Earl of Bute, one of George III's Prime Ministers. Her husband, as Baron Wharncliffe, would himself serve as a Tory minister and play a crucial role in the crisis over parliamentary reform. In 1801, the young couple were living in Wharncliff Lodge on a spectacular ridge, while their main home, nearby Wortley Hall, 10 miles north of Sheffield, was put in order.

The aristocratic Lady Caroline was horrified by the squalour and grime of Sheffield, but did not pause to consider its causes. At the best of times, cutlery production made this a smoky and dirty place. Its industries, though growing, did not as yet make people rich enough to own a carriage. Moreover, in 1801 the war with France had curtailed trade, causing widespread poverty.

Sheffield's press had been gagged and its radical movement for parliamentary reform had been stifled. Gales had fled and his successor, Montgomery, editor of the *Iris*, was unnerved by his two spells in jail. Some working-class radicals remained defiant and had joined the revolutionary movement of the United Britons (see below).

In 1802, the Peace of Amiens was agreed with France to great rejoicing in Sheffield, but by May 1803 Britain was again at war with Napoleon. There followed a period like 1940, with widespread fear of an invasion of Britain's shores. Volunteer regiments were formed to defend the homeland. The mood in Sheffield was very different now from 1793, when most people had been against the war. In this new crisis, middle-class radicals like the ageing Samuel Shore[3] and the younger Thomas Rawson and Thomas Asline Ward (see below) became volunteer officers. A great beacon was established in Greno Wood near Wharncliffe to warn Sheffield if the French had landed. On 15 August 1805, the people of Sheffield saw that this beacon was blazing and believed that the crisis had come. A huge muster of volunteers took place. Hunter wrote that their 'determined and enthusiastic spirit … can never be forgotten by those who witnessed it'.[4] But it was a false alarm, due to an accidental fire.

This unity against a common threat did not last. The war lingered on until 1815, further damaging Sheffield's trade, and was followed by further economic privations. The Government was determined on repression rather than reform and their severity at Peterloo drove Whig leaders, like Earl Fitzwilliam, as well as the radicals, into opposition.

It was not until 1830 that the advent of a pro-reform Whig Government suddenly changed the climate. The quotation above shows how by 1831 Benjamin Sayle of the Sheffield Political Union could claim that the movement for parliamentary reform was as irresistible as two topical forces – infection and the railways. Yet it still took a bitter struggle to overcome the resistance of the House of Lords. In this struggle, Sheffield played a full part. Then, ironically, the first election for Sheffield's own MPs ended in bloodshed.

### Changes in Sheffield

Despite the war and economic instability, Sheffield continued to grow at an astonishing rate. The population of the parish doubled from 45,755 in 1801 to 91,682 in 1831.[5] Substantial new housing appeared on Park Hill, the Wicker, Shalesmoor, Broomhall, Broomhill and the Moor stretching out to London Road and Highfields.

**18**   Town hall in Waingate, opened in 1808. Now in need of a new owner.

Sheffield's expansion was due to its success in meeting the growing demand for cutlery, edge tools, silver plate and silver objects, not only in the UK but also abroad, notably in the USA,[6] even if trade was at times curtailed by war. Sheffield's infrastructure was improving, with the infirmary (1797), a new town hall in Waingate (1808), an Improvement Commission to clean and light the streets (1818) and an improved police force (1818). In 1819 the gasworks opened and the extension of the canal to the present canal basin was opened with great rejoicing. In 1823, next to the canal, Messrs Greaves opened their Sheaf works, the biggest in Sheffield at that time, converting and melting steel and producing a wide range of cutlery products, especially for the American market. However, most industrial enterprises remained small workshops.

Sheffield was becoming more cultured. There was a subscription library (which moved to Surrey Street in 1825), various literary societies and a Society for the Propagation of Useful Knowledge, superseded in 1822 by the Literary and Philosophical Society.[7] In James Montgomery and Ebenezer Elliott, 'the Corn Law Rhymer', Sheffield had two poets with a national reputation. The literary circles in which Montgomery moved were a 'mild and lady-like set, with their tea-parties, their verse writing, their respectable domesticity'.[8]

Montgomery's poem *The Wanderer of Switzerland* was savagely criticised by the *Edinburgh Review*. In 1808, Lord Byron, the most famous – or infamous – radical of the age, wrote a verse commiserating with him, ending:

> *Nipped in the bud by Caledonian gales,*
> *His blossom withers as the blast prevails!*
> *O'er his lost works let classic Sheffield weep;*
> *May no rude hand disturb their early sleep!*[9]

The reference to 'classic Sheffield' was a sneer, as few towns were less 'classic' in 1808. Yet, in the coming decades, 'classic Sheffield' appeared architecturally on both sides of the Porter Valley in western Sheffield as 'one monumental Neoclassical composition',[10] comprising the Mount (1830-2, where Montgomery went to live), Wesley School (1837-40, now King Edward VII School), the entrance to the General Cemetery (1836) and the Clarkehouse Road entrance to the Botanical Gardens (1836). In 1813, Byron visited Sheffield as a break from amorous intrigues at Aston Hall and 'thought the grinders very fine fellows and had acquired some of their slang'.[11]

**19**   The Mount in Broomhill. Built 1830-2 as part of a monumental neo-classical composition in the Porter Valley. Montgomery lived here in later life.

## Religion and Revolution

This period also saw changes in the religious character of the town. Methodism grew to become the biggest dissenting force in the town, but it also split. In 1797 the New Connexion, led by Alexander Kilham of Scotland Street Chapel, seceded from the Wesleyan Connexion. Most Sheffield Methodists must have seceded, as Wesleyan membership fell from 3,099 to 1,080 between 1796 and 1804. Kilham's followers were known as the 'Tom Paine Methodists' because their opposition to the autocracy of the Wesleyan Conference was influenced by Paine's writings. All this spilt over into politics. The Wesleyans were Tory, with Jabez Bunting, the national Wesleyan leader, declaring that 'Methodism hates democracy as much as it hates sin.' By contrast, the New Connexion Methodists were radical in politics and active in the trade unions. There were other Methodist splits. In 1819, the first Primitive Methodist chapel appeared in Sheffield, with a respectable working-class congregation, tending towards liberalism in politics.[12]

After the Napoleonic Wars, Parliament voted £1,000,000 for new Anglican churches. In Sheffield, four massive new Gothic churches appeared: St George's in Portobello, St Mary's in Bramall Lane, St Philip's at the foot of Shalesmoor and Christ Church in Attercliffe.

Ted Wickham once remarked[13] that the Government built churches like St Mary's Bramall Lane in order to prevent revolution. If this is so, it was misconceived. The operations of these new churches were largely financed by pew rents. 'Free sittings' were

20   St Mary's, Bramall Lane, built in 1830 – one of four Anglican churches built after the Napoleonic War. In 1839, Chartists tried to fire-bomb it.

provided, but radical artisans did not occupy them. Those artisans willing to come to a place of worship wished to be treated as equals and so would be more attracted to those Methodist chapels that had abandoned pew rents. Indeed, some workers were suspicious of the big new Anglican churches and in 1839 the Chartists actually attempted to firebomb St Mary's. The great French historian Elie Halevy argued that 'Methodism was the antidote to Jacobinism' and that it was Methodism that prevented Britain from suffering revolution in this period.[14] Sheffield's experience certainly confirms that Methodism, even in its Kilham version, was a far more effective moderating force than any steps taken by the Church of England. But a few Methodists became revolutionaries and most artisans did not attend church. In Sheffield, the Church and chapel influence on the working classes was probably too weak to have curbed revolution.

21   Thomas Rawson, founder of Pond Street Brewery and radical leader – 'one of our violent men'.

### Radical Leaders

In these years, Sheffield lacked an outstanding radical leader of the calibre of Joseph Gales. Thomas Rawson of Wardsend was described as 'the father of radical reformers in Sheffield'.[15] He came from an old Sheffield family and had founded the brewery in Pond Street. In 1816, he became president of a new Union Society in Sheffield.

T.A. Ward called him 'one of our violent men', implying that he did not rule out physical force. However, at his death in 1826, Ward praised his willingness to 'vindicate the poor and weak against the rich and powerful'.[16]

Among the more moderate radicals, the central figure was Thomas Asline Ward (1781–1871) – cutlery manufacturer, man of letters, magistrate, volunteer officer and civic leader, Master Cutler in 1816 and town collector from 1828 to 1847. Like Gales, Ward was a Unitarian convert and this may have been a big influence. R.E. Leader, from Congregationalist roots, wrote long afterwards that Ward 'lived in an atmosphere charged with the aggressive beliefs of "Rational Dissenters" – Hunter, Piper, the Shores, Nanson, Rhodes, Moorhouse, Thompson and others ...'[17]

**22** Thomas Asline Ward, Master Cutler in 1816, moderate radical leader, diarist, newspaper editor, chair of Sheffield Political Union 1830-2 and parliamentary candidate in 1832.

Ward campaigned not only for parliamentary reform but also for causes like the plight of child chimney-sweepers. He was a Benthamite and friendly with Thomas Bowyer, Bentham's secretary. He was prepared to take a stand for his principles as when, in April 1810, he helped to organise a 'very numerous' public meeting in Paradise Square to pass resolutions of protest against the imprisonment in the Tower of London of Sir Francis Burdett, a leading parliamentary reformer. Three hundred other prominent citizens subsequently expressed dissent from these resolutions.[18] Ward had his hand in everything – political, economic, cultural, social and philanthropic. From 1823-9, he edited the *Sheffield Independent*. In 1830 became chairman of the Sheffield Political Union and later stood for Parliament. Finally, he was an assiduous diarist and correspondent.

In 1810, Rawson, Ward and other middle-class reformers formed a loose association called the Friends of Reform. At times of crisis, they organised large public meetings, but they ceased to be active after May 1817, following the discovery of a revolutionary plot (see below).[19]

It is much more difficult to identify the working-class leaders. They are shadowy figures and records about their lives are sparse. Moreover, after the Sheffield Society for Constitutional Information (SSCI) was crushed, they may have lacked leadership. In 1796 a London radical, John Thelwall, visited Sheffield and afterwards commented: 'there is a great body of virtue, intelligence and well grounded principle among what may be called the Sans-culotterie; but it is a body without a head. They have unfortunately no leaders.'[20]

Despite this, Sheffield radicals contributed to the abortive 'Despard Plot' of 1803 (see below). Edward Thompson wrote: 'From Despard to Brandreth (1817), there stretches the illegal tradition. It is a tradition which will never be rescued from its obscurity.'[21]

This is true of Sheffield, even if historians like John Baxter and Fred Donnelly are doing their best to reduce the obscurity.[22] Thompson also believed in some continuity in working-class leadership in England between the 1790s and the 1830s. In Sheffield, some working-class leaders operated over a sustained period, like John Crome, the printer, who was active in the early 1790s and 10 years later, John Blackwell, a revolutionary journeyman tailor, repeatedly involved in Sheffield disturbances in the 1810s and the father and son team of William and James Wostenholme, who between them were involved in the Despard plot of 1803, the disturbances of 1817 and Chartism in 1839-40.[23]

Underlying this story is the fault-line in the parliamentary reform movement between middle-class and working-class reformers. Working-class reformers sought manhood suffrage, whereas most middle-class reformers wanted a property-based franchise.

## *The Working Classes and the Trade Unions*

While the local cutlery industry had greatly expanded, it had not undergone an 'industrial revolution', which Halevy defined as an 'entire transformation of the mechanism of manufacture'.[24] The techniques of the industry remained predominantly manual, even if steam power was increasingly replacing water power for grinding. It was a highly sub-divided craft-based industry, using skills that artisans had normally acquired through apprenticeship in a host of different occupations.[25]

Economic demand was highly variable and the artisans could be prosperous in one year only to face penury in the next. In the 1780s, the freemen had unsuccessfully sought to persuade the Cutlers' Company to protect them by tighter regulation of entry into their occupations. In 1814, the company raised no protest when Parliament legislated to strip the company of its legal powers of regulation of the trades.

These events had a profound impact on working-class opinion. They highlighted the need for working-class representation in Parliament – a major theme for the next half-century. They also led the Sheffield trade unions to 'believe that that they were the rightful heirs of the Cutlers' Company and its regulative functions abdicated in 1814'.[26]

So long as the Combination Acts forbade union activity, the trades were organised in friendly societies, which supported sick artisans and eased the ups and downs of the economic cycle, though they might also covertly act as unions and force up wages when prices shot up as in 1810 and 1814. After the Combination Acts were repealed in 1824, trade union activity could be pursued more freely and became a powerful factor in Sheffield life. Trade unions sought to raise wages in good times, prevent their reduction in bad times and restrict entry to the trade through controlling the number of apprentices and the entry of outsiders. Enlightened employers like T.A. Ward recognised that 'poor men cannot procure an advance in wages without some kind of combinations.'[27] But they did not condone unions' enforcement of their rules by violent means such as 'rattening' (removal or destruction of the grinders' bands that connected the grindstones with the revolving shafts).[28] Over the next half-century, the role of the unions would become one of the most hotly contested issues in Sheffield life.

## Disturbances

Repression drove anti-Government activity underground. Secret assemblies were held outside Sheffield. In December 1800, for instance, Captain Warris of the Sheffield Volunteers spied on a meeting of over 1,000 people near Sheffield. Once again, as in Gales' time, Sheffield became a centre for the production of pike heads.[29]

In 1801-2, a widespread conspiracy of the United Britons was developing. The Sheffield Committee included several former leaders of the SSCI, including the printer, John Crome. A total of 1,615 people in Sheffield were said to be involved. The national conspiracy, known as the 'Despard Plot', was to seize the King on his way to Parliament, take the Tower of London and the Bank of England and take control of towns up and down the country. On hearing from London, the Sheffield militants would seize the barracks, imprison the soldiers and then take possession of the town. In August 1802, the Sheffield men were acquiring pike heads and spear heads, which they later buried in a wood. But the authorities had spies planted among the conspirators in London and on 16 November 1802 swooped with great secrecy and arrested them. Similar arrests took place in Yorkshire and two Sheffield militants, William Lee and William Ronksley, were tried at York Assizes and sentenced to transportation.[30] This was the end of the Despard Plot.

The following years were punctuated by disturbances caused by economic distress and the high price of bread. For instance, on 14 April 1812 a crowd in the marketplace was manhandling a woman grain seller and James Montgomery chivalrously intervened to rescue her. He got her into the safety of the *Sheffield Iris* office in Hartshead, but he re-emerged when someone threw a potato through the window. The crowd was hostile but someone called out 'Nay, nay, sir, we won't hurt you – you were our friend once.'[31] It was an interesting comment on Montgomery's change of political stance since his second spell in York Castle.

The crowd proceeded to the local militia depot where the young men overcame the guards and began to seize weapons and other equipment. But the older men in the crowd warned them that they would be hanged if caught with arms in their hands, so they turned instead to wrecking the contents of the armoury until the Hussars arrived. John Blackwell was identified as a ringleader and, although he denied it, may well have been the revolutionary tactician responsible for turning a food riot into an attack on a barracks.[32]

On 18 August 1812, there were further disturbances over the price of grain. The magistrates and Lord Milton, young son of Lord Fitzwilliam, tried to restore order but Milton was stoned by the crowd when he suggested that they await the harvest. The military intervened to protect Milton. There were threats to march on Wentworth House. A group raided a mill at Attercliffe.[33]

The gap between the 'moderates' and the 'extremists' was illustrated a month later when Ward decided not to attend a dinner with Major Cartwright, a famous veteran radical campaigner. Ward noted that: 'Many of the most respectable gentlemen were so timid in consequence of the late riots here, being apprehensive of more, that they refused to take part in it.' Ward heard it was a 'disgraceful meeting'. The dinner tickets were priced so low that 'the company, with few exceptions, were of the lowest rank and serious squabbles ensued'. Ward noted that causes like 'The Annual Parliament and Universal Suffrage' were supported. However, the next day Ward's curiosity got the better of him, for he breakfasted with Cartwright at the home of Thomas Rawson (see above). Ward found Cartwright 'a talkative, good humoured, mild man, completely of the old school in dress and manners'.[34]

Ward's diary gives us an unusual insight into the unpatriotic and pro-French sentiments of some of the working class at this time. He records a conversation he had in a public house in 1812 with half a dozen poor men:

> It is their opinion that the kingdom cannot exist, without a change until Christmas, and they seemed scarcely startled at the idea of a revolution. Everything, they say, is wrong in this country, from the King to the Constable, and Bonaparte is an honest fellow. I insisted on the despotic nature of the French Government and the great freedom which we enjoyed. They would not believe me. Speaking of Lord Wellington, they said that he was driven from Madrid. I told them he was in advance of it and pursuing the retreating enemy. They said that the rich always pretended to know better than the poor, who had, or ought to have, equal rights with them – but George Foster (I suppose some alehouse demagogue) told that it would soon be 'all over' with Lord Wellington. I could not help smiling (though it is really grievous) to find them so obstinate in their ignorance and misconceptions.[35]

In November 1812, an incident at the Sheffield theatre illustrated the gulf between the classes. Officers from the garrison insisted on the audience singing *God Save the King*, whereas there were objections from those up in the gallery, including John Blackwell who became known as 'King of the Gallery'.[36]

After Napoleon's defeat at Waterloo, a brief economic recovery was followed by a deep depression in 1816. There was agitation in Sheffield. In October 1816, a petition for the redress of economic grievances was signed by more than 20,000 people in Sheffield, but turned down by Parliament.[37] A Sheffield Union Society was formed with Thomas Rawson as president. On 3 December 1816, following a meeting in the market, John Blackwell led a group round the town. He was carrying a long pole with a blood-stained loaf and a sign reading 'Bread or Blood'. When the group returned to the market, the magistrates read the Riot Act and Blackwell shouted out: 'Never mind, my lads, tomorrow shall be our day.' He was arrested and sent off to York.

This was a time of intense agitation for parliamentary reform and an end to corruption. A meeting in Paradise Square led to a petition of 21,500 signatures. But, to counter this, loyalists in the Church Burgesses, the Town Trustees and the Cutlers' Company produced an address of loyalty to the Prince Regent. This was far from unanimous. The Master Cutler at this time was T.A. Ward, who refused to sign.[38] Meanwhile, the working-class agitators held secret meetings, some of which were penetrated by Oliver, the famous spy employed by the Home Office. On 29 May 1817, the conspirators met at a grinding wheel and were planning an attack on 10 June on the local barracks, the arms depot at Doncaster and Wentworth House. The magistrates arrived and the conspirators fled. Several conspirators were subsequently arrested, including William Wostenholme, who 'boasted that he was a Despard's man and had been 28 years in the cause'.[39] His son, James, spent six months in Winchester Gaol at this time and would reappear as a Chartist leader in 1839. T.A. Ward was involved in the magisterial proceedings connected with these arrests and commented:

> Our Yorkshire riots or insurrections were wicked, though rash and absurd; and, notwithstanding it is asserted that they were organised before Oliver's appearance, yet it seems very doubtful. That fellow's motions were watched by our magistrates who had almost apprehended him; and it was not until after a long correspondence with Lord Sidmouth

(Home Secretary) concerning him that they learned he was an agent of Government. Hugh Parker (local magistrate and banker) was very indignant.[40]

Recent historians suggest that these Sheffield conspirators were part of a much wider plot, which included Brandreth's rising in Pentrich in Derbyshire on 10 June.[41]

### Sheffield's Response to Peterloo

On 16 August 1819, in St Peter's Field, Manchester, a massive demonstration was attacked by soldiers, causing the death of 11 people. The event was named 'Peterloo' by the radicals. The Prince Regent and Lord Sidmouth, the Home Secretary, both praised the actions of the magistrates and soldiers. Sentiments in Sheffield were very different. T.A. Ward 'attended a meeting at the *Angel Inn* (Mr Shore President), at which resolutions were passed preparatory to a public meeting on Monday respecting the Manchester ---------- -----'. He restrained himself from writing the word 'massacre'.[42]

There followed one of the largest public meetings ever held in Sheffield. The *Iris* estimated 40-50,000 were present. It began with a vast procession, which formed in the Wicker and included almost all the clubs and friendly societies with their banners and bands playing the 'Dead March' from *Saul*. The women wore black and the men had white hats with crêpe and green ribbons, and carried banners saying 'Beware, beware a plot, a plot' or 'The Rights of Man – Liberty, Truth, Justice'. The procession went to a natural amphitheatre near Broad Lane, known as 'the Brocco'[43] with the platform for speakers erected in Allen Street. The elderly Samuel Shore was the chairman. Thomas Rawson gave a fiery speech, ending 'I scorn bondage. I will be a freeman.' The speakers included Lord Milton, whose father, the Earl Fitzwilliam, had just been sacked as Lord Lieutenant for his part in a county meeting in York, which called for an inquiry into Peterloo. The Sheffield resolutions, like those from York, called for an inquiry and passed unanimously. The great meeting dispersed peaceably and in order.[44] It was a rare day of unity between the highest and lowest.

In February 1820, T.A. Ward went to Wentworth House for a gathering of some 130 prominent Yorkshire citizens for the presentation of an address signed by 6,000 people, expressing support for Fitzwilliam after his dismissal as Lord Lieutenant, marking a significant coming together of radicals and Whigs. Ward tried to persuade Samuel Shore to accompany him, but Shore was 'much affected at the death of the King (George III) who was younger a few months than he is. In consequence of this event, he could not summon resolution and spirits enough to accompany the delegation ...'[45] This story illustrates how Shore combined his zeal for parliamentary reform with a deep patriotism. Shore died in 1828, but Ward had already inherited his mantle as the radical leader in Sheffield best able to hold conflicting forces together.

On 11-12 April 1820, John Blackwell, released from York Castle, led a group of Sheffield insurgents as part of an attempted 'general rising' in the North. His para-military group of about two hundred men was highly organised and split into separate units to march down certain streets, like King Street and Apple Market, and then converge in the Haymarket. Members of the crowd called 'that's Jacky Blacker, the King' and 'the Revolution, the Revolution'. They then marched towards the barracks but decided to 'adjourn this perilous enterprise to the next day'. Blackwell was arrested the next day, tried at York and given a 30-month sentence at York Castle. This ended his career as an activist. He died in the Sheffield Poorhouse in 1839.[46]

## Newspapers

Gales had shown the importance of newspapers in promoting radical politics. However, by 1819, Sheffield radicals had lost patience with Montgomery's *Iris,* which was liberal/conservative with tepid and colourless opinions. The other Sheffield paper was the Tory *Sheffield Mercury* founded in 1807. In 1819 the *Sheffield Independent* was founded by the young H.A. Bacon. Middle-class reformers, including T.A. Ward, later took shares in the paper.[47] From 1823 until 1829 Ward was editor, pressing for parliamentary reform, free trade and particularly repeal of the Corn Laws, religious freedom including Catholic emancipation and schemes for all kinds of local improvement. For example, the Mechanics' Library was established in 1823 following Ward's advocacy in the *Independent.*

In 1829, the paper was bought up by Robert Leader Senior, heir of a family who, with the Tudor family, had built up Sheffield's silver plate industry, settling near Tudor Street (now Tudor Square). Leader House, the family home until 1817, still stands facing Arundel Gate. Robert Leader's son, Robert Leader Junior, took over as editor in 1833, when he was twenty-three. In this way, the Leaders, Congregationalist in religion, became influential Liberal newspaper owners and editors.[48]

## A Crisis over Religion

The position of dissenters of all kinds was improving. In 1816, 'a neat and handsome chapel' was erected at the corner of Fargate and Norfolk Row for Roman Catholics. In 1818-19, as a result of strong pressure from dissenters, Sheffield was one of the first towns in England to end the payment of church rates.[49] But in the 1820s Sheffield became caught up in a major national crisis over the civic position of Roman Catholics.

The political rights of Protestant dissenters were secured in 1828 when Parliament at last repealed the Test and Corporation Acts. But Catholic emancipation was a far more emotive issue and it was only unrest in Ireland that eventually forced a change in Government policy. In Sheffield, the petition in favour, promoted by Ward and other enlightened middle-class leaders, attracted 7,000 signatures. But the petition against, backed by Anglican clergy and Stuart-Wortley, now Lord Wharncliffe, of Wortley Hall, astonishingly attracted 30,000. Luke Palfreyman claimed that 40 people hawked the petition from house to house over a wide area and got children to sign. But even so it suggests that, among the non-churchgoing masses, 'No Popery' remained a strong rallying cry. There was, however, no great excitement in the town when the Bill was passed in 1829.[50]

## Sheffield and Parliamentary Reform

Sheffield's history in 1829-32 was closely linked to national events. Catholic emancipation split the Tories. The 1829 harvest failed, pushing up food prices and intensifying popular discontent. In 1830, George IV died and his successor, William IV, was more pragmatic than his two predecessors. Following a General Election, Wellington's Tory Government collapsed and the Whigs at last returned to power under Earl Grey.

Parliamentary reform would never have taken place but for popular pressure in the big towns, expressed through over 100 lobby groups known as 'Political Unions'. In January 1830, the first Political Union was established in Birmingham. Sheffield was slower off the mark, owing to divided leadership and uncertainty.[51] In January 1830, it had the stimulus of three lectures by William Cobbett. On 19 February, a meeting at the town hall discussed a petition on representational reform. But there was dismay that Lord John Russell had left Sheffield out of proposals for enfranchising major towns. John Parker, future MP for Sheffield, wrote a pamphlet pointing out that Russell had used the population figures for the central township, whereas he should have used those for the parish.

The 1830 election demonstrated Sheffield's strong support for the new Whig Government, with Henry Brougham, a formidable Whig candidate for the West Riding, attracting 10,000 to a meeting. But the classic split between moderates and extremists inhibited campaigning for parliamentary reform. In November, the extremists, led by the young Isaac Ironside, a fascinating political figure for the next 30 years in Sheffield, organised two meetings, described as 'excited, confused and futile', which identified four representatives, including Ironside, to work with the middle-class reformers.

### The Sheffield Political Union

In November 1830, a group of reform leaders issued a prospectus inviting people to register their support for a Sheffield Political Union. The leaders included T.A. Ward, Robert Leader, current editor of the *Independent*, Dr Arnold Knight, a Roman Catholic and founder of the public dispensary, Dr G.C. Holland of the School of Anatomy and Medicine, Luke Palfreyman, a solicitor and son of a 1790s activist who was imprisoned in York Castle, Benjamin Sayle, an ironmaster, Ebenezer Rhodes (Master Cutler in 1809), Edward Bramley, from a distinguished Unitarian solicitors' family, and Isaac Ironside.

In January 1831, they held their first meeting in the town hall under Ward's chairmanship. Ward ran through their objects. The first was the reform of the House of Commons to ensure 'a real and effectual representation of the lower and middle classes'. He did not use the words 'universal suffrage', but the union evidently supported some degree of working-class representation. There were nine other objects, including changing the system of taxation so that it 'presses less severely on industrious classes'. Several leaders stressed moderation. Bramley pointed out that their objects were 'conservatory and strictly legal … It is no agitating society, its members are neither turbulent nor dangerous.' Similarly, Knight said that 'There always had been distinctions in rank and property and probably always would be.' He would sooner 'lay his head on the block than join in any insane crusade against the aristocracy'. Luke Palfreyman persuaded the meeting to call for the secret ballot. Thirty-three members were elected to the union's council.[52]

While the union sometimes used strong rhetoric, it stood essentially for middle-class reformism. With a subscription of only 6d., it attracted artisans but unlike the SSCI in the 1790s did not form cells or classes. The Home Office was reassured that 'there are good names in it, and men you can trust … The Union's movements may do good by helping to push reform as a necessity … The Union's objectives are not incompatible with public security.'[53] The union's council included Ironside and his three 'extremist' colleagues, elected in November, who wanted annual parliaments and manhood suffrage, but, as conflict with the House of Lords intensified, the union supported the Whig agenda.

In March 1831, Grey's administration presented unexpectedly sweeping proposals for parliamentary reform

23   Lord Wharncliffe of Wortley Hall, a Tory peer, was very unpopular in Sheffield in October 1831 for his stance over parliamentary reform.

to the Commons. Opposition in the Commons led to another General Election, which was a Whig triumph. But in October 1831 the Second Reform Bill was rejected by the House of Lords. The Tory motion against the Bill was moved by Lord Wharncliffe of Wortley Hall. The Lords' rejection caused anger throughout the country and Britain was close to revolution. In Bristol, Nottingham and Derby there was rioting, but surprisingly not in Sheffield, perhaps because the Political Union now managed to channel the intense anger into huge meetings and a petition with 15,000 signatures. Wharncliffe was especially unpopular. At a Sheffield demonstration on 15 October, there was a gibbeted dummy dressed in the uniform of the West Yorkshire Yeomanry, with the inscription 'The dragon of Wortley: the enemy of King and People.'[54] In fact, Wharncliffe soon suggested a compromise, which his Tory colleagues rejected.

In May 1832, the Lords threatened major changes to the Third Reform Bill. Grey's cabinet refused to accept these changes but King William, instead of creating peers to overrule the Tories, asked Wellington if he could form a Government. There was a fevered reaction in Sheffield. The council of the Political Union went into permanent session and recruited 15,000 additional members.[55] There were two mass meetings in a week, one called in Paradise Square with only two hours' notice and 20,000 people present. The union secretary, Bramley, said he would rather 'lay my head on the block than submit longer to the odious tyranny of a factious unprincipled oligarchy'. He could not believe that 24 million would bow down in the dust before 150 Lords. There were 'three groans for the King', instead of three cheers. Massive petitions were sent to London. Not all reactions were constitutional. The *Independent* noted that 'some swords and some pike heads have been manufactured in Sheffield'. [56]

In March 1832, Wharncliffe and another Tory, Harrowby, split away from their party and the Bill at last went through the Lords. In Sheffield, the Political Union organised a public procession of celebration so vast that it took 45 minutes to pass.

Alongside the drama over parliamentary reform was a crisis over cholera. In February 1832, the *Independent*, in moralistic mode, said that cholera's 'ravages are still great where

**24**   Memorial on Park Hill to the 402 victims of the cholera epidemic of 1832.

poverty, bad living, insufficient clothing, filth and intemperance abound'. The epidemic reached Sheffield in the summer of 1832. The Society for the Betterment of the Poor, in which Ward was active, recommended cleanliness in persons' clothes and bedding, the white-washing of buildings, and plain food.[57] But the newspapers' tendency to blame immoral living among the poor for the outbreak was checked when Blake, the Master Cutler, fell victim. Before the epidemic spent itself in November, 402 bodies had been buried in the burial ground on Park Hill where the Cholera Memorial now stands.

### The Election of 1832

As a result of the Reform Act, Sheffield at last could elect two MPs. The electors were in the main adult males owning or occupying property worth at least £10 per annum. Their number was only 3,504[58] out of a population in 1831 of 91,000. The House of Lords' resistance had pushed the middle and working classes together in the struggle, but many in the working classes felt betrayed by the outcome. Nor was there a secret ballot, so the masses, who were in 'a state of great excitement', would know how individuals voted.

There was no system of party endorsement. Instead, a group of gentlemen put forward a candidate. 'Canvassing' was formally discouraged, though accusations were made that it was going on.

Four candidates came forward, significantly all reformists. The *Independent* noted that 'A few Tories still linger in this town,'[59] but there were not enough to put up a candidate. (When a Tory stood in 1837, he only got 665 votes.) The candidates were:

• Samuel Bailey, son of a cutler, who joined the family firm, was a founder of the Sheffield Banking Company, a subtle economist and philosopher, called by Brougham 'the Bentham of Hallamshire' and something of a recluse.

• James Silk Buckingham, an eloquent Cornishman, whose criticisms of the East India Company in a paper he edited in Calcutta had led to his expulsion from India. He was 'ready to do battle with existing and imaginary abuses' and promised great benefits to all classes of society.[60]

• John Parker, barrister son of Hugh Parker, the leading local magistrate and banker.

• T.A. Ward, who, as this chapter has shown, was Sheffield's best-known reformer, but he entered the election race late.

In July there was a public meeting in Paradise Square, at which all the candidates spoke from the steps of the Freemasons' Lodge to a dense crowd estimated at 16–18,000.[61] A similar meeting was held just before the election in December. The voting was as follows:

| | |
|---|---|
| Parker | 1,515 |
| Buckingham | 1,498 |
| Ward | 1,210 |
| Bailey | 812 |

It was an odd result. The electors rejected the two local candidates with roots in the cutlery trade. Parker had the strongest support in the local press. Perhaps electors expected him and Buckingham to make most impact in Westminster. (Parker later became a Minister in the Treasury and the Admiralty, while Buckingham wrote prophetically on town planning.) During the election, Ward thought that his Unitarianism and Bailey's suspected deism might be handicaps with the voters.[62] Again, Bailey's failure may have been to due to his family's reputation for exploiting workmen.[63]

The voteless masses deplored the choice of Parker, a Whig who represented law and order. The popular favourites were Buckingham and Ward. A crowd gathered in the Haymarket and threw stones at the *Tontine Inn*, where Parker's committee met and at the house in Queen Street of Luke Palfreyman, a solicitor in Parker's interest. Palfreymen got out his blunderbuss and fired in the air. The local coroner read the Riot Act, special constables patrolled the streets and a detachment of the 18th Irish Foot came over from Rotherham and formed in the courtyard of the *Tontine*. The crowd threw stones at the soldiers as soon as they arrived and, when a stone hit a magistrate called Bosville, the order to 'fire' was given. Five people were shot dead and many wounded before the magistrates persuaded the soldiers to desist. The verdict of the coroner's inquest was 'justifiable homicide'.[64]

The editor of the *Independent*, presumably Robert Leader Senior, was just penning his editorial congratulating Sheffield on its peaceable election, when he was interrupted 'by the shouts and hootings of a riotous mob, by the discharges of musketry and the shrieks of the frightened multitude'. When he resumed his editorial, he was very emotional:

> Alas, alas, our eyes have seen five of our … townsmen, all pale and ghastly and bloody, lying dead upon the floor of our Town Hall; and others who have been wounded more or less severely, may … be lying in the agonies of death or groaning in pain. Oh, horrible, most horrible event, ever to be remembered with feelings of shame and sorrow.[65]

The next edition argued that the magistrates' order to fire had been given too quickly.

The Political Union collapsed in December 1832 following Ward's withdrawal and as a result of dissension between various extreme factions. T.A. Ward was presented with a service of plate financed by a voluntary subscription of 10,000 citizens. He withdrew from active politics until his death in 1871.

Sheffield now could participate in national decisions. But the terrible end to the first election and the disintegration thereafter of the Political Union showed how unstable the political situation remained, with only 3,500 having the vote. The next phase was a massive new struggle by the working class to obtain the civic privileges now granted to the middle class.

*Chapter 4*

# The Age of the Chartists

Sacred to the memory of Samuel Holberry, who at the early age of 27 died in York Castle after suffering an imprisonment of 2 years and 3 months. June 21st 1842. For advocating what to him appeared to be the true interest of the people of England.

Inscription on Samuel Holberry's gravestone in the General Cemetery, Sheffield

> *Avenge the plundered poor, oh Lord!*
> *But not with fire, but not with sword,*
> *Not as at Peterloo they died,*
> *Beneath the hooves of coward pride.*
> *Avenge our rags, our chains, our sighs,*
> *The famine in our children's eyes!*
> *But not with sword – no, not with fire,*
> *Chastise Thou Britain's locustry!*
> *Lord, let them feel thy heavier ire;*
> *Whip them, oh Lord, with poverty!*
> *Then, cold in soul as coffin'd dust,*
> *Their hearts as tearless, dead, and dry,*
> *Let them in outraged mercy trust,*
> *And find the mercy they deny!*

From 'The Jacobin's Prayer' by Ebenezer Elliott

The 1830s and 1840s were a time of ferment in Sheffield. The Chartists represented the biggest working-class challenge to traditional government that Britain had ever seen.

This period produced a rich crop of Sheffield troublemakers and this book focuses on three of them. The two Chartist leaders were at opposite poles. Samuel Holberry, a young revolutionary who died in York Castle aged only 27, has become a legendary figure in Sheffield history. Isaac Ironside, a democratic or 'moral force' Chartist, is less well known, but was perhaps the most colourful and flamboyant figure ever to be involved in Sheffield's local politics.

While the working class was struggling for the vote, the middle class was struggling for the repeal of the Corn Laws. No one was more eloquent in support of this cause than Ebenezer Elliott, the Poet of the Poor, who was briefly a Chartist but is remembered as the Corn Law Rhymer, the impassioned advocate of the repeal of the Corn Laws.

## Sheffield acquires Rail Links and a Town Council

The population continued to increase, from 92,000 in 1831 to 135,000 in 1851. Sheffield was the leading steel and cutlery town in the world. Links with the outside world improved with new railways. George Stephenson had left Sheffield out of his original rail network plans because of its hilly terrain. But in 1838 Sheffield gained a rail link to Rotherham, in 1840 a link to Derby via Rotherham and in 1845 a link to Manchester via Woodhead. The North Midland line opened up opportunities for rail travel to London and the whole elaborate system of coaches and horses from the *Tontine Inn* collapsed overnight.[1] Even if there was no direct line to Chesterfield until 1870, the new rail links would make possible the development of Sheffield's great steel works after 1850.

In 1842, Sheffield at last acquired a town council, which was initially dominated by Liberals like Thomas Dunn, a coal owner.

## *Vital Statistics*

We have a fascinating picture of Sheffield in this period thanks to G.C. Holland, Physician to the General Infirmary, who was persuaded by Thomas Ward to produce 'Vital Statistics of Sheffield'[2] in 1843. Holland argued that in Sheffield:

> The labouring classes are higher in intelligence, morality and physical condition than where machinery is extensively used as in Manchester, Leeds, Nottingham or Stockport. The middle classes are a greater proportion of the population than in these towns. The merchants and manufacturers among us are not men of large capital, exercising immense influence. They are far from treading on the heels of the aristocracy.[3]

Thus there was less misery, destitution and ignorance among the artisans and also less at the other extreme – opulence and extravagance – than in these other towns.

Holland also noted the middle class flight to the western suburbs with 'numerous villas, which adorn the neighbouring hills – the expensive establishments – the costly equipages – the manifest command of luxuries and comforts unknown to the same class of manufacturer forty years ago'.

As regards health, infant mortality was well above the national average. The mean age of death was 24.12, about the same as in Birmingham but well below the England and Wales average of 29.11. Reasons included the nature of Sheffield industry, which was 'extremely destructive of human life, perhaps to a much greater extent than the staple manufacture of any town in the Kingdom'. He refers to bronchitis, pleuritis, asthma, catarrh and phthisis and the special hazards faced by grinders. Another cause was 'dissipation', encouraged by the independent position of many workmen. Some artisans did not save for the bad times, but there was now a savings bank with 5,257 depositors. He deplored the employment of women and children in factories and the lack of a comprehensive system of education.

Holland was reassuring about housing. There were on average five people to a house and in general people occupied separate houses unlike other manufacturing districts. But he also referred to 'the crowding together of the working classes into narrow streets, filthy lanes, alleys and yards'. There was a need to attend to paving, drainage and sewerage.

## *The Poor Law Amendment Act, 1834*

Sheffield was used to running its own Poor Law arrangements. The Overseers of the Poor collected local rates and supported the poor either by 'outdoor relief' or in the workhouse, which in 1829 had been transferred from West Bar Green to the old cotton mill near Kelham Island. Being an Overseer of the Poor could be time consuming; in 1816 T.A. Ward often spent eight hours a day at the workhouse.[4]

Sheffield's Overseers of the Poor were disturbed by the Poor Law Amendment Act of 1834, which combined Benthamite reorganising zeal with Malthusian pessimism about over-population. Under the new law, the overseers were to be replaced by two new Poor Law Unions of Guardians – one for Sheffield and the other for Ecclesall. The overseers' anxieties were about the 'less eligibility' principle – the conditions of those on public relief were to be less attractive than the worst conditions elsewhere. The poor should no longer receive outdoor relief, but be compelled to enter the workhouse, thus breaking up families. Moreover, the bastardy clause imposed the responsibility for an illegitimate child on the mother unless she could prove paternity in court.

Sheffield's manufacturers were split about the new Poor Law. Some thought it less wasteful than the old Poor Law. Others, like Samuel Roberts, silver plate manufacturer, were deeply critical. Roberts wrote a series of angry pamphlets. The new law was both heartless and impractical. Local trades were subject to trade cycles. At times of depression, unemployed artisans could not be coerced by the threat of the workhouse into finding work, since there was no work to be had. Forcing families into the workhouse and splitting them up was socially destructive and made recovery much more difficult when trade picked up.

Working-class people were outraged. In April 1837, 5,000-6,000 people met in Paradise Square under Thomas Dunn's chairmanship. A clergyman described the new law as contrary to the spirit of Christianity, subversive, unconstitutional and oppressive. A resolution was passed saying in effect that the new law should not be implemented in Sheffield.

In May 1837, Mr Gulson, Assistant Poor Law Commissioner, came to Sheffield. An astute operator, he used flattery to disarm the opposition. He said that Sheffield had 'the most perfect specimen of the administration of the Poor Law I have seen'. He insisted that the overseers must be replaced by new Boards of Guardians but otherwise 'virtually no alteration' would be necessary. In other words, in times of bad trade such as obtained in 1837, the guardians could go on using outdoor relief. This was reassuring pragmatism.[5]

**25**   Nether Edge Workhouse. Drawing of 1840 by architect William Flockton, following Sheffield's reluctant decision to implement the 1834 Poor Law Amendment Act.

The Poor Law Commissioners then ordered the creation of the two new Poor Law Unions. The Overseers of the Poor were torn between this order and the resolution passed at the public meeting. They feared 'considerable odium' if they carried out the order. They put their dilemma to local magistrates. Hugh Parker, senior magistrate and a strong figure who had been involved in the arrest of revolutionary conspirators in 1817, took charge of the situation, becoming chair of the guardians of the new Sheffield Union.[6] From then on, the two unions for Sheffield and Ecclesall administered the new Act but they continued extensive outdoor relief. For example, in March 1843, a time of extreme depression, there were 594 in the Workhouse and 6,488 on outdoor relief,[7] but G.C. Holland noted that many people out of work were not claiming public relief, partly because of trade union support.

### Ebenezer Elliott – Corn Law Rhymer

In some ways, Elliott was in the tradition of Joseph Mather, the acerbic alehouse poet who lashed the Sheffield establishment in the 1780s and 1790s. But, unlike Mather, Elliott was a businessman rather than an artisan. Known as the 'Corn Law Rhymer', he was obsessed with a single political cause.

26   Ebenezer Elliott, 'Corn Law Rhymer', was involved for a time in Chartism but is mainly remembered as one of the most eloquent opponents of the Corn Law.

Elliott was born in 1781 in Masbrough, Rotherham, the son of a radical ironmonger and foundry owner. From his youth, Ebenezer loved the countryside, was drawn to poetry and was deeply moved by cruelty, as when he saw a lad publicly flogged for stealing a chicken.

Elliott became a partner in his father's business and then went bankrupt in 1816. In 1819, he and his family moved to Sheffield, where he set himself up as an iron and steel merchant in Burgess Street, with a warehouse in Gibraltar Street. Meanwhile, Elliott was developing as a poet, encouraged by the Poet Laureate Robert Southey (who deplored his politics) but, when he approached Lord Byron outside a Rotherham bank in 1813, he was treated discourteously.

Elliott blamed the Corn Laws for pushing up the price of food. In 1830, he founded the Sheffield Mechanics Anti-Bread Tax Society, the first organisation committed to the abolition of the Corn Laws. In 1831 his 'Corn Law Rhymes' were published and he gained a national reputation as 'The Poet of the Poor'. Thomas Carlyle, prophetic writer of the time, said his poetry had 'more of sincerity and genuine natural fire than anything that has come my way in recent years'.

Elliott is a paradoxical figure. He was an early Chartist and at mass meetings the Chartists sang his hymns about the rich oppressing the poor. The middle classes saw him as a noisy upstart. Yet here is what he said in 1843 about the 'undeserving poor':

> in the lanes and footpaths adjoining the town you might meet group after group of boys and young men, playing at pitch penny, or fighting their bull dogs and insulting every decently dressed passenger … The horrid words of the incipient sages and legislators; their ferocious gestures; their hideous laughter; their brutal bloated mindless faces appal and amaze the stranger; and in their looks thoughtful men see a catastrophe which is too probably destined to cast the horrors of the first French Revolution utterly into the shade.[8]

Elliott opposed universal suffrage because he believed many working-class people were unworthy of it, unless they underwent economic and educational self-improvement. He worried about the rugged independence of the Sheffield working class, for many of whom the 359 public houses[9] were more important than the churches and chapels. Arnold Knight, an enlightened medical man like Holland, commented: 'far too little is done by the middle classes to entice and allure the working classes from their vices and errors'.[10]

In 1830–2, Elliott assumed that parliamentary reform would lead to the repeal of the Corn Laws, so he merged his society into the Sheffield Political Union and campaigned vigorously for reform. When the Whigs failed to repeal the Corn Laws, he set up the Sheffield Anti-Corn Law Society in 1834. He then became involved in the early stages of Chartism. He was Sheffield delegate at a great Chartist public meeting in Westminster in September 1838 and then presided at a meeting back in Sheffield at which the charter was presented to local people. But when Parliament rejected the charter and some Chartists favoured violence, Elliott withdrew. He was always against violence: 'I would not hurt a fly, not even if it stung me.'

From 1834, Elliott lived in the house (which is still there) at the top of Blake Grove Road in Upperthorpe. It was built by John Blake, the Master Cutler who died in the cholera epidemic. Then in 1841, because of ill health, he retired to the obscurity of Great Houghton, about eight miles from Barnsley. He died in 1849, having seen the repeal of the Corn Laws in 1846. His life's work had not been in vain. His sonorous poetry had influenced events. The working people of Sheffield and Rotherham raised £600 for a statue of him, which was placed very centrally in Market Place where the High Street now is. Sadly, it is now far from the centre in Weston Park.[11]

**27**  Ebenezer Elliott's home in Blake Grove Road, previously the home of Blake, the Master Cutler who died of cholera in 1832.

**28**   The monument to Elliott as it was originally, in the Market Place looking towards High Street. It was removed in 1875 and placed in Weston Park, where it is today.

### Chartism

Chartism was extraordinary in drawing together the working classes to pursue democracy through the famous six points.[12]

In Sheffield,[13] Chartism drew on a variety of strands – the Jacobin tradition of the 1790s, the left-wing Methodism of the New Connexion and the resentment among working-class people at the outcome of the parliamentary reform movement. The growing trades unions in Sheffield were another strand, but they were ambivalent about whether Chartism, with its political focus, was the right way forward as opposed to more narrowly based trade union action.[14]

In late 1837, a group of local journeymen and others formed the Sheffield Working Men's Association (SWMA), which was soon in conflict with the middle-class liberals. On 1 December 1837, a meeting was convened at the town hall by the Master Cutler to petition for the secret ballot.[15] The SWMA's amendment calling for universal suffrage was defeated. The aggrieved SWMA issued an address in January 1838 that showed a working-class self-consciousness and sense of grievance that became characteristic of Chartism. The association was formed:

> because the members despair of ever obtaining social and political equality except by their own exertions. The working classes of this Kingdom produce the wealth that is at the disposal of the capitalists … and yet they are oppressed by unjust and unequal laws, and injured by the degrading forms and customs of the existing system of society.[16]

In 1837 a prolonged economic depression began, which continued with ups and downs until the mid-1840s. The apparent failure of capitalism to deliver prosperity added to the anger that drove the Chartists. Thus, one of the Sheffield Chartist leaders, William Gill, a scale cutter, said to the middle classes: 'Let them look to the streets, and say whether the present state of society had not the tendency to make the world a hell ... The capitalists of the country were producing misery.'[17]

In May 1838, the People's Charter was promulgated in London and Chartism took shape as a national movement. The SWMA remained weak, despite a visit from Feargus O'Connor, the charismatic Chartist leader and editor of the Leeds-based *Northern Star*.

On 25 September 1838, the SWMA organised a public demonstration of over 20,000 people, attracting people not only from Sheffield but also from nearby villages and Rotherham, Birmingham and Manchester. Speakers included Isaac Ironside and Ebenezer Elliott. The hard-line William Gill was elected Sheffield delegate to the national convention. In its determined proselytising among the working class, the SWMA was more like the SSCI of the 1790s (chapter 2) than the Sheffield Political Union of 1830-2 (chapter 3). In early 1839, the SWMA organised 'district' meetings in various public houses and boosted the weekly 'rent' collections to £50.

1839 was a year of intense Chartist activity. On Whit Monday, the two associations for Sheffield and Rotherham held a joint rally of 15,000-20,000 in Sheffield in Paradise Square, chaired by James Wostenholme, who had been jailed for six months in 1817 for his part in the group apprehended at a grinding wheel (chapter 3). By now, he was a small master file maker in his mid-50s.[18]

On 27 June O'Connor spoke again in Sheffield to speak at another meeting chaired by Wostenholme. A Female Radical Association was formed in the town − a sign of the growing politicisation of women.

In July, the Chartists' National Petition was rejected by Parliament, leading the Chartists into a crisis, with acute tensions between the advocates of physical force and those advocating 'moral force'. In Sheffield, the 'physical force' party were increasingly dominant. Ebenezer Elliott and Isaac Ironside ceased to be active Chartists around this time. The national convention reconvened in Birmingham. At a meeting in Paradise Square on 15 July, James Wostenholme was elected to replace the exhausted Gill as Sheffield's representative at the national convention.

More and more meetings took place, creating an atmosphere of confrontation in the town. There were calls to boycott 46 tradespeople who had refused to pay the Chartist 'rent'. On 20 July Sheffield magistrates banned the use of Paradise Square for meetings, whereupon the Chartists defiantly organised a sequence of meetings elsewhere and then held several 'illegal' meetings in Paradise Square.

The idea of striking for a 'sacred month' in August had been dropped by the convention but other activities continued in Sheffield with increasing intensity. Monday 12 August was a day of extraordinary disturbances, starting with a rally in Paradise Square at 9 a.m., followed by a march through the town and past the town hall, where Hugh Parker, the senior magistrate, warned them they were acting illegally. There was then a rally outside the Corn Exchange, followed by a further meeting in Paradise Square. On the next day, two Chartist leaders, Peter Foden and Charles Fox, were arrested and the magistrates banned all meetings. A huge crowd assembled outside the town hall, where their leaders were imprisoned. The Dragoons were called in and over 70 arrests were made as the streets were cleared. The magistrates sent Foden, Fox and a few others to York to await trial.

The Chartists then adopted a new tactic − churchgoings − reflecting their hostility to the established Church. On Sunday 18 August they attended morning service at the parish church en masse. They marched the short distance from Paradise Square singing one of Ebenezer Elliott's Corn Law hymns. They filled the church 'to the exclusion of the majority of respectable seat-holders'. They had asked the vicar to preach on the Epistle of St James Chapter 5 verses 1-6, which begin: 'Come now, you rich, weep and howl for the miseries that are coming upon you.' Instead, an assistant minister preached from Proverbs 24: 'My son, fear thou the Lord and the king: and meddle not with them that are given to change.' He warned the workmen of their wickedness and the desperate hazard they were pursuing.

On the following Sunday they came again. This time the sermon was on the text from James's Epistle, but adding verses 7-11, which include the exhortation to be patient for the coming of the Lord. The preacher told them that 'The troubles were sent by God and they must endure them. If they were poor, they must be contented, for if they were rich their responsibilities would be greater.' On the third Sunday, there was trouble when a seat-holder asked Chartists to vacate his pew for which he had paid £6 a year and they refused. The vicar and churchwardens asked the magistrates for protection the next Sunday. On Sunday 13 September, the police were at the church gates with cutlasses and 'only decently dressed individuals' were allowed to pass.[19] The Chartists could claim a moral victory.

In August and September, the SWMA had continued to expand with 700 new members. When the authorities banned Chartist meetings, they held small 'class' meetings on the Methodist pattern and then a 'silent meeting' in Paradise Square. On 11 September, as club-bearing contingents came out of neighbouring villages like militant Ecclesfield, there was fighting with the Dragoons, leading to the arrest of dozens of Chartists. They adjourned to Doctor's Fields to the south east of the town. Later on, they resorted to a disused quarry on Sky Edge – a symbolic meeting place of the early 1800s. Faced with repression, Wostenholme and several other leading Sheffield Chartists emigrated to the USA, as Gales had done.

On 22 September, they held the first of three 'Camp' meetings. Some 10-15,000 Chartist sympathisers gathered on Hood Hill, eight miles north of Sheffield. They sang a hymn by Ebenezer Elliott. Earl Fitzwilliam and his men from Wentworth watched from a distance. Other meetings were held at Attercliffe and in Loxley Chase. O'Connor addressed one last public meeting of SWMA but after this their public activity was confined to 'classes' and to educational and social activities at their Fig Tree Lane meeting rooms. But what was happening beneath the surface was far more significant.

### Samuel Holberry's Plot

More than any other of this book's troublemakers, Samuel Holberry[20] has become a cult figure in Sheffield. The cascades in the Peace Gardens have been dedicated to his memory. A street in Broomhall and an historical society have been named after him.

The key to Holberry's story is that, unlike most Chartist activists, he was an ex-soldier. Born in 1814 in a village near East Retford in Nottinghamshire, the son of an agricultural labourer, he enlisted at the age of 16 in the 33rd Regiment of Foot. In Northampton, he attended a night school and became disgusted with army life. In 1835, he bought himself out, destroyed every memento of his army past and moved to Sheffield, where he worked for a time as a rectifying distiller. Following redundancy, he worked for 10 months in a London distillery until his Sheffield employer invited him back. During this time in Sheffield and London he became immersed in working-class politics.

In the autumn of 1838, Holberry returned to Sheffield and joined the local Chartists at a time of growing activity. In August 1839, after the national petition had been rejected,

Holberry, a Baptist by origin, was a leader in the Sunday churchgoings. But the ex-soldier soon shifted to much darker designs.

The national plans of the physical-force Chartists at this time remain mysterious. They may have been disrupted by the arrest of numerous Chartist leaders across the country. Instead of co-ordinated nationwide action, there were sporadic outbreaks, notably the Newport rising of 4 November 1839. Armed men from the South Wales valleys marched into Newport, but troops opened fire and killed 22 of the Chartists. The rest fled. John Frost and two other leaders were arrested and sentenced to death, later commuted.

After Newport, Holberry was involved in efforts to mount a rising in the West Riding of Yorkshire. Later, in November, the Chartists tested out explosive shells in the nearby countryside and firebombed St Mary's, Bramall Lane, though the church was not seriously damaged. Holberry was one of a group of activists, including a bricklayer called Boardman, who represented them at meetings in Newcastle and London in December and chaired some of the sessions. Holberry toured South Yorkshire and the north Midlands mobilising support. On 9 January, he attended a final planning meeting in Sheffield with other leaders from Sheffield, Dewsbury and Barnsley and James Allen from Rotherham. They decided to act on the night of 11–12 January. At least eight 'classes' were to rise in Sheffield, supported by 'friends' from Eckington, Attercliffe and Rotherham. Dewsbury would rise independently and the Barnsley men would rise once they knew that the Sheffield rising was successful.

Holberry, the ex-soldier, made a careful military plan. The rising would begin with diversions on the outskirts of town – firing isolated magistrates' houses and the barracks,

**29**   Bust of Samuel Holberry now in Weston Park Museum. Holberry, a Chartist ex-soldier, led the last attempted military uprising in Sheffield in 1839.

placing a bomb in the police office – and similar diversions in Rotherham. They would assassinate any magistrates seen riding into town. The diversions would draw the military out of town, whereupon two Chartist assault groups of four classes each would seize the town hall in Waingate and the nearby *Tontine Inn* and barricade themselves in these 'Chartist forts'.

But Holberry had a traitor in his ranks. Some weeks earlier, John Bland, police chief of Rotherham, had heard rumours of an uprising and approached James Allen, a Rotherham Chartist, stove-gate fitter and at the time keeper of the *Station Inn* beerhouse in Westgate, Rotherham. Allen said he was in regular touch with the Sheffield Chartists and promised to inform Bland of the plans as they developed. He later reported the plan to seize the town hall and the *Tontine Inn*. With Allen's consent, Bland reported to Lord Howard of Barbot Hall, a West Riding magistrate and then informed Hugh Parker, a 67-year-old senior magistrate in Sheffield. Parker pooh-poohed this information.

The conspirators had suspicions about Allen and began to leave him out of their counsels. Desperate for information, Bland at length persuaded him to tell the plotters that he was now fully converted to the cause and would mobilise 150 men in support. This device worked. Allen attended secret meetings on three successive days and on 10 January reported to Bland that the uprising would take place the following night. Bland urged him to attend the final meeting and obtain details of the timing, the leading conspirators, their meeting places and their arms and ammunition stores. Allen went to this meeting. Bland and Lord Howard waited until after 7 p.m. for Allen to return, breathless and trembling with fear, but with the information.

Lord Howard galloped at full speed to Sheffield Police Office where he arrived at about 10 p.m. The police swung into action. A detachment of soldiers was called out. Holberry and his pregnant wife Mary were arrested at his home, 10 Eyre Lane. Some of the other leaders were arrested. The 'classes' were found and fled, hiding or throwing away their weapons – many in the dams and Crookes Moor. The plot had been foiled. Police ringed the town hall where the captive conspirators were held.

Following approaches by the Earl Fitzwilliam to the Home Secretary, Allen, whose life was thought to be in danger, was resettled in the South of England under an assumed name, until spotted there by someone from Rotherham, whereupon he disappeared. In order to protect him, the role of Rotherham police was hushed up until 1864, when the Sheffield press began to reveal the truth.

In March 1840, Holberry and seven of his associates were tried at York for 'seditious conspiracy' and found guilty. Holberry was given a four-year sentence in Northallerton House of Correction. The others got lesser sentences. Holberry was badly and illegally treated at Northallerton with five weeks on the treadmill and several months in solitary confinement. Chartist groups, particularly in Sheffield, petitioned for the release of these prisoners. Holberry's health deteriorated and in September 1841 he was moved to York Castle. By now, he was suffering from consumption and went into a hospital ward but, in June 1842, he died.

On 27 June 1842, Holberry was given a public funeral in Sheffield. Shops shut as a mark of respect or fear. Between 20,000 and 50,000 people lined the routes through the centre of the town to the General Cemetery, where his grave still can be seen.

Holberry's life and death became a Sheffield legend, inspiring new generations of Chartists. A poet called J. McOwen produced a poem entitled *Father, who are the Chartists?*:

> And they've sworn at a Holberry's grave, my child,
> That martyr so noble and grave, my child,
> That come weal or come woe,
> Still ONWARD they go
> Till freedom be won for the slave, my child!

For a young man of 27 to die in this way is full of pathos and it was understandable that the Chartists should build up Holberry as a martyr. But any more objective assessment of Holberry's actions needs to ask two questions.

First, was the use of force morally acceptable? Although some argued that the rejection of the national petition left Chartists with no option other than force, others felt that to resort to this was unacceptable and would discredit the movement. James Montgomery called Holberry's plot 'a scheme of murder, conflagration and pillage'. Others far more friendly to Chartism, like Ebenezer Elliott and Isaac Ironstone, moved away from it once violence was contemplated.

Secondly, did Holberry's plan have any chance of success? Even a sympathetic historian, John Baxter, referred to Holberry being 'lured into the blind alley of Blanquist-type insurgency', though he later qualified this as a value judgement.[21] Certainly, Holberry's plot

**30**   Holberry's grave in the General Cemetery. More than 20,000 people lined the streets for his funeral procession.

looks far more sophisticated than previous Sheffield plots in 1802, 1817 or 1820 and very nearly went into action. Holberry was unlucky to be up against a police chief as persistent as Bland and a turncoat as conscientious as Allen. But for these chance factors, the plot would have gone ahead and the town hall and the *Tontine Inn* might have been successfully seized. But what would have happened then? Even if there had been supportive risings in Barnsley, Dewsbury and a few other places, it seems unlikely that resistance could have been sustained for long. It was indeed a 'blind alley'. Holberry might have died not in a prison cell but in the heat of battle.

### Sheffield Chartism after Holberry's Plot

Following the failure of Holberry's plot,[22] Chartism went into abeyance. But in 1841–2 there was a revival with the arrival in the town of George Julian Harney (1817–97) as correspondent of the *Northern Star* and militant missionary. Harney orchestrated Holberry's funeral to foster a Chartist revival. Sheffield had joined the National Charter Association, whose local membership exceeded 1,000.

Chartist support was strengthened by the economic depression that was at its most severe in 1842–3, described as the 'the worst two years of the century'.[23] These were the years chronicled by Engels in his *Condition of the Working Class in England* (1845). In Sheffield in 1843, the bank bearing the names of two of the town's most distinguished families – Parker and Shore – collapsed.

Among the Sheffield Chartists, the big issue was how to respond to Parliament's rejection of their 1842 petition. There were intense debates in Paradise Square about whether to join parts of Lancashire in political strikes. Conscious of the weakness and hesitancy of the local trades unions at the time, Harney, formerly a militant, successfully advised against. Between 1842 and 1848 Chartists supported various industrial struggles, there was an increase in industrial violence, Chartist or Democrat councillors were elected and Chartist Land Plan ideas were launched. In 1843, Harney departed to Leeds to become sub-editor of the *Northern Star* and then editor in 1845.

In 1848, the French Revolution gave new heart to the Chartists and there was a series of great rallies and camp meetings. In June, there was a huge rally of 10,000 at which O'Connor spoke, but Briggs, a local Chartist leader with trade union links, had a nervous breakdown and died shortly afterwards. After this, the various Chartist organisations disappeared apart from the Democrat Party on the council, which is discussed below.

## Isaac Ironside

Isaac Ironside (1808-70)[24] had no sympathy with the physical-force Chartists. His brand of Chartism went far beyond the six points into education and democratic participation in decision-making.

Like Ebenezer Elliott, Ironside was born in a poor family in Masbrough. But soon after his birth in 1808, his family moved to Sheffield, where his father became a Congregationalist lay preacher and a successful estate agent. After education at Neepsend Lancasterian School, Isaac left school at 12 to become an apprentice stove-grate fitter. He attended the night school run by John Eadon and won a mathematical prize in the *Edinburgh Review*. Owing to ill health, he gave up his apprenticeship, joined his father's estate agency and became a successful 'accountant', so that by 1848 he was said to be worth several thousand pounds. He also became a rationalist.

Ironside was a precocious and irrepressible young man. Chapter 3 showed how in November 1830, at the age of only 22, he led the ultra-radicals calling for universal suffrage. Moderate liberal leaders like T.A. Ward accepted him as a council member of the Sheffield Political Union. In the 1832 election, he became T.A. Ward's campaign secretary, because of Ward's commitment to education. Ironside's passion for education led to his involvement in the Mechanics' Library and in 1833 in the foundation of the Mechanics' Institute.

Ironside continued to collaborate politically with the moderate liberals until December 1837, when he and other radicals despaired of Whig support for an extended franchise. Elliott observed: 'What is a Whig but a Tory and what is a Tory but a wolf?' At Sheffield's first full-scale Chartist demonstration in Paradise Square on 25 September 1838, Ironside spoke impressively, accusing the parliamentary reformers of betraying the people, calling for the six points in order to achieve national regeneration, including 'a thoroughly efficient system of education' as 'democracy to be successful must be intelligent'.

As the Sheffield Chartists became more violent, Ironside withdrew and focused on educational reforms. He had become frustrated by middle-class control of both the Mechanics' Library (where he was sacked as secretary for acquiring irreligious books) and the Mechanics' Institute (where controversial subjects were banned from the curriculum). He was converted to Robert Owen's rationalist socialism, which called for co-operation rather than competition. Ironside was prone to hero worship and Owen was the first of three heroes to whom he attached himself. Soon he was writing to Owen, beginning 'Dear Father' and saying, 'I am working hard and fast for the cause. I glory in it. May we soon prosper.'

In March 1839 Owen opened the Hall of Science initially in Buckingham Street and later in a new building in Rockingham Street.[25] Very much Ironside's project, the hall provided a day school for children and adult education and was also a church for the Universal Community of Rational Religionists (with Ironside as president of the Sheffield branch). It was registered as a place of worship and for the solemnisation of weddings. Finally, there was a social side. Ironside also wanted the hall to be a second home for its members, with festivals, balls, parties, soirées, masquerades, dancing classes and free instruction in choral singing.

G.J. Holyoake (1817-1906), later famous as a rationalist propagandist, joined the staff as 'social missionary', teaching at the day school and giving three lectures a week. Holyoake and his friends went to Barnsley to see Elliott who teased Holyoake with an anti-Communist poem:

> What is a communist? One who hath yearnings
> For equal division of unequal earnings.
> Idler or bungler, or both, he is willing
> To fork out his penny and pocket your shilling.[26]

Under Owen's influence, Ironside became interested in agrarian communities. In the 1840s, despair at the prolonged industrial depression led some Sheffield trade unions to acquire land that their members could work. Feargus O'Connor launched a Chartist Land Company to which 620 Sheffield Chartists subscribed. Similarly, in 1848, the Sheffield Poor Law Guardians leased 48 acres of moorland in Hollow Meadows for paupers to reclaim and grow crops – an unusual and short-lived experiment that Ironside staunchly defended against its critics.

It was a rural experiment that caused Ironside to break with Owen. As a board member of the Owenites' Queenwood agrarian community in Hampshire, Ironside smelled financial impropriety, called his fellow directors 'a nest of swindlers' and resigned in 1843. Owen accused Ironside of a want of common sense and honesty.

The Hall of Science continued to exist for several decades (see chapter 6). Its creation in 1839 probably stimulated other notable educational developments. The first was the Church of England Educational Institute. Then in 1842, the Rev. P.S. Bayley, Minister of Howard Street Congregational Chapel, set up the People's College in 1842, which in turn formed a model for F.D. Maurice's London Working Men's College. After Bayley left Sheffield in 1848, 16 young men determined to keep it alive and it survived until 1879.[27]

Meanwhile, Ironside returned to the Chartists when they saw opportunities for Chartist participation in the new town council. Cottage tenants who paid rates through their landlords could qualify to vote provided their names were registered.

In 1846, Ironside and a Chartist farmer called Briggs were elected to the town council as 'Democrats' in Ecclesall and Brightside respectively. Ironside enjoyed the irony that a Chartist should represent Ecclesall – 'the most powerful, wealthy, aristocratic and popular ward in Sheffield'. Thereafter, the Democrats built up to nine councillors in 1847, 15 in 1848, 22 in 1849 and 26 in 1852 out of a total of fifty-six. They had a Central Democrat Association to organise their elections, in contrast to the informal gentlemanly practices of the Liberals. Also, from 1851 onwards, the Democrats had their own newspaper, the *Sheffield Free Press*, which Ironside eventually dominated. Altogether, the Democrats were such a threat to Liberal dominance of Sheffield that Robert Leader, voice of the Liberals, accused them of 'arrogant demagoguism'.[28]

When Ironside joined the three-year-old council in 1846, it was regarded with 'indifference' in the town. Ironside soon changed this perception. He immediately began to 'smell out abuses' on the part of the councillors themselves, the police, the Poor Law Guardians, the Church Burgesses, the magistrates and the Midland Railway. His fellow councillors voted down the numerous motions he put forward, for example, that everyone in Attercliffe should be given a lollipop. But he saw his mission as educational, even, as he said, 'religious'. He was using the council forum to spread his Owenite philosophy. He did not see himself as a 'party leader' in the modern sense and in his early years on the council refused to vote. He had an anarchist belief in resolving issues by rational discussion.

Not surprisingly, Ironside acquired a reputation as 'Sheffield's Don Quixote'. But some of his campaigns were beneficial. At a time when public health desperately needed attention, he persuaded his fellow councillors to create a health committee, with himself as secretary. This committee appointed two surveyors, whose report showed Sheffield 'sitting on a dunghill'. Sheffield's working-class houses were not badly built; but there was a problem of badly sited rarely emptied privy middens (serving as many as 20 houses each) and unpaved yards whose surface was little more than hard-trampled excrement. The sewers were mostly made of rubble (which had helped to spread cholera) and the water supply was grossly insufficient.[29] These conditions were a challenge to the council which it was ill-equipped to tackle, but Ironside had helped to make the council more health conscious.

In 1848, Ironside played a valuable role in keeping Sheffield Chartists in constitutional channels. He was as excited by the French Revolution of 1848 as Gales had been by that of 1789. At a meeting in Paradise Square in March 1848, he obtained endorsement for an extraordinary communistic address that called on the French people to introduce 'a state of justice, peace and happiness', including a welfare state (with guaranteed employment, free education and provision for sickness and old age), the taking over of all wealth and a federation of all European states into one free republic. It was a mixture of Chartism, Owen, Proudhon, Mazzini and other influences. Ironside then went to Paris and presented the address to the French Parliament.

In the 1850s, Ironside's weaknesses – his uncritical hero worship, his indiscriminate inquisitorial tendencies, his impulsiveness and lack of consistency – gradually undermined the Democrat party. Having fallen out with Owen, his new guru was Joshua Toulmin-Smith, Anglo-Saxon scholar and constitutional lawyer, who was bitterly critical of the 'centralising' tendencies in British Government and called for 'Saxon' devolution to local communities. This appealed to Ironside because local assemblies would 'cause men to feel the want of intellectual discipline and to be desirous of learning how to think and speak'. He began promoting local assemblies or 'Wardmotes', which could be seen as forgotten precursors of today's area panels. In November 1851, the Ecclesall Wardmote began to meet with 40 people at its second meeting. Others were set up in St Philip's and St George's wards. They were to select and brief Democrat councillors and make pronouncements on domestic and foreign policy.

He tried to install Toulmin-Smith as parliamentary candidate, unwisely dropping his previous support for the fierce radical MP, John Arthur Roebuck, on grounds of alleged corruption. Roebuck vehemently denounced the 'loathsome patronage of a petty democratic chieftain'. Toulmin-Smith withdrew from a distasteful situation and Roebuck and a wealthy local Liberal, George Hadfield, won the election.

In the early 1850s Ironside became entangled in a succession of controversies. His Democrats conducted an illegal election for new aldermen. Then they helped to kill a local improvement Bill that would have given the town council wide-ranging powers over sewerage, building regulations, smoke pollution, markets, gas, cemeteries and so on. Ironside, who had been on the drafting committee for this bill, was accused of 'strangling his own baby'.

As chair of the Highways Board, his most notable – if illegal – achievement was to install deep drains in the city centre. He criticised the local gas company and set up his own rival company without parliamentary sanction. In scenes resembling an Ealing comedy, rival teams of navvies dug up and filled in trenches in the roads. There was a big explosion in Spital Hill. Eventually, his venture was quashed by the Court of the Queen's Bench and the two gas companies merged.

By now, Ironstone's erratic behaviour was seriously damaging the Democrats and they fought their last municipal election in 1854. But Ironside did not pull back. On the contrary, he found a new hero, David Urquhart, who promoted debate all over the country on foreign affairs from a platform of pathological Russophobia. Under Urquhart's and Ironside's influence, in September 1854, the first really big demonstration attacking the conduct of the Crimean War was held in Sheffield, probably stimulating Roebuck's later motion calling for an enquiry (chapter 5).

Ironside's newspaper, the *Sheffield Free Press*, became full of wild accusations that prominent people, including Lord Palmerston, the new Prime Minister, were Russian spies. One of its columnists was Karl Marx, who wrote articles on diplomatic history that were so long that Ironside said he was 'entombing the newspaper'. Unfortunately this remark was passed on to Marx, who took it as an insult, declined to provide further articles and was justifiably indignant when Ironside failed to send his fees. Marx's commented to Engels: 'Money is the only interesting point for me in my intercourse with these Calibans.'[30] This appears to be the only comment the great Communist philosopher made on the people of Sheffield. In June 1855, Ironside established the Sheffield Foreign Affairs Committee, which encouraged working men to study foreign policy and root out scandals.

After the Crimean War, Ironside and his causes went into decline. When he died in 1870, the local press recognised his honesty, energy and business acumen but found his public career beyond logical comprehension. There is something tragic about his frenetic energy being wasted through lack of judgement. But for this, his Democrats might have taken over the council 70 years before Labour eventually did so. Enthusiasm for devolution was unhelpful at a time when public health and other challenges required concentrated local authority action, as Birmingham under Joseph Chamberlain was soon to demonstrate. But Ironside's educational initiatives helped to pave the way for Sheffield's impressive educational advances later in the century.

In Ironside's latter years, working-class activism declined. Chartism and the Democrats belonged to the past. Sheffield politics was developing in new ways.

## Chapter 5

# The Age of John Roebuck

That a Select Committee be appointed to enquire into the condition of our army before Sebastopol and into the conduct of those departments of the Government whose duty it has been to minister to the wants of that army.

House of Commons Motion proposed by John Arthur Roebuck, MP for Sheffield, January 1855

Even as late as 1936 the phrase 'Don't John Arthur Roebuck me' was still used in Sheffield if one felt that a person was getting the better of one somewhat tendentiously in a heated argument.

Asa Briggs[1]

By the early 1850s, the working-class struggle for Chartism was largely spent, both nationally and in Sheffield. This chapter begins by considering the reasons for this decline. It goes on to look at a middle-class radical, John Roebuck, who was MP for Sheffield from 1849 until his death in 1879, except for the period 1868-74. His most famous moment was in January 1855 when, during the Crimean War, he tabled the Commons motion (see above), which brought down Lord Aberdeen's Government. This won him national fame and Sheffield was proud of him.

Roebuck, however, was by no means a typical radical. An unusually pugnacious man, who gave himself the canine nickname 'Tear'em', he went out of his way to upset the nonconformists who formed the backbone of the local Liberal Party. Nor did he reach out to the trade unions, which became increasingly important after the Parliamentary Reform Act of 1867. Instead, he helped to instigate the Sheffield Outrages Inquiry, which laid bare the activities of William Broadhead, the least savoury of the troublemakers described in this book.

Roebuck gradually became a Conservative in all but name, helping to shift the town's politics towards Conservatism. He was in conflict with rising radical Liberal politicians like Samuel Plimsoll, A.J. Mundella and H.J. Wilson. They were all successful businessmen fighting for humanitarian causes and sympathetic with the working classes. Despite their efforts, the Sheffield Liberals lost the initiative to the Conservatives. This chapter concludes by discussing why this happened.

## What happened to Working-Class Radicalism?

This book has traced a militant working-class radical movement in Sheffield right from the 1790s through to the huge Chartist demonstrations of 1848. But only a few years later in the mid-1850s, all the Chartist political organisations had disappeared or been merged into middle-class liberalism/radicalism.[2] Sidney Pollard writes: 'Few independent political working-class movements can be discerned during the generation following the defeat of

Chartism … by and large the leadership of the Liberal Party was meekly accepted until the middle 1880s.'[3] How are we to explain this?

It was not just a Sheffield phenomenon. Nationally, Chartism's defeat had created disillusionment, so that most Chartists ceased to be active working-class rebels. A penetrating historian, W.L. Burn, describes the period from 1852-67 as the 'Age of Equipoise',[4] an era of newly found stability after a time of troubles. Stability was bolstered by greater economic prosperity.

In some ways, Sheffield remained more radical than other towns. Until 1854, Ironside's Democrats offered a radical alternative to the middle-class Liberal establishment that ran municipal politics. Ironside's influence lingered on until 1864 through his chairmanship of the Highways Board. Moreover, Robert Leader's *Sheffield Independent* continued to provide a strong radical voice in Sheffield:

> the *Sheffield Independent* was more radical than either of its two contemporaries (the *Manchester Guardian* and the *Leeds Mercury*), just as Sheffield was more truly radical than either Manchester or Leeds. After 1846, most of the middle – and many of the working – classes in Manchester and Leeds settled down to a period of comparative conservatism. Peel had solved many of their problems and they made him their hero … In Sheffield the structure of the cutlery trade encouraged a more genuine and persistent radicalism. Sheffield welcomed Peel's work but did not make a hero out of him and it continued a radical city throughout the mid-Victorian years. Significantly, no statue of Peel was erected in Sheffield.[5]

But the working-class radical movement had undoubtedly declined. There are many possible explanations:

- The evident failure of Chartism
- 'Respectability': more prosperous working-class people were diverted by middle-class ideas of 'respectability', fostered by church and chapel, adult education, new savings institutions, middle-class political parties and so on[6]
- The attractions of the individualist ideology of 'Self Help', promoted by Samuel Smiles and others
- Workers were distracted from domestic issues into foreign affairs – a preoccupation with Britain's place in the world – by politicians such as Ironside and Roebuck from the time of the Crimean War
- The ambiguous political position of the trades unions, which had regarded its industrial role as more vital than Chartism; some Sheffield unions were rooted in the past and determined to maintain traditional practices; Sheffield unions formed an Association of Organised Trades, which they sought in 1866 to make nationwide, with a Sheffield base; but they then became engulfed in the scandal of the Sheffield Outrages.

Whatever the reasons for the decline of working-class radicalism, the flame never went out. There remained working-class radicals in the unions and elsewhere. Ironside's rationalist Hall of Science still existed. When, in 1876, Ruskin looked for people for St George's Farm, he was introduced to a group of 'Communists' ('Secularists, Utilitarians and Quakers') from a mutual help group established in the Hall of Science (chapter 6). Moreover, changes in Sheffield's industrial structure would in time help to promote a new wave of left-wing radicalism and trade unionism.

*Sheffield's Industrial Revolution*

From the 1850s onwards, Sheffield experienced an industrial revolution. As recently as 1843, G.C. Holland had said that 'The merchants and manufacturers among us are not men

**31**    Rolling armour plates for ships of war at John Brown's Atlas Works.

of large capital, exercising immense influence.' (Chapter 4.) This now began to change. The new Sheffield to Rotherham railway, opened in 1838, made possible the development of the large flat area of Attercliffe and Brightside as a centre for iron and steel production. Partly stimulated by the demands of the Crimean War, several great steel manufacturing firms emerged during the 1850s and 1860s. By 1872, John Brown employed 2,000 workers, Cammell 4,000 and Firth over 1,000. By 1890, Vickers employed 2,000 and Jessop's 1,200. Overall employment in Sheffield's 'heavy trades' quadrupled from 5,200 in 1850 to over 21,000 in 1891.

Conforming to the ideas of Samuel Smiles, these new princely manufacturers were mostly self-made men, though from fairly comfortable backgrounds.[7] They came from Yorkshire and several were from Sheffield trades. For example, Sir John Brown, son of a slater, in 1848 invented the conical steel buffer for railway coaches and wagons. In the 1850s he established the Atlas Works in Savile Street. In the 1860s he exploited Henry Bessemer's new steel-making process and developed rolling mills to produce smoother and more satisfactory armour plate for the Navy. Sheffield's growing importance in armaments production was indicated by the visit in August 1862 of the Prime Minister, Lord Palmerston, to Brown's home, Shirle Hall in Nether Edge. Palmerston was taken to see armour plate manufacture for himself.

Another example was Mark Firth, son of the head melter at Sandersons, a leading crucible steel producer. Mark, with his brother and father, set up a new steel business, which quickly became one of the largest in Sheffield, with premises again in Savile Street. By the 1860s, Firth was producing puddle steel for the major armaments manufacturers, particularly for large guns produced by Armstrong and Whitworth. By now, Firth was a very rich man who built a palatial residence for himself at Oakbrook in Ranmoor. These great manufacturers were public spirited, serving on the town council, the Cutlers Company and the school board and helping to promote higher education.

While steel manufacturing grew by leaps and bounds, the cutlery trades were also expanding in the prosperous period after 1850. The result was that the population grew from 135,000 in 1851 to 240,000 in 1871 – an extraordinary demographic surge.

The council and other local institutions could not cope with this transformation. The water company's efforts to supply more water led to disaster in 1864. There was much overcrowding in unsanitary slums in the central areas. In 1860, the council resolved that 'it is not expedient to consider the most efficient means for improving the sanitary condition of the borough.'[8] Effective drainage and sewage arrangements had to wait until the 1880s and 1890s.[9]

This, then, was the town which Roebuck was to represent for the best part of three decades – a town of hectic expansion, inadequate infrastructure, growing national awareness, middle-class radicalism and an uncertain mood among the working classes after the failure of Chartism.

### J.A. Roebuck's background

John Arthur Roebuck[10] (1802-79) came from an old Sheffield family. His grandfather, Dr John Roebuck, a pioneer of the Industrial Revolution, grew up in Sheffield and moved to Falkirk to found the Carron Iron Works. John Arthur Roebuck grew up in the outback in Canada, without a systematic schooling, but he read extensively. He was small and lame from an accident but self-confident and independent.

**32**   J.A. Roebuck, MP for Sheffield 1849-68 and 1873-9. At first seen as a radical, in later years he was dropped by the Liberals and backed by the Conservatives.

In 1824 he arrived in London to read for the bar and struck up a friendship with John Stuart Mill. This brought him to the hub of one of the most influential intellectual movements of the time – the utilitarians – just at a time when reform was in the air. J.S. Mill was tutor as well as friend, having 'a remarkable influence on my intellectual character'. Roebuck became an ardent utilitarian, dismissive of religion and sentiment and suspicious of 'sinister interests' like the aristocracy and the established church. In principle he favoured representative government, but with universal education as a prerequisite. Although initially involved in the drawing up of the Charter, on reflection he opposed movements like the Chartists and the Anti-Corn Law League as sectional or class-based.

Roebuck and J.S. Mill were not entirely bookish and intellectual. When revolution broke out in France in 1830, they rushed to Paris, met Lafayette and led the singing of the *marseillaise* at the opera in the presence of the new King, Louis Philippe. But relations between Roebuck and J.S. Mill cooled – according to Roebuck, over his questioning of Mill's relationship with Mrs Harriet Taylor, though Mill claimed the differences were literary and linked to Roebuck's lack of imagination.[11]

At the time of the Reform Bills, Roebuck worked for Francis Place, the famous radical campaigner. From 1832-7 and from 1841-7, Roebuck was radical MP for Bath. He also worked for greater autonomy for Canada. In the 1840s, he stood for *laissez-faire* radicalism, opposing action to alleviate the Irish famine and factory legislation designed to safeguard adults. In 1847, he lost his Bath seat to Lord Ashley.

### Roebuck Becomes MP for Sheffield

Roebuck wanted to return to Parliament. In 1849, a vacancy appeared in Sheffield. Leading liberals in Sheffield formed the Sheffield Reform Freehold Association to campaign for the secret ballot, free trade, extension of the suffrage and opposition to the extension of religious endowments. Alderman William Fisher, a Unitarian, who was to be Roebuck's closest supporter, invited him to Sheffield and he was adopted as candidate. He had the valuable support of Robert Leader Junior, owner and editor of the *Sheffield and Rotherham Independent*. One of the Chartist leaders, Thomas Clark, was suspicious of Roebuck's unwillingness to support payment of MPs and annual Parliaments but decided not to stand against him. His colleague, Ironside, supported Roebuck as an 'honest man'. However, Roebuck shrewdly commented to his wife: 'I am a sort of bulwark here by which the masters hope to be defended; the men fear while they are compelled to elect me.'[12] The election was uncontested and Roebuck was returned.

On election day, Roebuck made it clear that he would accept truth and knowledge wherever he found them and would not act at his constituents' beck and call. Most Sheffielders, including artisans, accepted him as a 'character' with strong principles. He was proud of his reputation for ferocity in debate: indeed, it was in a speech at the cutlers' feast in 1858 that he compared himself with 'Tear 'em' – the faithful guard dog in Walter Scott's Guy Mannering. By then, his actions during the Crimean War had made him a hero in Sheffield.

### The Crimean War

In 1854 Britain, France, Turkey and Russia blundered into the Crimean War. In Britain, war fever was fanned by paranoid propaganda from people like David Urquhart (chapter 4). The British and French armies, ill prepared for winter, became bogged down outside Sebastopol and beset by disease. The public was informed of this parlous situation by W.H. Russell, the *Times* correspondent.

Radical attitudes to war were divided. Back in Gales' time, radicals had strongly opposed the French Revolutionary War. In the 1850s, some radicals like George Hadfield, Roebuck's fellow Sheffield MP, were uneasy about the Crimean War, but this made them unpopular in Sheffield. The more common radical view was to see Russia as reactionary – the country that oppressed the Poles and had helped to suppress the Hungarian revolution in 1849. Thus, many radicals supported military action to curb Russia and in September 1854 Ironside, under Urquhart's influence, organised a meeting in Sheffield to challenge the conduct of the war (chapter 4). Roebuck himself was strongly patriotic and deeply critical of the incompetent administration of the armed forces.

In January 1855, Roebuck put down his motion calling for a Select Committee into the condition of the Army before Sebastopol and Hadfield seconded it. The motion had an electrifying political impact, prompting the resignation of Lord John Russell, a former Prime Minister. At the end of January, the debate took place. Roebuck was not well and collapsed when delivering his speech. Despite this, the motion was carried by 305 votes to 148, a staggering majority that caused Aberdeen's Government to resign.

The Sheffield press was ecstatic about Roebuck's patriotic action. The *Sheffield and Rotherham Independent* declared: 'we are glad that the public voice has found a spokesman in the House of Commons so able and fearless as our member.'

The *Iris* asserted:

> Let Mr Roebuck take heart; his burning words cannot express the deep seated shame with which the disgraceful past is viewed in Sheffield; nor the firm resolve which exists to bring the authors of our loss to exposure and punishment. We trust he will persevere, be the consequences what they may.[13]

Palmerston took over as premier. Roebuck insisted on going ahead with a Committee of Inquiry under his chairmanship, but was disappointed with the outcome. Like Ironside he was inclined to conspiracy theories, for he later declared that:

> There was brought before me a scheme of imbecility and corruption of which I can give you no idea. I felt, as I walked, the very ground palpitate under me with putrefaction; but things were so artfully managed – and we had no power to make men speak out – that we could not discover it … Though we felt it at every step we took, we could not bring it out.[14]

Roebuck put forward to the Commons a series of stinging resolutions, attacking Government administration, but these resolutions were voted down. Roebuck became chair of the Administrative Reform Association, which campaigned for reform but was overly focused on competitive examinations for civil services clerks. Roebuck helped to stimulate administrative reform but his lack of administrative experience made him ill-equipped to mastermind it.

Sheffield had other links with the Crimean War. Nearly all the steel used by British troops in the war came from Sheffield. Moreover, Florence Nightingale came from the Sheffield family of the Shores. Her grandfather was William Shore, a Sheffield banker who lived in Shore Lane at old Tapton Hall. (Its successor, built for Edward Vickers in 1855, is now a masonic hall.) Her father, William Edward Shore, changed his name to Nightingale to receive an inheritance. He was a nephew of the radical Unitarian and parliamentary reformer Samuel Shore, whose grandchildren caught George III's eye on the beach in Weymouth (Introduction and chapter 1). Florence knew Sheffield well. During her childhood, her family spent part of each year at their home near Matlock and had holidays with relations in Sheffield, both at Tapton Hall and at Norton Hall where her

**33**  The Crimean War Memorial, 1890, in its original position at Moorhead, at the junction of Sheffield Moor and Union Street. Florence Nightingale was one of the subscribers. Without its column, it is now in council storage.

uncle, another Samuel Shore, lived. She and her family donated money to the memorial to Sheffield soldiers who died in the Crimean War. This memorial initially stood on a column in Moorhead. In 1957 it was cut off from its supporting column and was installed for a time in the botanical gardens, but is now in council storage.[15]

### Roebuck – The National Figure

The Crimean War made Roebuck a prominent national figure, but did not change his style. Nominally Liberal, he increasingly sympathised with the Conservatives on controversial issues. He focused on foreign affairs and took a consistently patriotic stance, rather like W.S. Gilbert's satire of patriotic complacency *The Englishman*.

Roebuck was contemptuously indifferent towards liberal views on foreign affairs. He had no sympathy with Italian unification. In Vienna in 1860-1 he expressed support for the Emperor of Austria's occupation of Venetia. *Punch* published an amusing cartoon showing the Emperor stealing a dog called 'Tear-em', a 'Sheffield terrier'. During the American Civil War, unlike virtually all radicals, he called for the recognition of the Southern Confederate states, because of his disillusionment with North American democracy. He even described the sufferings of aborigines in the colonies as a necessary evil.

The positions he took up on foreign affairs alienated his Sheffield supporters, including the influential Robert Leader, editor of the *Sheffield Independent*.

### The Battle of the Newspaper Editors

In 1819-20 local radicals founded the *Sheffield Independent* to promote their kind of politics in Sheffield. In 1833 the 23-year-old Robert Leader Junior[16] (1809-85) took over the editorship (chapter 3). Leader was grandson of a silver plate manufacturer and had served an apprenticeship under Montgomery on the *Iris*. He edited the *Independent* for 42 years, making it an influential Liberal newspaper that fought strongly for free trade and against state interference in education, which Leader, as a Congregationalist, feared would strengthen the Church of England. After ceasing his editorship in 1875, he became president of the Liberal Association and joined the town council, but long before that he was a leading figure in the Sheffield Liberal Party, trying to hold its fissiparous elements together. On his departure, neither of his sons wished to take on the editorship.

By 1864, Leader had edited the *Independent* for over 30 years. It must have been a shock for him when in that year William Leng (1825-1902) took over the *Sheffield Daily Telegraph* as part-owner and managing editor which he remained until his death in 1902. Under Leng, the *Telegraph* built up a larger circulation than the *Independent*. From his beginnings as a Wesleyan Methodist and Liberal from Hull, Leng had become an evangelical Anglican and Conservative, 'because of his love of order and stability'.[17]

Leng transformed the *Telegraph* into an influential voice for Conservatism. Complementing Leader's role in the Liberal Party, he became the voice of the local Conservative Party. He was behind both the return of Roebuck in 1874 and the selection of Stuart-Wortley as his successor. He created the Conservative organisation in Sheffield and promoted working-men's clubs. After his death, a council colleague said that Sheffield Conservatives had lost 'almost the author of their

**34** Robert Leader Junior, editor of the *Sheffield Independent* from 1833 to 1875, was a leading figure in the Liberal Party in Sheffield until his death in 1885.

existence'.[18] He was knighted in 1887. Following the model of Joseph Chamberlain's Birmingham, he preached a 'civic Gospel' and was 'not ashamed to say he was a Socialist'. This did not mean that he was an egalitarian, but that he favoured municipalising services that could bring in an income to the authority.

From 1864 to Leader's retirement in 1875, Sheffield had two editors who 'preferred bare knuckles to gloves when fighting'.[19] The Sheffield flood and the trade union outrages enabled Leng to display his talent for investigative journalism and his crusading zeal.

## The Sheffield Flood

The disastrous Sheffield Flood of 1864 occurred when the embankment of the new Dale Dike Reservoir gave way, causing the deaths of 240 people. The Board of the Waterworks Company included various prominent Liberals. Leng, though new to Sheffield, quickly seized the opportunity to undermine the Liberal establishment dominating the town council. He accused the town council of culpably failing to act effectively against the water company despite its gross neglect. The town council in fact wanted to take over the supply of water from the company, but received no help from Roebuck, a believer in *laissez-faire* economics, who opposed municipal aggrandisement of this kind. It was not until 1888 that the council eventually, after many vicissitudes, took over the waterworks.

## The Sheffield Outrages

Deep in Sheffield's past lay a practice called 'rattening', which meant disciplining an errant grinder by removing or destroying the bands, which connected his grindstone with the revolving shaft.[20] Sometimes union members went beyond 'rattening' into violent attacks.

**35**   Sir William Leng, part-owner and editor of
the *Sheffield Telegraph* from 1864 to his death in
1902. He built up the Sheffield Conservative Party.
During the Outrages Inquiry, he had a loaded
revolver on his desk.

These incidents included the murder, with a shot from an air gun, in 1859 of James Linley, a saw-grinder, and a gunpowder explosion in 1861 in the house of George Wastnidge in Acorn Street, causing the death of a woman lodger. The last straw was the explosion in October 1866 in the house of Thomas Fernehough, a saw-grinder, in New Hereford Street off the Moor. This triggered an outcry among manufacturers, who offered £1,000 for information. The trade unions protested their innocence and offered £100.

Even more than Roebuck, Leng played a key role in calling for a Government inquiry. He showed courage in suggesting in his paper that the man behind the outrages might be William Broadhead, secretary of the Saw-Grinders' Union and proprietor of the *Royal George Hotel* in Carver Street; Leng himself received threatening letters from 'Mary Ann'. Broadhead was one of the most prominent trade union leaders in Sheffield and was treasurer of the Sheffield 'Association of Organised Trades'. Far from admitting guilt, Broadhead wrote letters to the press deploring violent incidents. Contemporaries noted that Broadhead 'had no resemblance to the common idea of an assassin or a conspirator, but is a jolly corpulent man, apparently satisfied with life'.[21]

In November 1866 the two MPs, Roebuck and George Hadfield, led a deputation of civic leaders and employers to Spencer Horatio Walpole, the Home Secretary, to call for an inquiry. Later, the MPs joined a similar trade union deputation. The Government decided to hold a Royal Commission on the trade unions, including an inquiry into the Sheffield outrages. Roebuck served on the Royal Commission, aggressively interrogating union representatives, but was not on the Sheffield inquiry.

As it was going to be difficult to break down trade union secrecy, Roebuck persuaded the Home Secretary that, most unusually, a certificate of indemnity should be given to any lawbreaker who made a full and truthful confession. This proved critical to the inquiry.

The inquiry into the outrages was extraordinarily dramatic. Various artisans and union officers spoke about the prevalence of rattening. Gradually, the evidence began to point to Broadhead. George Shaw, threatened with prosecution for perjury, admitted that, after receiving instructions and gunpowder at Broadhead's *Royal George Hotel*, he had blown up 'Old Topsy' Helliwell, a non-union member, at the Tower Wheel. Even more telling was the evidence from Joseph Hallam, a saw-grinder. He was reluctantly persuaded by the chief constable, John Jackson, to appear in court but then his courage then failed him. He was committed to gaol for six weeks for Contempt of Court. When, after further persuasion by Jackson, he returned, he fainted in court and then attempted to strangle himself in his cell. Jackson prevented this and got him back into court. With Broadhead watching him closely, Hallam then described how, on Broadhead's instructions, he and

Samuel Crookes had blown up Wheatmen and Smith's works and had shot Linley. Samuel Crookes confirmed this story in every detail.

After these revelations, Broadhead confessed to his involvement in various violent incidents. The number of rattening cases he had arranged ran into three figures. He was, as promised, given immunity by the commission. The vicar of St Matthew's, Carver Street, raised a collection to enable him to depart to the United States, but Broadhead was unable to secure employment there and returned in 1870 to Sheffield, where he was 'a very lonely and much avoided man'.[22] He died in 1879.

The commission reported that, of 60 trade unions in Sheffield, only 12 had resorted to outrage. However, these 12 had been very active: altogether, the commission heard of 166 rattenings, 20 outrages, 22 threatening letters and 12 cases of intimidation in 10 years. There was a shocked reaction among the middle classes and in the press. The *Sheffield Independent* reported: 'the deep impression of shame which every Sheffield man must feel that the good old town should have been placed in the pillory of public scorn and made a scoffing and a bye-word not to England only but to the whole civilised world.'[23]

But this was not the universal reaction. Isaac Ironside argued that 'all the trades outrages, strikes and rattenings are the inevitable consequences of the one-sided and unjust laws.'[24] In a letter to Thomas Hughes, author of *Tom Brown's Schooldays*, he wrote:

> all those who get a living from a trade are bound to obey the laws of the Union of that trade. After entering a trade, it is not a voluntary act of theirs to become a member of that Trade's Union. It is their duty to thrash all into submission who get their living by the trade and who will not obey the laws of their union without thrashing ...[25]

Many working men agreed with this view.

What are we to make of these events in Sheffield, coming several decades later than the similar violence of Luddism in other industrial centres? Sidney Pollard's 1954 analysis of the 'ethics' of the outrages[26] followed the maxim '*Tout comprendre, c'est tout pardonner.*' He argued that: 'A study of the Sheffield outrages is not so much a study of crime as a study of social relations.' The Sheffield light trades were a throwback to the 18th-century guild tradition – 'a hermetically sealed world uninfluenced by the world around'. These skilled manual workers were vulnerable to fluctuations in trade. The Cutlers' Company had ceased to protect their position (chapter 1), so the artisans sought protection through the strength of their trade unions.

The most violent union was the Saw-Grinders' Society, whose members had only recently emerged from isolated waterwheels in the river valleys to steam-driven wheels in the town. In the 1840s and 1850s, the society had 200 members and high pay rates. When a recession began in 1857, the union under Broadhead's leadership decided to preserve high wage rates by excluding newcomers and paying 50 to 80 of their 200 members to be 'on the box' or unemployed for long periods. This system required increasingly tough enforcement. Thus Linley was shot because he had offended union rules by switching from scissor-grinding into better paid saw-grinding and then by taking on seven or eight apprentices, who became an added burden for the union to carry. Pollard reports that: 'Among Sheffield craftsmen, not only were the agents of violence not considered criminal, but the victims were held in opprobrium as convicted offenders.'[27]

Roebuck had no sympathy with these arguments. In January 1868, he gave a lecture on 'Capital and Labour' in which he criticised the unions for interfering with the working-man's right to support his family by honest industry and said that most strikes were 'conspiracies'.

**36**  William Broadhead, secretary of the Saw-Grinders' Union and proprietor of the *Royal George Hotel* in Carver Street. He was exposed as responsible for the Sheffield outrages.

Rattening did not die out after the Royal Commission. Fifty-six cases were reported in the next 20 years, about a third of which involved saw-grinders. The practice only died out with the decline of the old type of trade society.[28]

### Parliamentary Reform and the General Election of 1868: Roebuck, Plimsoll and Mundella

Alongside the drama over the outrages, there was a national debate about extending the franchise. Sheffield Liberals were split between those like the veteran Liberal Thomas Dunn, who opposed manhood suffrage, and others who favoured it, like Samuel Plimsoll[29] (1824-98), a rising businessman and Liberal politician, who was president of the local branch of the Reform League.

Plimsoll's family had moved to Sheffield in 1838. He left school at 15 and later became clerk to Thomas Birks, managing director of Rawson's Brewery, who in 1850 became Mayor of Sheffield. The young Plimsoll organised the Sheffield Court at the 1851 Exhibition in Crystal Palace. A natural entrepreneur, he also devised plans for new rail transport arrangements to bring South Yorkshire coal to London, but was thwarted by the existing monopolists and became bankrupt and destitute. His spell in a London lodging house gave him a lasting sympathy with the underdog that may have motivated his support for parliamentary reform.

His fortunes improved when, in 1857 in Ecclesfield Church, he married Eliza Railton, stepdaughter of John

**37**  Samuel Plimsoll made a fortune in coal transporting and became leader of the reform wing of the Sheffield Liberals before he began his famous campaign about safety at sea.

Chambers of Newton Chambers, who owned Thorncliffe Colliery. Chambers's backing helped Plimsoll to build up an enormous coal transporting business, aided by his own inventions. By 1866, he and Eliza had a London house and a country house – Whiteley Wood Hall on the edge of the Mayfield valley in Sheffield. Plimsoll led local campaigning for parliamentary reform with great energy.

On 21 January 1867, a big reform demonstration was held in the Haymarket, at which Ernest Jones, former Chartist leader, spoke. Roebuck was absent through genuine illness, but was suspected of betrayal. On 6 May Plimsoll chaired a big meeting in Paradise Square, which condemned Roebuck and praised Hadfield, Sheffield's other Liberal MP. Two weeks later, the Prime Minister, Disraeli, astonished everyone by proposing and then accepting an opposition amendment to a Bill that led to a form of household suffrage far more radical than anything that the Liberals had proposed.

As a result of the 1867 Act, the Sheffield electorate trebled from 9,000 to around 28,000,[30] so that many workers could vote for the first time. The ensuing General Election of 1868 was the most gripping election in Sheffield since 1832. It was a duel between Roebuck and a new Liberal champion, A.J. Mundella.

A.J. Mundella (1825-97) was a rising Gladstonian Liberal. He was the son of an Italian émigré, grew up in Leicester, left school at 11 and was apprenticed to a hosiery firm. From these humble beginnings, he became a highly successful hosiery manufacturer in Nottingham. He was deeply interested

**38**  Mundella, a radical Liberal from Nottingham, who challenged Roebuck in Sheffield in 1868. Cartoon by Spy from *Vanity Fair.*

in education, industrial relations and improving the conditions of working people. He pioneered the use of industrial arbitration to resolve disputes. William Dronfield of the Association of Organised Trades identified him as a potential Liberal candidate for Sheffield, capable of reconciling capital and labour after the damage done by the outrages. He was a shrewd choice.

The selection of Mundella reflected not only trade union views but also the exasperation of leading Sheffield Liberals, like Robert Leader, with Roebuck's illiberal views on foreign policy, his closeness to the Conservatives over parliamentary reform, his criticism of teetotallers as 'canting hypocrites' and his opposition to the disestablishment of the Irish Church – an attractive cause to nonconformist Liberals who wanted general disestablishment. Finally, Roebuck accused the Liberal leader, Gladstone, of 'disregard of political honour'.

Plimsoll and his branch of the National Reform League called on Roebuck to resign. The Sheffield Liberals decided to switch their support to Mundella, while retaining support for Roebuck's fellow MP George Hadfield, a conventional and wealthy nonconformist Liberal.

The election was hotly contested and aroused national interest. The meeting in Paradise Square on 20 July 1868 was said to be the largest since Brougham came to Sheffield in 1830.[31] Much mud was slung on all sides. Leng vilified Mundella as a foreigner and bad employer. The Liberal press accused Roebuck of corruption. The brewers pledged £500 towards Roebuck's expenses. Among his supporters was, of all people, William Broadhead, who claimed wrongly that Roebuck endorsed a policy of making union dues 'recoverable in the courts'.[32] Plimsoll opened up his Whiteley Wood home to the South Yorkshire miners, so that they could hear Mundella speak.

For the first time, Roebuck was rejected by Sheffield. The voting was as follows:

| | |
|---|---|
| Mundella | 14,793 |
| Hadfield | 12,212 |
| Roebuck | 9,571 |
| E.P. Price (Conservative) | 5,272 |

**39**  'The Sheffield races' – the jockeys are the candidates for the 1868 election in Sheffield. Mundella is shown as fallen from his horse, but in fact won the election.

## The General Election of 1874: Roebuck, H.J. Wilson and Joseph Chamberlain

After this defeat, the 66-year-old Roebuck was expected to retire to spend his last years with his wife and daughter. But he still accepted Sheffield engagements, sounding less and less like an iconoclastic radical. At a banquet in honour of the Duke of Norfolk, he praised the benefits that distinguished families conferred on the community. At a Church of England Educational Institute soirée, he called the established Church 'an instrument for doing good'.

The next General Election was due in 1874. The Liberals were content for Mundella to continue as one of their candidates, but faced a dilemma as to who should succeed George Hadfield, who was standing down. They had no wish to recall Roebuck, but Leng and other Conservatives shrewdly persuaded him to stand as their candidate, even if his name still appeared on the voting paper as 'liberal'.

The Liberals suffered a serious split over the succession to Hadfield. This was due to Henry Joseph Wilson[33] (1833-1914) – a true troublemaker who possessed an unresting nonconformist conscience. He was grandson, through his mother, of the Sheffield smelter Joseph Read. His aunt was the ardent Sheffield anti-slavery campaigner Mary Anne Rawson (chapter 9). He grew up in an intense Congregationalist household in Nottinghamshire.

THE AGE OF JOHN ROEBUCK

In 1866, he moved to Sheffield to join his brother John Wycliffe in reviving the Sheffield Smelting Company. They diversified into standard silver with great success. He fought for nonconformist causes such as Temperance, placing a notice outside his house inviting people to sign the pledge. He did much to build up Sheffield's schools, but bitterly opposed state support for Anglican and Roman Catholic schools and refused to pay local rates.

Wilson disliked Roebuck, whom he called 'Beelzebub's envoy extraordinary'. But Wilson also fell out with Robert Leader, head of the Sheffield Liberals. The reasons are interesting. Wilson and his wife, Charlotte, had joined Josephine Butler's fight against the Contagious Diseases Act and campaigned for more humane treatment of prostitutes. Much to Wilson's chagrin, Leader in the *Independent* criticised Charlotte for 'meddling with a subject too nasty to be touched'.

Robert Leader backed A.J. Allott, a local accountant, as Liberal candidate. But Wilson and others formed the Sheffield Reform Association and persuaded Joseph Chamberlain to stand. Chamberlain was a rising radical force in Birmingham and stood for 'Free Church, Free Schools, Free Land and Free Labour'. Mundella was disturbed by the split in the Liberal ranks and suggested an umpire or a test vote. Eventually, a test vote took place

**40**   H.J. Wilson MP. From a smelting family, he was a passionate Liberal who fought for many causes.

at a huge meeting in Paradise Square on 29 January 1873 and Chamberlain was successful. Allott withdrew, but his name still appeared on the ballot paper. The voting was:

| | |
|---|---|
| Roebuck | 14,193 |
| Mundella | 12,858 |
| Chamberlain | 11,053 |
| Allott | 621 |

Roebuck and Mundella were successful, with Roebuck top of the poll, thanks to strong support from the Conservatives – the big manufacturers, the breweries and many of the moderate middle classes. This election began the Conservatives' success in parliamentary politics in Sheffield. Chamberlain returned indignantly to Birmingham and never stood again in Sheffield.

### Roebuck's Last Years

In his last Parliament, Roebuck still sat on the Liberal benches but supported Disraeli's Conservative Government. Mundella described Roebuck as 'the delight of the Tories'. Roebuck said: 'I am in politics a Liberal but I am an Englishman first and *then* a politician.' In 1878, he was appointed to the Privy Council. In 1879, he died.

In a fragment of autobiography, Roebuck gave a gloomy verdict on his career. He had taken part 'in the most important transactions as regards the country, yet perhaps having little influence'.[34] His former friend, J.S. Mill, was more damning: 'he gradually ceased to be the champion of any important progress; he became the panegyrist of England, a conformist to the Church and in short merged in the common herd of Conservative liberals.'[35]

Roebuck's mature political philosophy, combining *laissez-faire* economics with patriotic imperialism, bears some resemblance to that of Margaret Thatcher, but he lacked her political adroitness. Nor could he point to the solid legislative achievements of his younger rival Mundella. Roebuck had his finest hour in 1855. His very curmudgeonliness made him popular with Sheffield people who, except in 1868, tolerated his eccentricities and admired his courage and independence. But by the 1860s he had ceased to be a force for radicalism.

### The Radical Liberals and the Decline of Liberal Sheffield

The aged Roebuck was very different from younger radical Liberals like Plimsoll, Mundella and H.J. Wilson, who energetically supported 'reformist' causes at home and abroad and reached out to the trades unions and working classes.

Plimsoll ceased to be a force in Sheffield politics. In 1868 he became MP for Derby and in 1870 he took up the cause of the safety of merchant seamen, which made him internationally famous but also forced him to sell Whiteley Wood Hall to pay for litigation.

Mundella remained one of Sheffield's Liberal MPs from 1868 until his death in 1897. He became an extremely active private member, then in effect education minister and finally President of the Board of Trade, responsible for important legislation. He was too busy in Westminster to play a major role in Sheffield. But his achievements were such that he was probably Sheffield's most distinguished MP.

After the fiasco of the 1874 General Election, H.J. Wilson continued to be influential in the Sheffield Liberal Party, but henceforth he tried to collaborate with Robert Leader. He was MP for Holmfirth from 1885 to 1912. He sided with Gladstone rather than Chamberlain over Home Rule for Ireland, turning Chamberlain's picture to the wall and writing 'Judas from Birmingham' on the back. He attacked the opium trade in India and the Boer War. Like Mundella, Wilson was sympathetic with the trade unions and favoured 'Lib Lab' candidates in working-class constituencies.

H.J. Wilson's family home was a hive of political activity, dominating Liberal politics in the east end of the city. In 1883, he moved to Osgathorpe Hills between Pitsmoor and Grimesthorpe. He had a drawing room big enough for a meeting of 70 people. He was anti-imperialist and a 'pro-Boer'. He led a family of political activists. His brother, John Wycliffe Wilson, was a leading city councillor and his sons and daughter would become politically active (chapters 8, 9 and 10). However, his moral crusades did not necessarily strengthen his party. Unlike the pragmatic party manager, Robert Leader, he expected potential Liberal candidates to support all his numerous causes.[36] Temperance policies helped the Conservatives, who used public houses as recruiting grounds. Opposition to the Boer War was highly unpopular in Sheffield.

By the 1880s, Sheffield's once-mighty Liberal Party was not in a healthy state. Roebuck's switch to the Conservatives had taken many supporters with him. Leng was a brilliant propagandist and organiser for the Conservative cause: Mundella called him the Conservatives' 'evil genius'. The new princely manufacturers supported the Conservatives because they felt that Liberal free trade was threatening their businesses.

The Liberals had also failed to promote Sheffield's civic development. Mundella wrote to Leader:

> I see a pretty state of things in your Municipality. Everything is mean, petty and narrow in the extreme … Sheffield would do well to spend half a million on improvements. A better town hall might be followed by better Councillors and more public spirit … I wish you would preach the duty of the wealthy intellects of Sheffield that they share in the elevation of the town.[37]

**41**  H.J. and Charlotte Wilson and their children and grandchildren at the family home, Osgathorpe Hills in Pitsmoor in 1908. They were a highly political family.

Unfortunately for the Liberals, it was the Conservatives who would take this message on board, though the Liberals did fight for a new town hall.

Robert Leader, who had done so much to hold the party together, died in 1885. His successors faced the overriding dilemma of the party's stance towards the working classes. The radical Liberals were sympathetic with the trade unions and the aspirations of working people. But a new generation of Liberals, led notably by William E. Clegg, saw things differently (chapter 10).

This chapter began with the decline of working-class radicalism after 1850 and ends with the decline of middle-class radical Liberalism. But under the surface a new socialist radicalism was emerging.

*Chapter 6*

# Ruskin, Carpenter
# and Early Sheffield Socialism

There is no wealth but life.

John Ruskin, *Unto this Last*

To establish, instead of a National Debt, a National Store.

John Ruskin, *Fors Clavigera*, July 1876

From the first I was taken with the Sheffield people. Rough in the extreme, twenty or thirty years in date behind other towns, and very uneducated, there was a heartiness about them, not without shrewdness, which attracted me. I felt more inclined to take root here than in any of the Northern towns where I had been.[1]

Edward Carpenter

> *England arise! The long long night is over.*
> *Faint in the East behold the dawn appear*
> *Out of your evil dream of toil and sorrow-*
> *Arise, O England, for the day is here;*
> *From your fields and hills, Hark the answer swells –*
> *Arise, O England for the day is here!*

Socialist Marching song by Edward Carpenter

Sheffield's serious socialist tradition dates back to the 1870s and 1880s. Up until then, Sheffield's radical movements had been mainly about liberty and democracy, though with a tinge of socialism all along. It was in the 1870s and 1880s that a more explicit socialism emerged in Sheffield, which owed much to John Ruskin and Edward Carpenter.

Whereas Roebuck strongly supported the *laissez-faire* economics of Victorian Britain, Ruskin and Carpenter were bitterly opposed to it. They sought fundamental changes in society through a form of socialism that was spiritual and cultural, concerned with individual fulfilment and personal relationships. Carpenter was an ardent egalitarian, whereas Ruskin believed in a hierarchical society.

They were both drawn to the city by the spirit and skill of its workers, but they experienced Sheffield in very different ways. Ruskin's actual presence in Sheffield was confined to a few short visits, yet he left the lasting legacy of the Ruskin Museum, which is still with us, and the memory of the 'communist experiment' in Totley. Carpenter lived in or near Sheffield for 44 years. He was largely forgotten for a time, but since the 1960s has been acclaimed for his early advocacy of sexual liberation, as well as his role as a founding father of British socialism.

The two men belonged to different generations. In 1879, when they first were in touch with each other, Ruskin was a famous national figure aged 60, whereas Carpenter was still an unknown man of thirty-five. Ruskin influenced Carpenter's thinking.[2] Both were drawn to rural life as an alternative to urban squalour and exploitation. Both were charismatic public speakers, who could attract audiences of thousands. Both were troublemakers who challenged the capitalist system. And, importantly, they both worked with a variety of less famous Sheffield socialist pioneers.

### The Origins of Socialism in Sheffield

The word 'socialism' did not come into use in Britain until the mid-1820s but, well before this in the 1790s, middle-class reformers like Rev. Christopher Wyvill were fearful that the Sheffield working-class movement wanted to 'plunder the rich' (chapter 2). This could be seen as a fear of 'socialism'. When the word 'socialism' first came into use, it was mainly identified with St Simon's ideas in France and Robert Owen's rationalist, philanthropic and communitarian philosophy in Britain. It was Owen's ideas that led Ironside to found the Hall of Science. One of the Hall's most famous lecturers, George Holyoake, was a kind of socialist missionary who described his hearers there as 'communists'. Although Ironside called himself a 'Socialist', his ideas for devolving authority were very different from socialism as it developed later in Victorian England (chapter 4).

Around 1848, the 'Christian Socialists' emerged, led by F.D. Maurice, who challenged Victorian materialism and sought to awaken the middle classes to their responsibilities. Maurice had indirect links with Sheffield in that his London Working Men's College (founded in 1854) was partly modelled on the People's College and his curate, Carpenter, came to Sheffield. But increasingly 'socialism' was becoming identified in the public mind with the much more revolutionary ideas of Karl Marx, particularly after Harney (the former Sheffield Chartist) published the *Communist Manifesto* in English in 1850. Marx's powerful critique of capitalism was far more relevant to the great new factories developing in Sheffield's east end than it was to the old Sheffield of small workshops and little mesters. Marx's links with Sheffield were unhappy. He contributed to the *Sheffield Free Press* but was disgusted when Ironside failed to pay his fees (chapter 4). The *Sheffield Free Press* was too idiosyncratic to be described as a 'socialist' newspaper.

After the collapse of Chartism, many working-class people in Sheffield gave up political activism (chapter 5), but the Hall of Science was still operating and there remained groups of utopian socialists and communists in the town. In 1877 George Harrison Riley arrived in Sheffield and produced the town's first truly socialist journal.

George Harrison Riley grew up in Manchester and was an engraver, a commercial traveller and a journalist. During the 1860s he lived in the United States, where he met Walt Whitman. He was a socialist, familiar with Marx's theories and from 1872–5 he edited the journal of the London section of the International Working Men's Association. By then, he was in Bristol where he led Mutual Help organisations. When this work ran out of money, he moved to Sheffield, where he produced a penny news-sheet called *Socialist*, which appeared from July to December 1877. This journal had a Christian Socialist slant: 'during the time of Jesus and his Apostles, no person was accepted as a Christian who was not a socialist.' Riley produced his own 'British Constitution', under which everyone had to work, the land belonged to the whole Commonwealth and food, fuel and clothing would be distributed to people according to their need. When someone sent Ruskin a copy of *Socialist*, he said he concurred but added that any attempt to 'communize' a neighbour's property ended in 'ruin and shame'.[3] Nonetheless, there appeared to be enough common ground between Riley and Ruskin for them to work together.

### John Ruskin and Sheffield

John Ruskin (1819-1900) became involved in Sheffield in 1875-6.[4] By then, he was aged 56, Slade Professor of the History of Art in the University of Oxford and England's most famous art critic. He admired skilled craftsmanship and disapproved of machine-based industry. He also had a deep concern for the poor. He founded a pamphlet called *Fors Clavigera* in which he addressed monthly letters to 'the workmen and labourers of Great Britain'.

Ruskin's politics are difficult to pin down. In his autobiography, *Praeterita*, he declared: 'I am and my father was before me, a violent Tory of the old School.' But in 1871, writing shortly after the Paris Commune, he described himself as a communist 'of the old school – reddest also of the red'[5], though he gave a very narrow and aesthetic definition of communism. He certainly rejected liberalism in economics and politics. But he differed from most socialists and communists in that he believed in a traditional hierarchy in which the masters cared for the less fortunate. Like Riley and Carpenter, he deplored the immorality and ruthlessness of capitalism. His eloquent book *Unto this Last* became one of the classic texts of British socialism.

In order to give expression to his ideas, he founded the Guild of St George in 1871. It was a mysterious organisation, vaguely medieval, but adapting to the changing concerns of the Master. It was hierarchical, with Ruskin as Master and various kinds of Companions, mostly friends or admirers of the Master, some of whom subscribed a tithe of their wealth. There were also to be Marshals, Landlords and Labourers. Among other things, the guild aimed to spread cultural enlightenment and improved conditions for the workers through museums and agricultural schemes.

**42**   John Ruskin admired Sheffield's cutlery tradition and planted a museum and a 'communistic experiment' in the Sheffield area. Photograph at Brantwood by F.W. Sutcliffe 1873.

Why did Ruskin choose to plant these initiatives in Sheffield? His first answer was a simple one: 'that I acknowledge Ironwork as an art always necessary and useful to man, and English work in iron as masterful of its kind'. Ruskin admired Sheffield's individualistic cutlery tradition and the 'spirit of co-operation and discipline'.[6] He had no time for massive new industries like those emerging in the lower Don Valley. He liked the geographical setting of Sheffield – apparently coining the phrase 'a dirty picture in a golden frame'. He felt that Yorkshire people were 'old English and capable therefore of the ideals of Honesty and Piety'. But there was another more practical reason: one of his followers, Henry Swan, had settled in Sheffield as an engraver, working on plated goods or silver.

Ruskin came to know Henry Swan as a pupil in 1855, when Ruskin was teaching drawing at the London Working Men's College. Swan had then moved to Sheffield to seek work. He has been described as 'a crank'[7] and had an extraordinary range of interests – photographer, illuminator, shorthand expert, vegetarian, Quaker, spiritualist, pioneering cyclist and boomerang thrower.

Whereas capitalism created a national debt, Ruskin's idea was to create a 'National Store', which would include a museum to show artisans 'what is lovely in the life of Nature, and heroic in the life of Men'. In September 1875, he and Swan identified a cottage and land in Bellhagg Road, Walkley, for his museum and it was bought by the guild for £600. He appointed Swan curator right from its opening in late 1875 to Swan's death in March 1889. The museum was just one room with the rest of the cottage occupied by Swan and his family. Ruskin explained to the *Times*: 'The mountain home of the museum was originally chosen, not to keep the collection out of smoke, but expressly to beguile the artisan out of it.' The Museum contained pictures, illuminated manuscripts, minerals and books from Ruskin's own collection. It succeeded in attracting artisans as well as middle-class visitors.

**43**   Interior of Ruskin's St George's Museum in Walkley.

The museum suffered from lack of space, even after a wooden shed was built in the garden to house the bigger exhibits. Nor was the Walkley site well chosen. A journalist commented that: 'the people for whom Mr Ruskin had done so much refused to climb the painful slope, flanked by unsightly blocks of brick and mortar, to reach the little temple of art.'[8] In 1890, the museum was moved to Meersbrook House, the former home of Samuel Shore, provided by Sheffield Corporation.[9] In 1953 it was closed because visitors were only a dozen a day and the contents removed to Reading until 1985, when they were transferred into Sheffield's new Ruskin Museum in Norfolk Street. Finally, in 2001 they moved to their present home in the Millennium Galleries.

### The 'Communist' Experiment at St George's Farm

The experiment at St George's Farm is one of the stranger stories in this book. It ended in acrimony. Accounts of what happened differ and are not easy to reconcile.

In the Chartist period, many people saw a return to the land as a way out of the growing problems of urban life (chapter 4). This kind of thinking did not die out. In the 1870s, a group of Sheffield 'communists' had a long-term intention of buying land for a farm.[10] Similarly, one of the aims of Ruskin's Guild of St George was agricultural: 'simply the purchase of land in healthy districts, and the employment of labourers on the land, under the carefullest supervision, and with every means of mental instruction. That is the only way of bettering the material condition of the poor.'[11]

In April 1876, a meeting took place at the Walkley Museum between Ruskin and these Sheffield 'communists'.[12] A report subsequently appeared in the *Sheffield Telegraph*[13] under the intriguing heading 'Communism and Art'. These 'communists' whom Henry Swan introduced to Ruskin were an already existing group of 'Mutual Helpers' – 'Secularists, Unitarians, and Quakers, who professed Communism'.[14] Many had roots in Chartism. They belonged to the Mutual Improvement Society in Sheffield, which was part of a movement promoted by Riley to enable people gradually to make themselves independent of present civilisation by mutually exchanging their products.[15] The Sheffield group had started meeting in 1874 in Ironside's Hall of Science.

The *Telegraph* reported that at this meeting with Ruskin: 'Primarily, the subject of communism came up and its most extreme principles were freely and enthusiastically advocated by one or two of those present.' Somebody suggested establishing a community in Sheffield engaged in co-operative manufacture, like making boots. This idea then developed into a farming experiment.

Later in the month, Ruskin reported the purchase of land in Totley for St George's Farm:

> A few of the Sheffield working men who admit the possibility of the St George's notions being just, have asked me to let them rent some ground from the Company, whereupon to spend what spare hours they have, of morning or evening, in useful labour. I have accordingly authorised the sale of £2,200 worth of our stock, to be re-invested on a little estate, near Sheffield, of 13 acres, with a good water supply. The workmen undertake to St George for his 3%. I have no knowledge of the men's plans in detail, nor … shall I much interfere with them. But here at last is a little piece of England given into the English workmen's hands, and heaven's.[16]

Ruskin felt this was a safe investment because the men were to repay the guild and the land could always be sold, but his action none the less triggered the resignation of his fellow trustees. With characteristic hyperbole, he described the working men as 'Life Guards of a New Life … in the spirit of a body of monks gathered for missionary service'.

**44**   St George's Farm, Totley. Here Ruskin's unhappy 'communistic experiment' was launched in 1876. It ended in mutual recriminations.

Swan provided Ruskin with a list of potential tenants for the farm. There were several bootmakers, together with ironworkers, opticians and suchlike who knew little about agriculture. They carried on in their occupations and engaged a man to work on the farm and then another. Eggs, fruit and vegetables were produced. But Ruskin deplored the fact that 'The tenants tried at first to get on by a vote of the majority,' whereas Ruskin believed that progress could only be made under a 'simple and orderly tyrant'.[17]

Carpenter was intrigued by the experiment and sent Ruskin a gift of £2. Ruskin's reply reflects an understandable puzzlement as to Carpenter's social position:

> I cannot guess what position of life you are in – though I see you to be a gentleman and scientific &c in 'connection' with Cambridge – but what not? – but it is curious you don't tell me more, and that you should have worked with me so much without telling me so much![18]

But Carpenter remained elusive, not wanting perhaps to be drawn too much into Ruskin's schemes.

The group were angry when the bootmaker member who had first suggested the commune accepted £100 from Ruskin. They ordered him to return it, but Ruskin refused to accept it back. Then, early in 1878, Ruskin brought in William Harrison Riley as 'retainer'. Presumably, Riley was Ruskin's 'simple and orderly tyrant'. Riley fitted the bill as he proved to be very heavy-handed, telling the communists that he was 'master' and that they had no power. According to W.H. Malloy, one of the communists, Riley 'met their remonstrances with sneers and in one case with threats of personal violence'. The committee wrote twice to Ruskin to complain about Riley but, getting no reply, they informed Ruskin that they declined any further responsibility for the farm.[19]

Carpenter, who around this time moved into a farm in nearby Bradway, said that in the end 'Peace and fraternity were turned into missiles and malice' and: 'The wives entered into the fray and the would-be Garden of Eden became a scene of such confusion that

Ruskin had to send down an ancient retainer of his (with a pitchfork instead of a flaming sword) to bar them all out.'

Ruskin's 'ancient retainer' was David Downes, from Scotland – according to Carpenter, a 'very old-fashioned and John Bull-like retainer of the Ruskin family'.

Carpenter was friendly with Riley and interceded with Ruskin on his behalf but got nowhere. Ruskin declared that Riley 'liked smoking better than digging'. Carpenter was not attracted to utopian communities. He wrote: 'Personally, I would not like to belong to a community of under a million people! I think that with that number one might feel safe, but with less there would be a great danger of being watched.'[20]

Riley, resentful of his treatment by Ruskin, emigrated with his family to Massachusetts and resumed a career in journalism.[21]

The commune came to an end and one account suggests that Downes died there.[22] Another account says that, around 1886, Ruskin removed Downes and let the farm 'to a company of Communists whose head-quarters is another farm with quarry not far distant … Its founder is a remarkable and noble kind of man.'[23] This was John Furniss who is discussed further below. There is agreement that the guild let the farm to George Pearson, a young friend of Furniss and Carpenter, who worked it for 50 years and bought it in 1929.[24]

The abortive experiment left all the participants feeling scarred. Ruskin's nervous breakdown in 1878 was connected with this failure. The underlying problems were that Ruskin's aims were incompatible with those of the original committee of working men and that Riley was ill-suited to act as mediator.

## Carpenter and Sheffield

No wonder Ruskin found it difficult to place Carpenter socially for, over the previous 10 years, he had been trying to de-class himself. Edward Carpenter (1844-1929) was a man of striking appearance and extraordinary breadth – poet, mystic, social thinker, mathematician, practical man and propagandist. In contrast with James Montgomery, Carpenter's early life was highly respectable but, from 1868 onwards, he became increasingly unconventional. He felt deeply alienated by his bourgeois Brighton background, writing later of 'unexpressed hatred … for the social conditions in which I was born'.[25] He read Mathematics at Trinity Hall in Cambridge and was awarded a college fellowship. He was also ordained by the Bishop of Ely and around 1869 was curate to the Christian Socialist, F.D. Maurice, at St Edward's Church in Cambridge. Maurice and Carpenter were at very different stages in their lives. Maurice was in his sixties, a sick man who died in 1872. Carpenter was in his twenties and losing his faith. He found Maurice's theology opaque and unconvincing. Moreover, he had been exposed to a powerful new influence.

In 1868-9, Carpenter read Walt Whitman's *Leaves of Grass* and *Democratic Vistas* and 'a profound change set in within me'.[26] Over the next few years, Carpenter gradually reappraised his whole life, being at times near to a nervous breakdown. His reappraisal had four inter-related strands: sexual, religious, social and political.

Whitman's celebration of 'the manly love of comrades' helped Carpenter to accept his own homosexuality. As regards religion, he rejected Anglican Christianity, but he remained an intensely religious writer and later developed an interest in Eastern religion (visiting Ceylon and India in 1890-1). In his poetry, he wrote mystically of the whole universe coming together in the great self, the universal ego, the world soul or cosmic consciousness. Socially, he rejected Victorian middle-class values, which he later described as:

**45**   Edward Carpenter at his
home in Millthorpe.

cant in religion, pure materialism in science, futility in social convention, the worship of
stocks and shares, the starving of the human heart, the denial of the human body and its
needs, the huddling concealment of the body in clothes, the 'impure hush' on matters of
sex, class-division, contempt of manual labour, and the cruel barring of women from every
natural and useful expression of their lives.[27]

Politically, he gradually became a socialist. In 1871, he visited Paris soon after the fall
of the Commune – like Gales, Roebuck and Ironside he was fascinated by revolutionary
France. On returning in 1874 from another visit to France: 'it suddenly flashed on me,
with a vibration through my whole body, that I would and must somehow go and make
my life with the mass of the people and the manual workers.'[28]

He extricated himself from his fellowship and his holy orders and became from 1874 to 1879 a university extension lecturer in Northern towns, teaching astronomy and other subjects. He found this life emotionally exhausting and was disappointed that his pupils were middle class rather than working class. Eventually, he settled in Sheffield, finding lodgings, first at the top end of Glossop Road, then, after a spell in Chesterfield, in Holland Terrace, Highfields. He liked Sheffield people (see the opening of this chapter) and began to make good friends among manual workers. In 1877, he sent Walt Whitman a classic description of Victorian Sheffield:

> Sheffield is finely situated, magnificent hill country all around and on the hills for miles and miles (on one side of the town) elegant villa residences – and in the valley below one enduring cloud of smoke and a pale-faced teeming population and tall chimneys and ash heaps covered with squalid children picking them over, and dirty alleys and courts and houses, half roofless and a river running black through the midst of them. It is a strange and wonderful sight. There is a great deal of distress just now – so many being out of work

and it is impossible to pass through the streets without seeing it obvious in one form or another. (A man burst into floods of tears the other day when I gave him a bit of silver). But each individual is such a mere unit in a great crowd and they go to hide their misery easily enough.[29]

By 1879, Carpenter felt 'the absolute necessity of an open-air life'.[30] One of his pupils, a scythe-maker called Albert Fearnehough, invited him to visit him, his wife and children and his landlord, a bright young bachelor farmer called Charles Fox. They lived near to each other in the countryside around Bradway. After some reflection and discussion, Carpenter arranged to lodge with Fearnehough, first in Totley and then in Bradway and to help with the farm-work. His health improved. He read the *Bhagavad Gita*. In a mood of exaltation and inspiration, he composed his Whitman-esque prose poem *Towards Democracy*.

In 1882 his father died, leaving him £6,000, enabling him to buy seven acres in Millthorpe in Derbyshire as a market garden. He had a cottage built on the land and in 1883 moved in there with the Fernehoughs. It was an isolated life, some nine miles

from Sheffield and four miles from a station. For a time, he only saw his Sheffield friends about once a week.

Carpenter was strongly drawn to a rural way of life not, he claimed, on grounds of ideology, but as a way of improving his health and well-being. He experimented with agricultural work in Bradway and then acquired his land in Millthorpe. Some time after, he read Thoreau's *Walden*. This book 'took the bottom out of my little bucket', by advocating a far more radical simplification of life than was possible at a time when he and Fernehough were struggling to make a commercial success of their market garden. But he was sufficiently captivated by Thoreau to lay a stone on his cairn when visiting the United States in 1884. Moreover, his country life fulfilled his wish to quit his urban middle-class background.

From 1887, Carpenter left most of the market gardening to Fernehough and focused on communicating new ideas.[31] Around 1893, George Adams, one of Carpenter's socialist friends, and his wife took the place of the Fernehoughs.

Carpenter was famous for his 'simplification of life.' Stimulated by a friend in Kashmir, he had a passion for sandals. A socialist bootmaker called W.H. Lill taught Carpenter to make sandals, but he increasingly delegated the work to Adams, who made about 100 sandals each year at Millthorpe. William Morris, who enjoyed an affluent lifestyle, admired Carpenter's simple way of life.[32] Carpenter made Millthorpe a centre at which advanced thinkers of all kinds congregated, often staying in nearby cottages. But there was a downside to fame. He said that 'Faddists of all sorts and kinds considered me their special prey' and arrived uninvited at Millthorpe.

The Adams stayed until February 1898. On the day after their departure, the 32-year-old George Merrill[33] arrived,

**46**   The distress in Sheffield – queuing up for poor relief, 1879.

'trundling a hand-cart over the hills and through a disheartening blizzard of snow'. Carpenter had met Merrill some years before in a train between Sheffield and Totley and 'had recognised at once a peculiar intimacy and mutual understanding'. Merrill, who had grown up in the Sheffield slums, had a 'singularly affectionate, humorous and swiftly intuitive nature' that greatly appealed to Carpenter. Carpenter received many well-meaning letters telling him that it was an unwise arrangement, but he ignored them and Merrill was Carpenter's lover, companion and housekeeper until he died.

Eventually in 1922, the death of another Sheffield friend, Hukin, removed for Carpenter any reason for staying in the North. They moved to Guildford,[34] where Merrill died in 1928, with Carpenter's death following 18 months later in July 1929.

### Carpenter and Sheffield Socialism

Carpenter's socialism was very different from Ruskin's. He disliked hierarchical relationships. He became a socialist in 1883 when he read Hyndman's *England for All,* which popularised Marx's teaching. He attended a committee meeting of Hyndman's Social Democratic Federation (SDF) and donated £300 to Hyndman's magazine *Justice*[35] but did not join the SDF. He recalled that: 'From that time forward, I worked definitely along the Socialist line; with a drift as was natural towards Anarchism.'[36] While he accepted Marx's theory that the capitalist classes lived off the surplus value generated by the workers, his was an 'ethical socialism' about ending domination, whether between rich and poor, between master and servant, between races or between people in their personal relationships. In *Towards Democracy,* he wrote of a utopian dream:

> I conceive a millennium on earth – a millennium not of riches, nor of mechanical facilities, nor of intellectual facilities, nor absolutely of immunity from disease, nor absolutely of immunity from pain; but a time when men and women all over the earth shall ascend and enter into relation with their bodies – shall attain freedom and joy.[37]

Carpenter's focus on freedom and fulfilment did not capture the labour movement but it was influential, for instance, in the novels of E.M. Forster, who was one of many visitors to Millthorpe. Carpenter took an eclectic view of the various competing strands of the labour movement, saying that it had taken on an 'oceanic character'.[38] He and his friends expected a 'Socialist Revolution' or 'SR' but were vague about how this new order would come about.

Carpenter became involved in Sheffield politics. In the 1880s, most politically active workers were Liberal, but the Chartist tradition of independent working-class action still survived. In 1884, the Sheffield Working Men's Radical Association was formed,[39] affiliated to the Social Democratic Federation. It soon built up a membership of two hundred. Its treasurer was John Furniss, an eloquent quarryman, Christian socialist, former Methodist preacher and, according to Carpenter, 'perhaps the first man to preach Socialism in the streets of Sheffield'.[40] Furniss was involved in a split in the association triggered by the General Election of 1885. In Sheffield Central constituency, the majority supported Samuel Plimsoll, the Liberal candidate, but Furniss and others, with Carpenter's support, put forward Mervyn Hawkes as an independent candidate. They were ahead of their time in seeking direct labour representation and Sheffield was not yet ready. The Conservative candidate won, with Plimsoll second and Hawkes only had 140 votes.[41]

In 1886, Morris broke with Hyndman's Social Democratic Federation and set up the Socialist League. Carpenter worked with Furniss and other enthusiasts to establish an autonomous Sheffield Socialist Society, following meetings in February 1886 at which

**47**    Sheffield socialists in 1886. Edward Carpenter is seated first on right.

Morris spoke. Carpenter's colleagues included Mrs Usher, an excellent publicist for the cause, J.M. Brown, an affable and persuasive tailor, Raymond Unwin from Chesterfield, later architect of garden cities, Fred Charles, who was later sent to gaol for an anarchist plot (see below) and George Hukin, a Dutch razor-grinder and intimate friend of Carpenter. Soon the Sheffield Socialists had a membership of a hundred or more and an active element of a dozen or twenty. They held weekly meetings at the Wentworth Café in Holly Street. They organised lectures, addresses, pamphlets and street-corner propaganda, often at the Monolith, then at the corner of Fargate and Surrey Street – a location that is still used for open-air meetings. Furniss would walk five or six miles over the moors to speak at the Monolith or at the Pump in West Bar. It was at this time that Carpenter composed his Socialist Marching song *England Arise* (see opening of this chapter).

In his memoirs, Carpenter reflects on the contrast between outsiders' fears of the socialists as revolutionary and subversive and the reality of their 'most simple fraternity and idealism'. His experience of the British masses was that, far from being too inflammable, they were too slow to move.[42] Carpenter drew up a manifesto for the Sheffield Socialist Society, in which their main object was the abolition of the present class society and the attainment of 'a regenerate society in which every one who can shall work and receive the due reward for his work'. The land and the public utilities would belong to the people. Labour representation would be pushed forward.[43]

In 1887, the Sheffield Socialists established the Commonwealth Café in the former debtors' jail in Scotland Street, then a poor part of the town. They used the large room above for meetings and lectures. The sentiments expressed at the opening meeting were more akin to the ideas of William Morris than those of Marx. John Furniss spoke about 'the common well being of the common people', adding that by that he did not mean one class. Charles Peach, a radical Unitarian minister, echoed this and commended Furniss's community at Totley. Carpenter said that socialism was 'the entire regeneration of society

**48**   The monolith where Carpenter's socialists held meetings. The view is from 1890 near the location of the new town hall and with St Paul's Church in the background. The monolith, which marked Queen Victoria's Golden Jubilee in 1887, was later moved to Endcliffe Park.

in art, in science, in religion and in literature the building of a new life in which industrial socialism was the foundation'.[44] The society brought in distinguished speakers like Mrs Annie Besant and Prince Kropotkin, a leading anarchist. They gave teas to local slum-children, but had to give these up because the children were tearing each other to pieces to gain admittance.

Carpenter slept in a large attic in the Commonwealth Café for the greater part of 1887. He describes the area as follows:

> In the early morning at 5am there was the strident sound of the 'hummers' and the clattering of innumerable clogs of men and girls going to work and on till late at night there were drunken cries and shouting. Far around stretched nothing but factory chimneys and foul courts inhabited by the wretched workers. It was, I must say, frightfully depressing.[45]

Carpenter had provided the financial backing for this café, but they could only keep it going for a year as it was not sufficiently patronised amid such poverty. They shifted to the *Temperance Hotel*. Later on, they renamed themselves the Socialist Club and acquired premises in Blonk Street.

After 1887, Carpenter was an active propagandist, not only in Sheffield but much more widely, writing books, pamphlets and articles on socialism, sex, prisons, vivisection and much else besides and engaged in public speaking, lecturing up to 12 times a month to trade union branches, socialist societies, labour churches and other bodies. His books ran into many editions and were translated into many foreign languages. His ideas touched many people in Britain and all over the world.

Carpenter also fought specific campaigns. He anticipated the campaigns of the Edwardian period (chapter 11) by drawing attention to the injustices of the enclosures. In 1889, he published a pamphlet arguing that the parishioners of Holmesfield were poor because they paid £2,200 in annual rent to the Duke of Rutland and because Parliament had deprived the people of 2,570 acres of common land by the enclosure of 1820. Another campaign was Sheffield-based. It was against the 'smoke nuisance' that made Sheffield 'a byword ... throughout the civilised world'. Looking down from the hills, Sheffield was blotted out by 'a vast dense cloud, so thick that I wondered how any human being could support life in it'. He visited London firms that had found ways of tackling the smoke problem and recommended practical remedies. Carpenter was well ahead of his time. His campaigning had some impact in and beyond Sheffield, but it was not till the 1950s that Sheffield seriously tackled its smoke.[46]

## Anarchism in Sheffield

Despite Carpenter's prominent role in the socialist movement of his day, he was arguably more an anarchist than a socialist.[47] He certainly feared state bureaucracy and red tape and wrote optimistically of the time when 'the state, qua state, and all efficient Government, are superseded by the voluntary and instinctive consent and mutual helpfulness of the people – when of course the Anarchist idea would be realised'.[48] Some anarchists followed Bakunin in practising violence. Carpenter's anarchism was pacific, though he was prepared to defend more extreme anarchists if he felt they were being unfairly victimised by the state.

In the late 1880s, anarchism was an expanding movement in Britain. In 1888, anarchists took over the Socialist League and in 1890 its journal *Commonweal*. William Morris withdrew. The Sheffield Socialist Club was similarly exposed to anarchist influence, particularly from Robert Bingham, a local grocer, and Fred Charles, aged 25, recently arrived from London and Norwich, who worked for Bingham. In 1889 Charles and Bingham supported a strike at John Brown's. There was much emotion about blacklegs and Bingham was prosecuted for an 'inflammatory address' at a Socialist Club meeting at the Monolith at which he said that killing a traitor was not murder. He narrowly escaped being convicted for incitement to murder.

The Socialist Club published an anarchistic manifesto, *An Appeal to Workers*, calling for 'the resumption by the People, for their own use, of the Land and Capital of their respective countries'. It made no mention of Parliament. Carpenter apparently endorsed this and may have drafted it. But he cannot have felt that the revolution was imminent for in October 1890 he left Sheffield for the East. In November, the Sheffield Socialist Club held a meeting to commemorate the Chicago Anarchist Martyrs. In a letter to Carpenter, Hukin reported disapprovingly that one speaker dropped upon his knees and called on everyone to vow not to rest until the murder of their comrades had been avenged. Nearly all those present held up their hands for the vow.

A new anarchist leader then appeared in Sheffield – John Creaghe, an Irish doctor, recently returned from Buenos Aires, where he had been connected with a revolutionary movement. He opened a dispensary for the poor and a branch in Attercliffe for the sale of literature. When Charles was sacked by the Binghams, he went to stay with Creaghe to help him. The Socialist Club became dominated by Creaghe and Charles. Bingham and others resigned. Hukin absented himself from meetings and wrote to Carpenter saying that 'I think the whole thing will collapse very soon.'

Early in 1891, Creaghe launched a no-rent campaign, citing in support the great Sheffield tradition of William Broadhead. An 'Anti-Property Association' was formed. He was prosecuted for assaulting a policeman and a bailiff with a poker when they came to secure the rent he owed to his landlady. He was fined £25 and bound over. Creaghe also launched a poachers' raid in the grounds of Chatsworth. Creaghe established the Sheffield Group of Anarchistic Communists, with the mottoes 'Neither God nor Master' and 'Anarchy' on the banners they unfurled on Attercliffe Common in commemoration of the Paris Commune.

Creaghe launched a journal *The Sheffield Anarchist*, perhaps thanks to help from a mysterious French anarchist called Auguste Coulon, who appeared on the scene and had access to funds. Creaghe was becoming more extreme, advocating the use of dynamite. In November, Creaghe left Sheffield for Liverpool. He seems to have attributed his lack of progress in Sheffield to the hold that Carpenter had on local activists. Carpenter, he claimed, produces 'very pretty verses' advocating anarchy and contempt for law and authority, but 'in conversation disavows all connexions with anarchists, belauds Fabians and Trades Unionists'. Carpenter replied in his eclectic way, claiming that he supported anarchists, Fabians and trades unionists alike. He asked: 'Why should we be snarling at each others' heels?'

Carpenter became involved in the unhappy sequel to this story – the Walsall anarchists' trial. In July 1891, Fred Charles moved to Walsall, where he worked in an iron foundry. He was involved with Victor Cailes, another anarchist and protégé of Coulon, in a plan to make bombs supposedly for use in Russia. But Coulon, a police agent provocateur (rather like Oliver the spy in 1817 – see chapter 3), was behind the whole plot. Coulon disappeared but Charles, Cailes and others were tried at Stafford Assizes, with the attorney general leading for the Crown. Carpenter had the moral courage to appear as a witness to Charles's character. He admitted to the attorney general that he was himself an anarchist. The sentences were severe – Charles faced 10 years' penal servitude.

This trial helped to crush the growing anarchist movement. On New Year's Day 1893, Creaghe came back to Sheffield for a last meeting at the Monolith before returning to South America. 1893 was the year of the miners' lock out, when the owners tried to reduce wages. Lord Rosebury intervened on behalf of the Government and they went back at their old rates.

## Carpenter and Sexual Liberation

In the Victorian age, Carpenter was exceptional in being open about his homosexuality, which he believed was innate, and in writing honestly about sexual issues.[49] The remarkable change in his way of life, which began in his mid-twenties, was driven initially by his wish to come to terms with his sexuality. But he was in his fifties before he formed his stable relationship with George Merrill. Before that, he seems to have had briefer relationships with other working men in his Sheffield circle, notably George Hukin. He was deeply distressed when Hukin got married.

The climate was against open homosexual relationships. In 1885, the Labouchere amendment to the Criminal Law Amendment Act made all male homosexual acts illegal. The trial of Oscar Wilde in 1895 created an atmosphere of panic. Yet Carpenter was straightforward on sexual matters. He and his friend Havelock Ellis were among the

**49**    Edward Carpenter and George Merrill.

very few writers on sex in England at the time. Carpenter's book, *Love's Coming-of-Age* (1896) discussed the oppression of women, which he linked to the introduction of private property. The book went through 16 editions in Britain and was translated into many foreign languages, with an international circulation of some 100,000 copies.[50] He wrote a succession of works on homosexuality, including *Homogenic Love* and *The Intermediate Sex*. He was an early advocate of birth control.[51]

Anyone in Carpenter's position was at risk of personal disaster.[52] This risk was greatest in 1908-10 when an Irishman called O'Brien, living in Dronfield, began a personal campaign to discredit him, starting with a letter in the *Sheffield Telegraph*. O'Brien followed him to socialist and suffrage meetings, interrupting and denouncing him in the 'grossest terms'. O'Brien produced a pamphlet called *Socialism and Infamy. The Homogenic or Comrade Love Exposed. An Open Letter in Plain Words for a Socialist Prophet to Edward Carpenter.* The author abhorred both socialism and homosexuality. He wrote of a 'putrid cesspool' and 'vile prophets of Sodom and Gomorrah'. He accused Carpenter of corrupting the morals of 'thousands of persons of both sexes' who had visited him in his 20 years in Millthorpe and of advocating naked dancing on the hilltops. O'Brien appeared in Holmesfield with a satchel of these pamphlets to spread them around. Local people on the whole supported

Carpenter. The local vicar said that he had no reason to believe that Carpenter 'lived anything but an absolutely clear life'. Hukin argued that Merrill's uninhibited behaviour was to blame. Carpenter was voted off the parish council. O'Brien's onslaught went on until 1910, but then he was imprisoned for some offence and never seen again. Disaster had been averted.

Many of Carpenter's socialist comrades were embarrassed by his writings on sexual matters, which they felt could bring the movement into disrepute. But his views on the oppression of women fed into the women's suffrage movement (chapter 9).

### Ruskin, Carpenter and the Sheffield Labour Movement

Ruskin's influence in Sheffield was more aesthetic than political, but his vehement criticism of the dominant Victorian capitalist ethos encouraged local socialists. Civic leaders valued Ruskin's museum and provided it with new premises at Meersbrook Park. But Ruskin's influence in Sheffield waned until the 1980s, when his museum was resurrected.

Politically, Carpenter was far more influential than Ruskin. Henry Pelling argued that Carpenter's 'anarchist ethics' were 'too subtle, too amorphous and intangible for the ordinary mind to grasp'.[53] Yet his books sold in large numbers and, in Sheffield and elsewhere, he was an extremely popular speaker. Fenner Brockway described his charismatic qualities. He was:

> the great spiritual inspiration of our lives. His *Towards Democracy* was our Bible ... We read it aloud in the summer evenings, when tired by tramping or games ... Carpenter came one evening. I remember him vividly. His head and features were of extraordinary beauty: his face was a chiselled statue clearcut and of perfect outline; his eyes bright and kindly; there was refinement in his every movement and the tone of his voice. One admired him and loved him at once.[54]

After his death, an Edward Carpenter Fellowship was formed, which held an annual memorial service near his home in Millthorpe. At the 1947 service, for example, the fellowship's chairman, G.H.B. Ward (chapter 11) could hardly have pitched his praise higher:

> Now and then in our human society one arises who does not conform in any sense to pattern. It is not that such are rebels or revolutionaries so much as that they appear to live in a world of their own, largely unhampered by the mundane affairs that get in the way of so many of us. They are men of quiet strength and purpose who seem to speak and act unmoved by the transient emotions and reactions of the crowd about them − St Francis, Tolstoy, Thoreau, Gandhi ... Perhaps their greatest achievement was self conquest ... Edward Carpenter was such a man.[55]

Carpenter helped to make socialist ideas acceptable in Sheffield and elsewhere. Even the conservative *Sheffield Daily Telegraph* in 1905 recognised this, calling him 'the most engaging personality of the socialist movement and by his intellectual eminence the most dangerous opponent of the existing order of society'.[56]

There were of course other important influences in Sheffield, particularly the trades unions, with whom Carpenter was not close, and also the co-operative movement, the Clarion ramblers, the labour church and renegades from liberalism. There were numerous left-of-centre organisations that waxed and waned. Carpenter's Socialist Society, having slid into anarchism, was relaunched by him in 1896 and finally merged with the SDF in 1908.[57] A further influence was the Fabian Society, which believed in 'the inevitability of gradualness' and the permeation of existing power structures, like the Liberal Party, with socialist ideas. In 1893, the Unitarian Minister, Rev. Charles Peach, a founder of the Socialist Society, founded a Sheffield Fabian branch, which he then revived in 1896.[58]

Morgan Phillips's famous statement that the Labour Party owed more to Methodism than to Karl Marx applied to Sheffield. Nor is this surprising. John Wesley visited Sheffield on at least 32 occasions and Methodism became deeply embedded in Sheffield culture. By contrast, as we have seen, Karl Marx's links with Sheffield were tenuous in the extreme (chapter 4).

Many of Sheffield's trade unionists derived their fervour and their organisational and oratorical skills not from reading Marx, but from the nonconformist chapels. According to Helen Mathers, leading local historian of this period, Christian faith often preceded conversion to socialism in Sheffield but seldom survived it.[59] Socialism offered 'the revolution' as a millennial alternative to the kingdom of heaven. Later on, Joseph Pointer, Sheffield's first MP, illustrated the shift from Christianity to socialism. He was a former Wesleyan Reform Minister who, as a result of attending Ruskin College, Oxford, had adopted socialism as his religion.[60] Once he became an MP, Pointer adopted a typically moderate brand of socialism. But there was also a small but significant band of revolutionary Marxists.

Thus in Sheffield, there were many influences on the developing labour movement, including not only Ruskin and Carpenter but also liberalism, Owenism, Marxism, Methodism, Christian socialism, the ideas of William Morris and anarchism. But the strongest single force was trade unionism. From the 1850s onwards, trade unionists in Sheffield's traditional cutlery trades (including the notorious William Broadhead – see chapter 5) joined together in federations, partly with a view to influencing politics. In 1872, the Sheffield Federated Trades Council (SFTC) was founded, followed by the Sheffield Labour Association, founded in 1883. Both sought 'Lib–Lab' trade union representation on public bodies and met with some success. Four Lib–Lab leaders were elected as councillors. Sidney Pollard argues that workers from the traditional light trades were becoming increasingly 'respectable' in the 1850s and 1860s. But this was not true of workers in the new steel industries of Brightside and Attercliffe, who were suspicious of the Liberals and more inclined to socialism.[61]

By the early 1890s, it was becoming clear that, if the various strands of the labour movement worked together, they might ultimately take power. In Sheffield, this would be achieved but would take 30 years. Before recounting this story, this study looks at some of the other movements active in Sheffield in Carpenter's time – Anglo-Catholicism, settlements and women's suffrage.

*Chapter 7*

# Turbulent Priest:
# Father Ommanney

He went to Sheffield under a cloud of suspicion and hostility; he died the most respected and beloved priest in the Diocese.

F.G. Belton on Ommanney

Carpenter and Ommanney[1] were roughly contemporaries in the Sheffield area, both active there from the 1880s to the inter-war period. Ommanney twice had the 'poet', Carpenter, to speak at evening meetings in a former public house in Holly Lane. But while Carpenter, a former priest, was a socialist prophet of the future, Ommanney, a serving priest, was recreating his vision of the pre-Reformation church.

For the Church of England establishment in Sheffield, Father Ommanney was a far more dangerous troublemaker than Carpenter. He occupied far more column inches in the local press. Sheffield had been a Protestant stronghold for centuries. In 1828 a Sheffield petition against Catholic emancipation attracted 30,000 signatures.

Since then, the Oxford Movement had generated a formidable Anglo-Catholic revival elsewhere, but this had hardly penetrated Sheffield. There had been a growth of Roman Catholicism in the town through the advent of Irish immigrants, living particularly in the area around Solly Street. To many Protestants, whether Anglican or nonconformist, Ommanney's position as Vicar of St Matthew's, Carver Street, threatened Catholic subversion from within the Church of England. They decided on strenuous opposition.

*Sheffield's 'religious boom'*

By 1882, when Ommanney arrived in Sheffield, religion in Sheffield had changed considerably from the days of James Wilkinson when, according to Wickham, the Church of England 'moved slowly, massively, and ponderously, a dinosaur among smaller livelier mammals'.[2] By contrast, between 1850 and 1900 both the Anglicans and the nonconformists were enjoying a 'religious boom'.[3]

The Church of England's building programme between 1820 and 1882 was remarkable. It began with the four large Anglican churches created in the 1820s under the Million Act (chapter 3). Then the huge unitary parish of Sheffield was at last split up into separate parishes. Between 1832 and 1862, 13 new churches with 8,800 additional sittings were built. By 1882, Sheffield had some 36 Anglican churches.[4] Similar building programmes took place among the nonconformists.

The table below draws on two censuses, which give us a statistical picture of religious observance.

CHURCH ATTENDANCE IN SHEFFIELD 30 MARCH 1851 AND 1881

|  | 30 March 1851 | 20 November 1881 |
|---|---|---|
| Church of England | 14,881 | 33,835 |
| Misc Methodist Churches | 15,803 | 29,648 |
| Independent | 4,550 | 7,847 |
| Baptist (Partic and General) | 2,344 | 3,206 |
| Unitarian | 1,000 | 1,188 |
| Roman Catholic | 4,000 | 5,473 |
| Salvation Army | 0 | 4,054 |
| Other | 843 | 2,505 |
| TOTAL | 43,421 | 87,756 |
| Borough Population | 135,310 | 284,410 |

Source: Wickham, *Church and People in an Industrial City*, Lutterworth (1957), PP. 109 and 148.

This table shows that, when those attending two services are taken into account, just under a quarter of the population attended church on each date (this excludes those attending Sunday Schools) – by modern standards an extraordinarily high figure, but contemporary commentators were full of woe about non-attendance. Moreover, it was impressive that churchgoing levels were roughly maintained while the population doubled between 1851 and 1881. Working-class people were under-represented, put off by the 'respectability' of many churches, by pew rents and unattractive 'free sittings'. By 1881, the Salvation Army had appeared on the scene with a very different appeal to working people.

Nonconformists still exceeded Anglicans but the Anglican proportion increased from 34 per cent in 1851 to 38 per cent in 1881. Roman Catholics remained a relatively low proportion of the population even in 1881.

The Church of England in Sheffield remained staunchly low church. But whereas Wilkinson was latitudinarian, early in the 19th century evangelical clergy, like the Rev. Thomas Cotterill at St Paul's, became influential. Thomas Sutton, who was vicar of the parish church from 1805 to 1851 – almost as long as Wilkinson – ensured generally evangelical appointments to the new churches in the town. The advowson (patronage) of the parish church was kept in evangelical hands to ensure continuity in churchmanship there.[5] In 1872 the young William Odom, not yet ordained, and others founded the Sheffield Young Churchmen's Protestant Association to defend the Church against disestablishment and Popery.[6] In 1882, apart from two Anglo-Catholic churches – St Michael's, Neepsend and St Luke's, Moorfield – Anglo-Catholicism had been successfully held at bay.

**50**    Canon William Odom, Vicar of Heeley, local historian and defender of Protestantism. Before he was ordained, he set up a Young Churchmen's Protestant Association to defend the Church against disestablishment and 'popery'.

## George Campbell Ommanney (1850-1936) – His Early Life

George Campbell Ommanney[7] was the son of Octavius Ommanney, a banker and naval agent, who lived in Mortlake and East Sheen. The Ommanneys were a distinguished family and

included several admirals. George's Anglo-Catholicism came from his mother, Helen Gream, daughter of a high church rector. John Mason Neale, ecclesiologist, hymn writer and a prominent Anglo-Catholic clergyman, was a close friend of the family. Helen's sister Katherine worked with Neale in setting up the Sisters of St Margaret of East Grinstead, one of the first orders of nuns in the Church of England since the Reformation. She became Superior of the order.

George went to Wadham College, Oxford, and then became a curate in Bristol. He had long felt a vocation to a celibate priesthood. He was a member of the Confraternity of the Blessed Sacrament,[8] an organisation that by the 1870s had 800 priest members.[9] Ommanney was untroubled by intellectual doubts. He saw himself as a loyal son of the Church of England and was distressed when clergy friends went over to Rome.

**51**   Father Ommanney outraged local Protestants with his 'popish practices' at St Matthew's, Carver Street.

### Ommanney's Appointment to St Matthew's, Carver Street

The parish of St Matthew was created in 1846, bounded by West Street, Sheffield Moor, Cambridge Street and Trafalgar Street. Today, it is a prosperous west end area, but in the 1880s it was a poor area of 'wretched courts and lanes', with a population of some 5,000, mostly living in crowded back to back houses of three rooms – a ground-floor living room, a first-floor bedroom and an attic. There were 10 houses to one tap. Many workshops belched out smoke. Sanitary conditions were appalling. The streets and courts were unpaved. Carver Street itself was almost impassable in a hansom cab. Within the parish were Ironside's secularist Hall of Science and William Broadhead's *George Hotel*, from which he had planned his 'outrages'. The Rev. Witty, Vicar of St Matthew's, had collected money to enable Broadhead to emigrate, but by the 1880s he had returned and was to be found in local public houses, reciting 'the infamous methods he had adopted, receiving money from the publicans and collections from the hearers'.[10]

As Ommanney's opponents repeatedly pointed out, the church had been built with 'Protestant money' from donors like Mr Wilson, the snuff manufacturer. Ommanney retorted that medieval Catholic money had been diverted to 'bonnets for Deans' wives and perambulators for deans' children'.[11] St Matthew's, consecrated in 1855, was plain and dreary.

The church was not originally Anglo-Catholic. Its patronage was in the hands alternately of the Archbishop of York and the Crown. When C.R. Job resigned in 1882, it was the Crown's turn to fill the vacancy. The Crown's ecclesiastical patronage rested with the Prime Minister, William Gladstone, who sympathised with Anglo-Catholicism. His first choice for the St Matthew's vacancy was the Hon. Hanbury Tracy. However, Tracy was reluctant and persuaded Ommanney that his name should go forward to Downing Street instead. The Prime Minister then decided to appoint Ommanney.

Sheffield was part of the Diocese of York, headed by Dr William Thomson, the Archbishop of York. Thomson distrusted the Anglo-Catholic movement with every fibre of his being and 'did his vigorous best to turn back the ritualistic tide'.[12] A distinguished logician, he had no feeling for ritualism. He had made his own diocese largely a ritualist-free zone and regarded insubordinate clergy as 'a shame and a reproach' to the Church.

**52** St Matthew's Church, Carver Street, Sheffield, built in 1855–6.

**53** Archbishop William Thomson of York tried to discipline Ommanney.

At his first interview with Ommanney, Thomson told his eager new young priest that his appointment had been 'a great grief' to him – hardly an encouraging start.[13] But he met his match in Ommanney.

### The Conflict Begins

Long before Ommanney actually arrived in Sheffield, the local press was full of articles and letters about the impending storm. William Leng, editor of the *Sheffield Daily Telegraph*, spokesman for the 'rather sombre evangelicalism which at that time ruled the Church in Sheffield',[14] took a keen personal interest in the affair, attacking Gladstone for 'ritualistic' appointments. Leng's correspondent reported that Ommanney's church in Bristol had men on one side and women on the other, a draped altar, genuflecting clergy and Ommanney kissing his stole before he preached. The *Telegraph* buzzed with indignant letters. Leng's correspondent wrote: 'Here we have the case of a Parish Church built with Protestant money in a Protestant town handed over with deliberate and offensive ostentation to the control of a Ritualistic priest.'[15] The liberal nonconformist *Independent* found it difficult to defend this aberration of its hero, Gladstone, and called Ommanney a square peg in a round hole. As to the Sheffield clergy, Ommanney found that they 'were nearly all against me'. Before Ommanney arrived, the Sheffield Church Conference refused his request to maintain a grant for the stipend of a curate at St Matthew's.

Ommanney did have a few sympathisers – 'men who had maintained the faith' – but far more opponents. The most serious opposition came from within his new congregation, led by Walter Wynn, a churchwarden and devout Protestant. Battle commenced at Ommanney's first vestry meeting. Ommanney assumed that Wynn was people's warden and proposed Henry Longley, a newcomer to the parish, as vicar's warden. But in fact Wynn had been vicar's warden for 12 years. It was eventually agreed that Longley would be vicar's warden and Wynn people's warden. Wynn then declared: 'We have got a Protestant church (hear hear) built by Protestant money (applause) for Protestant worship (renewed applause) … We want no mummery in this church.'[16]

St Matthew's was packed for Ommanney's first service. He avoided provocative ritualism, but a zealous *Telegraph* reporter observed that he bowed his head every time Jesus's name was mentioned and that he and the choir turned to the east for the creed. Ommanney criticised the local press for painting him in dark colours: 'calumny and falsehood were the weapons used against me'.

### Conflict with Archbishop Thomson

Wynn reported to Archbishop Thomson on the practices of the new priest. Thomson wrote to Ommanney, but then went silent, perhaps because the Archbishop of Canterbury had died and Thomson did not want to alienate Gladstone by bearing down on his choice.

After learning that Benson, the Bishop of Truro, had been appointed Archbishop of Canterbury, Thomson issued a 'monition' to Ommanney. Among other things, he was required to use pure wine (not diluted with water), let the congregation see what he was doing, not prostrate himself or bow in celebration, make no sign of the cross and no ceremonial elevation of the paten and cup and not consume the remains of the sacrament during the service. Ommanney accepted all but two requirements – the mixing of water with wine and the consuming of the remains. Thomson regarded this response as insubordination.

At the Easter vestry meeting in 1883, Ommanney tried to replace Wynn with Bindley, one of his own supporters, as churchwarden. The meeting was packed, with people shouting and screaming. Eventually, Wynn was re-elected by 326 votes to 146, partly thanks to manufacturers with six votes. During Holy Communion, Wynn stepped between Ommanney and the server to prevent them from washing the vessels and a struggle ensued. Ommanney took out a summons for riotous conduct but the case was dismissed.

Wynn and his fellow Protestants set up 'St Matthew's Protestant Mission Room' in the parish with Sunday evening services and a Sunday School. This was a tactical error, for Thomson soon rebuked Wynn for setting up a 'dissenting chapel' and for 'brawling'.[17]

On 18 June 1883, the anniversary of his arrival at St Matthew's, Ommanney delivered an extraordinary sermon. He said that, during the past year, great things had been gained for God, who had allowed him to endure persecution, and went on:

> There is a choice between two religions, between the Catholic religion of the Church of England and the Protestant religion begun only 300 years ago. The choice is between a religion of 1800 years standing and a new religion only 300 years old, between the religion of Jesus Christ and a religion of men founded by men whose characters would hardly bear examination. The choice was between the religion which formed the Saints and Martyrs of old and a religion which appeared to produce no change in the lives of those professing it.[18]

Ommanney could not have been more provocative. He was challenging Protestantism and the Reformation. Canon Blakeney, a gentle evangelical, feared that Ommanney had come to Sheffield to do the work of the Church of Rome.[19] This sermon was quoted in the press all over the country and caused great indignation in Sheffield. The local Church Conference voted by a large majority to seek immediate action by the archbishop.

On 27 June 1883, Archbishop Thomson announced a Commission of Inquiry into affairs at St Matthew's, to be chaired by Canon Blakeney, Vicar of Sheffield and Rural Dean, with three other local clergy as members. Wynn gave evidence to the commission and made more moderate charges than Ommanney had expected. Ommanney defended himself on the basis of the prayer book. The commission presented its report to Thomson. Ommanney understood it was mostly favourable to him, but he felt a 'burning sense of injustice that has never quite gone' that Thomson never published the report or announced any decisions based upon it.[20] It was as though the commission was just a device to buy time.

## The Dispute about Pews

Ommanney, keen to attract working people into St Matthew's, disliked the pew rents and 'free sittings' that he had inherited. He advised his followers not to interfere with existing pew rights but not to seek them themselves. An incident soon occurred that brought the matter to a head.

**54**   Canon Blakeney, gentle evangelical Vicar of Sheffield from 1877–95, led a Commission of Inquiry into Ommanney in 1883.

A lady called Mrs Rose had acquired pew rights when she lived in the parish. She now lived in Crookes but insisted on her rights, requiring some ladies to move out of her seat and make way for her. She was probably one of Wynn's Protestant supporters. Two men resented her action and deliberately sat in her seat until they were forcibly removed on the orders of Wynn as churchwarden. They went to court and were awarded £5 for assault and costs. The matter went to Archbishop Thomson. In February 1884, he wrote to Wynn saying that no seats could be permanently assigned to non-parishioners. When Wynn complained that Mrs Rose was being 'expelled', the archbishop denied this and said that she could sit elsewhere. He accused Wynn of a 'grave assault on others committed under your orders'.[21]

In 1889, Wynn resigned as churchwarden, saying he wanted to devote himself to the Protestant mission in Ball Lane, but eventually he gave that up, saying, 'I have it on my conscience that our continuance here savours strongly of persecution towards the Vicar.'[22] A period of calm ensued. Wynn lived to an advanced age and made his peace with Ommanney, even contributing to his 70th birthday present.

## The Development of St Matthew's

Ommanney was a priest of boundless energy. With John Sedding as church architect, he had the east end of the church remodelled, with a new altar and reredos, created a lady chapel and had a new organ installed. Having been initially cautious about ritual because of the opposition, in 1886 he began to use Eucharistic vestments, in 1889 introduced High Mass with full ceremonial and in 1898 Reservation of the Blessed Sacrament.

Denied resources by the Church Conference, Ommanney found local donors who would finance an additional priest. But he was distressed when two assistants went over to Rome. Ommanney described the popular reaction: 'At that time when Church feeling was intensely Protestant, it was a very heavy (blow). There was excitement beyond anything we can now conceive.'[23]

## The Imposition of 'Discipline'

In 1900 the two archbishops, Frederick Temple and William Maclagan, decided to regulate advanced ritualistic practices, banning the ceremonial use of incense and the Reservation of the Blessed Sacrament in open church.

Archbishop Maclagan offered Ommanney as a compromise the 'still use' of incense – a big thurible would be hung up from the roof and left burning during the service. Characteristically, Ommanney declined this olive branch. Maclagan hardly spoke to him ever again and placed him 'under discipline'. Thus, St Matthew's children would be examined by a Bishop prior to confirmation. The Bishop of Scarborough asked the children 'To whom do you confess your sins?' They said: 'God.' But then the bishop asked them: 'Do you confess to anyone else?' and they said 'Yes, to the priest.' The children commented that the bishop 'must be dotty'. Ommanney complained to the archbishop and this bit of discipline was not applied again.

Another aspect of 'discipline' was that other priests were to withdraw from Ommanney as 'a brother that doth walk disorderly', but the clergy took no notice. By now, Ommanney was an accepted local character. He was banned from having clergy from outside the diocese to preach, but this was not enforced.[24] The bishop never confirmed in the church and never visited it. The curates were unlicensed and there was no grant from the diocese.

Maclagan's successor, Cosmo Lang, ordered Ommanney to give up the continual Reservation of the Sacrament. Ommanney refused, commenting: 'to get the Archbishop into the Church, I must turn Christ out.' So the discipline continued.

## The Assaults of the Kensitites

St Matthew's became a target for an extreme Protestant militant group called the 'Kensitites', led by John Kensit, founder of the Protestant Truth Society, who organised disturbances in ritualistic churches. Three young men came to the church door. Denied entrance by the wardens, they conducted a 'Gospel Service' outside, casting aspersions on Ommanney. The local people threw mud at them. In 1900, John Kensit and his son came to the church and, after the blessing, made a public protest. The younger Kensit was carried out of the church.

The elder John Kensit died in 1902, but his son continued the family vendetta. In 1912 the Kensitites removed a figure of the baby Jesus and of the Virgin Mary from St Matthew's and took them to Bishopsthorpe, the archbishop's palace in York. The archbishop refused to see them and his chaplain passed the missing statues, a little broken, back to a churchwarden. Ommanney reluctantly had the church closed for over a year except during services. When the church was reopened, a man broke both figures. Ommanney decided to prosecute. Although the Kensitites hired Thomas Inskip, a top lawyer, they lost the case at Leeds Assizes and were fined £10 and bound over to keep the peace.

## Ommanney and the Working Class

Ommanney felt a special sense of mission towards the working class, as indeed did two of the archbishops with whom he came into conflict. Thomson's biographer states: 'Sheffield people idolised Thomson. He was able to attract working men in their thousands to listen to his addresses.'[25] Cosmo Lang shared this concern. But the dispute about ritual prevented Ommanney from working with them.

Ommanney fought hard to improve sanitary conditions in his parish: 'I worried and kept on worrying till I got the whole Parish repaired and drains in every street and lane. It is the one thing I am a little proud of. Since that time, St Matthew's Parish has been fairly free of epidemics.'[26]

He joined with a Catholic priest and a Fabian in deputations to the council about social conditions. He made his church a remarkable social centre, with numerous clubs and social events. He and his assistants visited homes in the parish and were seldom turned away. He was especially fond of the children – 'dear little mucky pale things'. He organised trips to the cinema in Union Street for every child in the parish. Regular patrons were asked 'not to mind the noise as Mr Ommanney's children were there'.[27]

But towards the end of his ministry, he wrote that work in the parish 'has always been exceedingly disappointing'. There were changes for the better – less drunkenness, less rows in the street, or fights between women. But people remained indifferent towards religion.[28] He attributed this to the Church's historic neglect of the poor. It was a deep-seated problem and in chapter 12 we shall see how two very different Anglican clergy sought to tackle it after the Second World War.

### Ommanney's Last Years

In 1914, the new diocese of Sheffield was formed under Dr Burrows as bishop. But the 'discipline' imposed on Ommanney continued and it rankled with him. He felt that, despite his loyalty to the Church, 'I have nearly all the time been treated as if I were a person to be suppressed in one way or another.'[29]

He obtained recognition in other ways. He represented the clergy of the diocese at convocation. But it was not until 1931, when Ommanney was 81, that, following an appeal to Dr Burrows, the 'discipline' was at last removed. The bishop attended the Patronal Festival at St Matthew's. On the 50th anniversary of Ommanney's incumbency, the bishop presided at a ceremony at the Cutlers' Hall in his honour. He died in 1936.

In his later years, Ommanney had become a famous and revered figure in Sheffield, deeply respected even by those who disagreed with him. Young clergy would seek his advice on pastoral work. Maybe he was too fussy about minor aspects of ritual, but this is probably what the early martyrs were like. By his courage and persistence, he helped to broaden the Church in South Yorkshire, making it easier for other dedicated Anglo-Catholic clergy to work, for instance, in the new coalfield churches. He led by example in his deep concern for working people.

**55** Te Deum window in the Chapel of the Holy Spirit in Sheffield Cathedral. This window by Philip Webb is in memory of Ommanney and symbolises the diocese's belated reconciliation with him.

*Chapter 8*

# The Settlement Movement

Our work is not a trick to fill any churches but to help men and women living in hard circumstances to fulfil better, and with more hope, a normal human life.

Rev. William Blackshaw, Founder of Croft House Settlement. 1904[1]

To establish in the City of Sheffield the Kingdom of God.

The Object of Sheffield Educational Settlement, according to Arnold Freeman

Arnold Freeman is an exceptional character. Instead of devoting his very considerable abilities in the Sheffield industries, he has spent his life in an attempt to achieve the spiritual regeneration of the inhabitants and aesthetic cultivation of the inhabitants mostly at his own expense. In short, nothing is too crazy for Mr Freeman ...

George Bernard Shaw in the *Sheffield Star* on 2 August 1940

By 1901, Sheffield's urban squalor and poverty were on a massive scale. Father Ommanney and many other clergy struggled sacrificially day-to-day with the problems in their areas but could not offer any hope of transformation, except through a better life hereafter. Socialists like Edward Carpenter believed that the only remedy was a reconstruction of society.

There were, however, some progressive nonconformist clergy and laity in Sheffield who were looking for more immediate action. Early in the 19th century, the Unitarians of Upper Chapel had been in the vanguard of radical reform but by the 1870s they were tending towards conservatism,[2] though there were still radical Unitarians in Sheffield, like the Rev. Charles Peach, founder of the Sheffield Fabians.

Increasingly in the Victorian period, Congregationalists took an interest in social issues. Thus the Rev. R.S. Bayley, Minister of Howard Street Chapel from 1836-46, founded the People's College. The Rev. Robert Stainton, Minister of Garden Street Chapel from 1865 to 1877, despite threats against him, convened a mass meeting apparently of 30,000 people in Paradise Square to denounce the role of William Broadhead in the Sheffield Outrages.[3] Families like the Leaders and the Wilsons (the smelting Wilsons rather than the snuff Wilsons) with Congregational roots were influential in the Liberal Party and in many social causes.

In the 1890s it was these Sheffield circles that were particularly drawn to the idea of the 'settlement', which was pioneered by an Anglican, Canon Samuel Barnett, at Toynbee Hall, founded in 1884 in the East End of London. Barnett argued: 'Let those of us who belong to the nation on top make direct personal contact with those belonging to the nation beneath.' This contact between the educated classes and the urban poor could help to alleviate poverty through the provision of social activities and adult education and greater understanding of the issue on the part of influential people. The educated people were there not just to impart knowledge but to befriend poor people and to learn. Barnett said that 'He who has, even for a month, shared the life of the poor can never rest again in his old thought.' Two of the founders of Britain's welfare state, William Beveridge and Clement Attlee, learned about poverty from Toynbee Hall.

Barnett distinguished between settlements and missions: settlements were for building bridges, whereas missions were for proselytising.[4] Other settlement founders disagreed. This would prove a contentious issue for Arnold Freeman, the most extraordinary figure in Sheffield settlement history.

We look first at the Neighbour Guilds Association[5] and then at the contributions of Dr Helen Wilson and the Rev. William Blackshaw and finally at the work of Arnold Freeman and the Sheffield Educational Settlement.

## The Neighbour Guilds Association

In Manchester, Birmingham and Liverpool, civic universities established university settlements in the late 1890s. Sheffield followed a different course. Its earliest settlements were set up by a group of concerned citizens, mostly nonconformists, who joined together on 18 March 1897 to form the Neighbour Guilds Association. The president was Alderman George Franklin JP, lord mayor elect. The neighbour guilds were to be non-political and non-sectarian and their object was: 'to brighten the lives of the poorer citizens of Sheffield by various means such as: working men's clubs with temperance bars, boys' clubs, girls' clubs, evening entertainments, reading circles and classes and voluntary sanitation committees'.[6]

The term 'neighbour guilds' to describe settlements came from an American Minister, Dr Stanley Coit, who had launched the first one in 1886 in New York, influenced by Toynbee Hall, and had subsequently written a book about them.[7]

The honorary secretary of the new asociation in Sheffield was Frank Tillyard (1865-1961), a lawyer concerned with business issues, including unemployment, who later became a professor at Birmingham University and was knighted. He brought to Sheffield valuable experience of a Congregationalist settlement, Mansfield House, in Canning Town, London.

The association deliberately planted its settlements in areas of extreme deprivation. Their first guild was in Shalesmoor where the death rate was 25 per cent – twice that in better areas. The association acquired the Old Ebenezer Day School, where they held clubs for boys and girls. Then in 1899 they acquired Kingsley House, 134 Birley Street, roughly the middle of Woodside Lane in Pitsmoor, where Sisters Mary and Agnes did nursing and visiting and ran boys' and girls' clubs. Unlike Toynbee Hall, these settlements did not provide residential accommodation.

## Dr Helen Wilson

By 1900, a remarkable woman, Dr Helen Wilson (1864-1951), had increasing influence in the Neighbour Guilds Association. From 1904, she was its secretary and in 1906 she paid with her own money for the building of Rutland Hall Settlement in Neepsend. In 1918, she transferred the Shipton Street Settlement from the Neighbour Guilds Association to the YMCA and, in 1919, the association concentrated its activities at Rutland Hall. From 1927-48, the settlement also owned Derwent Cottage in Hathersage. In 1942, Rutland Hall was renamed the 'Helen Wilson Settlement' in 1942 'out of a deep sense of gratitude to Dr Wilson'.[8] In 1949, the settlement became residential, housing the warden and social science students. It continued to operate until the 1970s.

Helen Wilson[9] was the daughter of H.J. Wilson (chapter 5), leading Sheffield liberal radical and MP for Holmfirth, who helped to fund the Neighbour Guilds Association.[10] Thus Helen came from a background of high principles and tempestuous debate. She was an early pupil at Sheffield High School for Girls, then based in Surrey Street, which her father had helped to found, along with his brother, John Wycliffe and J.D. Leader. After obtaining the London MD in 1894, she returned to Sheffield where she was probably the city's first woman doctor. She practised privately and as medical officer and referee to insurance companies and friendly societies and in the school health services.

In 1905, at the age of 41, Helen Wilson retired from medical practice to devote more time to addressing the 'social evil', carrying on her parents' work concerned with prostitutes. In 1910, she became secretary of the British Association for Moral and Social Hygiene and editor of the association's journal *The Shield*. Like her parents, she opposed the legalisation of prostitution, believing that the remedies were better education, higher living standards and better recreational facilities. Her work for the neighbour guilds in some of the most squalid parts of Sheffield provided opportunities for 'rescue' work among fallen women and those in danger of falling into prostitution.

She joined in the struggle for women's emancipation but did not approve of militant methods (chapter 9). In 1920, she was the first woman magistrate appointed in Sheffield.

*Willam Blackshaw and the Croft House Settlement*

In 1899, the Rev. William Blackshaw[11] (1866-1953) became Minister of Queen Street Congregational Chapel. Queen Street was the most liberal of Sheffield's Congregational churches and its members included prominent Liberals like Batty Langley, MP for

**56**   The Rev. William Blackshaw of Queen Street Congregational Church and founder of Croft House Settlement.

Attercliffe from 1894. Journalists later wrote of the 'The Queen Street School of Liberalism.'[12] The 'civic gospel' of the famous Birmingham Congregationalist R.W. Dale was to be heard here.[13] Blackshaw was a Londoner, influenced, as was Arnold Freeman, by Highbury Quadrant Congregational Church. Like Canon Barnett, he was dedicated to working with the poor, not for purposes of evangelism, but in order to improve their lives (see opening quotation to this chapter). He did not join up with the Neighbour Guilds Association, but instead persuaded Queen Street Church to form its own settlement. This was a bold venture into the unknown for his congregation and it is to their credit that they took the risk.

Blackshaw chose to work in the Crofts area around Garden Street and Scotland Street, where Carpenter and his socialists had established the Commonwealth Café in 1887. Fourteen years later, the area was even more run down. It was said that 'from the Saturday to the Monday, no respectable person dare pass unprotected.' It was agreed that the settlement should be based in Robert Stainton's former chapel in Garden Street, which was no longer in use – itself a sign of the area's decline. In March 1901, Sheffield Congregational Association welcomed the new venture: 'The meeting rejoices that Queen Street Church has determined to grapple boldly and in the spirit of the Master with the sin, poverty and wretchedness of the Crofts and will do its best to support Rev. William Blackshaw and his friends in carrying out this great enterprise.'[14]

Blackshaw planned a residential block in Townhead Street to accommodate himself as warden and his family, and other paying residents, as well as housing work with women and girls. But he could not raise enough money and settled for a major restructuring of the Garden Street chapel, where a new floor was inserted to make an upper hall. In October 1902, the lord mayor opened the 'Croft Settlement Hall'.

The new settlement had a boys' club, gymnasium, musical and dramatic society (the mainstay of its finances and precursor of the well-known operatic society), Sunday School, Bible classes and much else besides. The Blackshaws had a house in Totley but the dedicated warden spent four nights a week staying at 107, Townhead Street. Blackshaw organised weekend summer camps for men and boys, holiday activities in August for poor children and free breakfasts and soup for some 24 families. In 1905 work with girls began in Garden Street.

By 1909, the pressures on Blackshaw of being both minister and warden were too great. He gave up his role as minister of Queen Street and devoted himself to Croft House on two-thirds of his former salary. In 1910, Queen Street severed its connection with Croft House and for many years it was run by a committee chaired by Oliver Wilson, Helen's younger brother. Croft House pioneered in the city Baden Powell's idea of a scout troop. Blackshaw eventually left in 1913. He did not lose his interest in settlement work for, in 1926, he became warden of Mansfield House in London. In 1938 he wrote *The Community and Social Science*, a description of the social services of the day.

From 1914 until 1940, Miss Edith Spencer − known as 'Sister Edith' − was warden of Croft House. Originally a Londoner like Blackshaw, she had considerable experience of social work with children. Hers was a sacrificial ministry, driven by her religious

**57** Court 15, Scotland Street − typical of the poverty in this part of Sheffield where Blackshaw opened his settlement.

**58**   Garden Street Chapel, founded by the Rev. Robert Stainton. This is an architect's drawing. In order to accommodate Croft House settlement, in 1902 a new floor was inserted. The Settlement operates in this building to this day.

convictions, living on a low income in the damp flat in Townhead Street, where Blackshaw had lived, and working among people impoverished by unemployment. Often Sunday ended with her stopping fights in the street outside. There was a succession of wardens after Sister Edith, of whom perhaps the best known was Joe Jepson from the early 1960s to his death in 1988, with a break in the middle. The area around the settlement became depopulated but the activities continued with club members coming from further afield. The astonishing thing is that Croft House settlement celebrated its centenary in 2002 and still operates today in the same premises.

### The Origins of the Shipton Street Settlement

One of the neighbour guild settlements founded by Helen Wilson was on the corner of Shipton Street and Oxford Street in the parish of St Philip's in Upperthorpe, near the Royal Infirmary. Helen Wilson installed Miss M.J. Wrigley as matron. This settlement provided classes for women and girls and also sought to raise the morals of the area: 'From here Dr Helen, Miss Wrigley and later on Miss Dorothy Arnold, Deaconess of St Philips Church, sallied forth with veiled threats on the delivery home of the girls so effectively that these three virtually cleaned up the district.'[15]

This settlement had a hostel with accommodation for seven university or

**59**   Sheffield Educational Settlement in Upperthorpe – another poor area. In the foreground is the Settlement Hostel (later Nurses Home) on the corner of Shipton Street and Oxford Street. Arnold Freeman's settlement was based in the humble cottages beyond, yet had a magical atmosphere.

business people. Residents included John St George Heath, a former president of the Oxford Union and for a time warden of the neighbour guilds, his successor, Henry Clay, Alan Mawer, lecturer in English and later provost of University College London and E. Curtis, later a professor in Dublin. There was also free legal advice provided by barristers and solicitors from the city centre.

### Arnold Freeman (1886-1972)

In 1913, Arnold Freeman[16] was appointed tutor for extra mural studies in Sheffield and started to live in the hostel. Freeman came from a remarkable nonconformist family of tobacco importers in the East End of London. Arnold's brothers were highly practical (Ralph, a consulting engineer, designed Sydney Harbour Bridge), whereas Arnold was more of a religious dreamer. Criticised for not going into engineering, he retorted: 'Our family swarms with engineers. They infect the house like rats.' He studied history at St John's College, Oxford, the high-minded college in which Barnett had originally floated his settlement ideas. After Oxford, he worked with Sidney Webb on the abolition of destitution, having been recommended by his senior tutor as 'an ardent Socialist, keen and capable'. He also spent a year at the Quaker settlement at Woodbrooke, Birmingham.

Like Carpenter, Freeman began his life in South Yorkshire as a university extension lecturer, teaching not only in Sheffield but also in the mining areas of Swinton, Maltby and Denaby. Very widely read, he introduced his students to extensive historical and cultural knowledge.

In 1916 Freeman embarked on some extraordinary sociological research in Sheffield. With echoes of Ebenezer Elliott's criticisms of the working class (chapter 4), he feared that post-war reconstruction would be impeded by the workers' unreadiness to exercise political power. With the help of Miss Wrigley, Lady Mabel Smith (a left-wing member of the Fitzwilliam family) and others, Freeman launched a study of 816 Sheffield working-class men and women. The study's patronising and moralistic tone is odd to modern eyes. Among other things, investigators recorded:

- 'any points that would serve to indicate X's goodness or badness'
- Is (the home) really a home? Is there love? Is it merely a sleeping and eating place?'
- 'Are there any vices eg drinking, gambling, laziness etc that militate against his industrial efficiency?'
- 'Love of Beauty' eg Who was Beethoven or Edward Carpenter?
- 'Love of Knowledge' eg Who was Aristotle?
- 'Love of Goodness' eg Is he a member of a church?

Analysis showed that one quarter of the working classes were 'well-equipped' (ie 'awakened ... to the splendour and seriousness of existence'), nearly three-quarters were 'inadequately equipped' (ie 'asleep') and one-fifteenth were 'mal-equipped' (ie by deficiency or perversion unable to discharge their duties). The report, *The Equipment of the Workers*, was published in 1919 and acclaimed by the press as 'extraordinarily interesting'.

Freeman was arguing for major public investment in adult education. He planned two more volumes – one on education (completed but unpublished) and a third on the environment (never completed). He could not foresee the devastating post-war slump, which would crush high-principled aspirations like these.

### The YMCA Settlement

In 1918, Helen Wilson's Neighbour Guilds Association was struggling to keep the Shipton Street Settlement open. Freeman persuaded the YMCA, then in an expansionist phase, to take it over, with himself as warden. Freeman wrote a booklet with his vision of 'Education through fellowship for service':

> in some senses a university, a church and a club, devoid of creeds and traditions, free to experiment, free to co-operate with any agency working for similar ideals ... We plead for a new university which will set itself to establish the Kingdom of God by distributing culture among the mass of the people ... Members pledge themselves to the amelioration of social conditions and the building up of a satisfactory system of national education ... the consummation of the activities of the settlement is the production of a play ...[17]

The YMCA was uneasy about Freeman's ambitious ideas, but agreed to a major reconstruction of the buildings with an expanded hostel (known as the Casa Giocosa), a club room elegantly designed by William Rothenstein (whose famous painting *The Buffer Girls* was executed and hung there) and the Little Theatre, which swiftly became the settlement's most famous feature, just as the Operatic Society loomed large at Croft House.

In September 1919, General Sir Arthur Yapp, national secretary of the YMCA, opened the improved settlement and over the next two years those staying in the hostel including Annie Besant, Sir Arthur Conan Doyle, Harold Laski, Arnold Rowntree and Edward Carpenter. The settlement's initiatives included a survey of the parish, a guild of help, a Sunbeam Club for 68 unfortunate neglected people, a Maternity and Child Welfare Association, a choir and orchestra, elocution classes, numerous study circles, legal and advisory services, a conference on Bolshevism and a series of plays at the Little Theatre.

This was an astonishingly creative period but the YMCA was unhappy about the financial losses and announced that it would withdraw in April 1921, handing the settlement over to Freeman on generous terms.

### Sheffield Educational Settlement

Freeman renamed the organisation 'Sheffield Educational Settlement'. It was a continual struggle to maintain viability after the departure of the YMCA. The choir and orchestra moved elsewhere. A key colleague, Stephen Tredinnick, departed, criticising the 'veneered spirituality' of the settlement, though later returning to the area as Minister of Tabernacle Congregational Church. Freeman wrote to many of the great and good and assembled a distinguished advisory council. In order to harness business acumen, Harry Brearley, the inventor of stainless steel, was persuaded to become treasurer, but he lived in Torquay and the extent of his contribution is disputed.

Later in 1921, Freeman read an article by Rudolf Steiner about anthroposophy and became an ardent convert, as did D.V. Butler, secretary of the settlement. The main conviction of the anthroposophy movement is that, 'through meditation and awareness, people can heighten their own spirituality and commune with a shared universal spirituality'.[18] A visit by the inner group of settlement staff to Dornach, the movement's centre, strengthened Freeman's new beliefs. He had been a Fabian and knew Sidney Webb, Shaw, Wells and other socialist thinkers. But he felt they were mistaken in thinking that society could be reformed by redistribution or nationalisation. Freeman shared Carpenter's view that reform had to be spiritual.

Freeman's conversion created great tensions in the settlement. The settlement was 'non-sectarian' and yet the warden wrote to its members to say that Steiner was the only hope. A swear box was introduced to deter people from mentioning the name 'Steiner'. Herbert Prentice, the talented theatre director, who had been to Dornach but remained unconverted, felt 'dropped' by Freeman: 'Needless to say, the trouble is Steiner and Anthroposophy.'

**60** Scene from Hardy's *Dynasts* at the Little Theatre, 1951, showing the Napoleonic Wars on a six-foot stage – much appreciated by the young Roy Hattersley.

Eventually, Herbert and Marion Prentice left to pursue their theatrical interests elsewhere, founding Sheffield Repertory Theatre. But the Little Theatre continued to produce plays until 1961. It was the first theatre to produce Gilbert Murray's translations of classical Greek tragedies. The young Roy Hattersley and his schoolmates witnessed an ambitious production of Thomas Hardy's *The Dynasts* on a six-foot stage: 'We all sat in complete silence as the Grande Armee, the Austrians and Austerlitz and the multitudes proclaiming Napoleon's coronation were successfully depicted by the same half dozen actors.'[19]

Freeman's decision to stand as Labour candidate for the Hallam constituency in the 1923 General Election caused controversy. He stood because he was 'aghast at the situation into which the affairs of the world are drifting'. But his candidature reinforced a perception that the settlement was 'a hotbed of Socialists and labour-cranks'. Moreover, Freeman was criticised for sending copies of the New Testament stamped 'YMCA' with letters urging people to support him. He came second in the election, ahead of the Liberal candidate. Several eminent people withdrew from the council and fund raising became more difficult.

Industrial recession and high unemployment increased the financial difficulties. In 1924, the hostel was sold off to the Royal Infirmary, who desperately needed it for nurses' accommodation. This cleared some debt, but also eliminated one of the settlement's great assets – its ability to accommodate supporters and visitors. Freeman himself lived in Fulwood, as his wife was unwilling to live over the shop. He caught the first tram in the morning and worked very long hours.

In 1925, returning from a trip to Greece, Freeman found that a section of the management committee demanded a general meeting in order to secure his replacement on grounds of 'intolerance' – a odd charge, since Freeman had recently incurred obloquy for allowing a communist Sunday School on the premises. They might have done better to focus on financial management. The general meeting referred the issue to the management committee, who split eight each way, leaving Freeman to cast his chairman's vote in his own favour.

After these 'shattering events', the settlement began to focus strongly on the unemployed, redefining its role as 'a College and Club for Poor People, especially those who are out of work'. Given the scale of unemployment in the Upperthorpe area, this was the right way to go, but it added to the tensions. Many of the unemployed students were communists; some later becoming prominent union leaders. Freeman felt that they 'regarded him as "the old fool"' because he represented obsolete religious views and was not a revolutionary communist. He got unemployed students to write essays on their experiences, which even now make painful reading. His craft scheme to provide work for the unemployed was a noble failure. The Little Theatre performed a stage version of the socialist classic *The Ragged Trousered Philanthropists*.

The settlement encouraged outdoor activities, like Arnold Hardy's ramblers' club, which played a leading part in Sheffield's mass trespass in 1932 (chapter 11). Freeman feared that it might be too much under communist influence.[20] Freeman organised summer schools in the Lake District and other beautiful areas and negotiated with the Ministry of Labour so that unemployed people could attend. Then he and two colleagues bought an outward-bound centre at Hollowford near Castleton for the use of the settlement and retained it until 1946 when it was sold at a profit to the Sheffield Diocese.[21]

In 1930, the financial position of the settlement was at last stabilised when the wealthy and enlightened Ward sisters, Gertrude, who became an anthroposophist, and her remarkable sister, Ethel (see chapter 11), bought the premises for £400 and rented them to the settlement. An historian comments: 'Without the generosity of these two ladies, the Settlement would never have survived.'[22]

Winifred Albaya gives a vivid account of the settlement in the 1930s:

I cannot explain the peculiar feeling of exhilaration and excitement with which we approached the green door in Shipton Street – in and up the steep stairs into the Club Room which had once been described as the most beautiful interior in Sheffield, a little faded then but still comfortable, relaxing and (usually) peaceful … we were taking part in a unique experiment in adult education. It was totally comprehensive, totally unstreamed and represented every grade of the educational process from the almost illiterate, unemployed, early school leaver to the Oxford graduate.[23]

She also describes Freeman, who embodied the Settlement:

Of medium height and build, his external aesthetic appearance belied a toughness and strength of character. Not only was his appearance aesthetic, it was ascetic … with his high-domed

**61**  Arnold Freeman producing Hardy's *Dynasts* in 1951.

forehead and medieval tonsure, he would have looked more at home in a monk's cassock
and hood, but he always lectured in a tweed jacket, flannels and comfortable carpet slippers
… He was always patient and courteous and possessed of a whimsical puckish humour with
which he could charm his opponents or turn in on himself. Yet he never altered his views
or compromised his deeply held convictions.[24]

In the 1930s, politics became ever more highly charged. In 1937, a branch of the
Left Book Club was founded in Sheffield, which attracted some people from the
settlement. A student called Joe Albaya went to fight in Spain and on his return became
secretary/caretaker of a new left-wing Unity Club in Gibraltar Street. Freeman was
profoundly aware of the worsening international situation. The settlement 'adopted'
Walter Woelhardt, a German refugee. In 1938 a Fund for Jewish Relief was established
and Freeman became chair of a Sheffield Co-ordinating Committee for Refugees. Mrs
Freeman helped support child refugees, three of whom lived in the Freeman home in
Fulwood. Hollowford became a retreat for refugees.

During the Second World War, D. V. Butler founded a highly profitable canteen. Freeman
felt that it got in the way of other activities and he eventually closed it in 1948, after
Butler retired. Freeman eventually retired in 1955 at the age of seventy. His able successor,
Christopher Boulton, committed the organisation more explicitly to anthroposophy.
When the council demolished the hallowed buildings in Shipton Street, Boulton moved
to Tintagel House in Meadowbank Road, Nether Edge, where the theatrical tradition
continued in the new Merlin Theatre. Freeman was not forgotten. The new theatre
included an Arnold Freeman Hall. Then, in 2006, the Ruskin Mill Educational Trust
founded Freeman College in Sheffield for young people with learning difficulties.

Freeman was a controversial figure. Winifred Albaya wrote: 'In the latter years of
the Settlement, the aura of mysticism and holier than thou spirituality became over-
powering.'[25] Grace Hoy, who was involved for 19 years, rejected this criticism as coming
from a Marxist viewpoint. She accused Albaya and another historian of the settlement,
John Roberts, of missing the settlement's 'heartbeat' – the warmth, the glow, the magic,
due to Freeman's personality. But, alongside his charisma, Freeman from his teens onwards
had an irritating tendency to preach. His anthroposophy cast doubt on the fundamental
aims of the settlement, which remained ambiguous until his retirement. To do him justice,
Freeman strongly believed in individual expression and was tolerant to a fault.

Freeman's persistence in keeping the settlement going through so many vicissitudes
was astonishing. To quote one of his students, he was an 'erratic, unpredictable,
loveable genius'.[26]

The settlements' contribution to Sheffield life has been important. Their founders were
driven by deep convictions to work with and among poor people. Planted in some of the
most desolate parts of the city, the settlements provided stimulation, education and support
to hard-pressed people, in conditions of abject poverty and demoralising unemployment.
It is fascinating that the settlements lived on long after the post-war creation of the 'welfare
state' – in Shipton Street until the early 1960s, at the Helen Wilson Settlement in Neepsend
until the 1970s and in Croft House, which is still functioning. One explanation is that
poverty has not disappeared. But, more broadly, the settlements reflected a conviction that,
as Carpenter and Freeman argued, social improvement is not just about economics but
also about social interaction and relationships. The development of community forums
and local voluntary centres as part of 'regeneration' from the 1980s onwards has drawn on
the work of the settlements over the last hundred years.

*Chapter 9*

# The Women's Struggle

Although women will ever look to Manchester as the source from which they drew much of their idealism and inspiration … they should not overlook the fact that the great Yorkshire city of Sheffield is rightly proud of the part which it played in these shadowy beginnings.

Roger Fulford, *Votes for Women*[1]

The 'lady', the household drudge and the prostitute are the three main types of women resulting in our modern civilisation from the process of the past – and it is hard to know which is the most wretched, which is the most wronged and which is the most unlike that which in her heart every true woman would desire to be.

Edward Carpenter, *Love's Coming of Age*, 1896[2]

There was an important 19th-century tradition in Sheffield of women playing a strong and independent role. In 1825, the Sheffield Ladies Anti-Slavery Society was formed, which, led by Mary Anne Rawson, campaigned vigorously. In 1838, a Female Radical Association emerged within the Chartist movement. In 1842, the pioneering People's College was set up to provide adult education for men and women alike (in contrast to the later London Working Men's College). Most importantly, as Roger Fulford indicated, a group of Sheffield women in 1851 set up the first organisation in the country to call for female suffrage. Half a century later, Sheffield women played their full part in the movement for women's suffrage right up to 1914. The city council supported enfranchisement from 1911.

Underlying the campaign for female suffrage was the much deeper question of women's place in society, about which Edward Carpenter wrote so passionately and provocatively (see quotation above). The formidable women described in this chapter managed to escape from the subordinate roles described by Carpenter. The third of Carpenter's categories – the prostitutes – were the special concern of Charlotte Wilson and her husband H.J. Wilson MP.

The developing role of women in Sheffield is too big a topic and too little researched to cover fully here. In this chapter, we look at the role that some women in Sheffield played in political movements like the anti-slavery campaign, the 'shadowy beginnings' of the female suffrage movement in the 1850s and the climax of the suffrage movement early in the 20th century.

## *Mary Anne Rawson and the Sheffield Ladies Anti-Slavery Society*

We start with the anti-slavery movement[3] since, as we shall see, this inadvertently gave birth to the female suffrage movement. Both movements were about challenging structures of domination.

When James Montgomery joined the Gales household in 1792, he found that the family was boycotting sugar as part of the anti-slavery campaign. Gales had written a pamphlet commending this boycott, but it depended on strong support from Sheffield women. Montgomery took readily to the anti-slavery cause as his parents had been Moravian missionaries to slaves in the West Indies. Gales, Montgomery and many others in Sheffield contributed to the great movement that led to the abolition of Britain's role in the slave trade in 1807.

But slavery persisted in the colonies. In the 1820s societies campaigning to abolish colonial slavery emerged. These societies were male-dominated and gave little scope to the crusading zeal of women. So female societies were founded, starting in Birmingham in 1824 and spreading to Sheffield in 1825 when the Sheffield Ladies Anti-Slavery Society was formed. This society called for total and immediate abolition. The ladies sought to educate local

**62**   Mary Anne Rawson, leader of Sheffield Ladies' Anti-Slavery Society – a formidable campaigner.

people about slavery by distributing information, advertisements and pamphlets, campaigning door-to-door, singing anti-slavery hymns, boycotting West Indian goods, notably sugar, organising petitions and even knitting muffatees (fingerless gloves) and babies' shoes.

The moving spirit in the Sheffield society was Mary Anne Rawson[4] (1801–87), daughter of Joseph Read of a smelting family (silver and gold refining), who were pillars of Queen Street Congregational Church. They were also radical enough to help pay Montgomery's legal expenses in 1794-5. The smelting business went into decline, to be revived in the 1860s by Mary Anne's nephews, John Wycliffe Wilson and H.J. Wilson MP (chapter 5). In 1828 Mary Anne married William Rawson of Nottingham, who died in 1829. The couple had had one daughter, Elizabeth. Mary Anne did not retreat into a quiet widowhood. She was a highly educated evangelical woman, much concerned with missionary causes and education. With her sister, she ran for a time a school at Wincobank. Thanks to inheritances, she retained Wincobank Hall, which became a propaganda centre for good causes, rather like H.J. Wilson's Osgathorpe Hills later in the century. She belonged to Montgomery's circle, though she felt that his companions, the Misses Gales, lacked refinement.[5] The cautious Montgomery thought she had 'such extreme notions, such ultra views', like total abstinence, removal of the death penalty and immediate abolition of slavery.[6]

In 1833, the Government abolished slavery in the colonies, but Rawson was unhappy about the transitional seven-year 'apprenticeship' for the slaves, which seemed to her to prolong slavery. She wanted to end the apprenticeships and to get slavery abolished in other countries. So, in 1837, she and her colleagues formed the 'Sheffield Ladies' Association for the Universal Abolition of Slavery'. Further petitions were launched, including one signed, remarkably, by 25,000 Sheffield women – three-quarters of the female population. The ladies would not let anyone sign until they understood what it was about. In 1838, the apprenticeships were abolished. The international movement against slavery got under way and held a convention in London in 1840. But women were not allowed to speak – leading to anger among many and the beginnings of the female suffrage movement. Rawson, who was satisfied with the role she was able to play in evangelical and political causes, did not share this indignation.[7]

One of Rawson's most constructive ventures was to raise funds for a school in Jamaica, which trained schoolteachers for other schools. The funds initially came just from Sheffield but later from ladies' societies elsewhere. The school opened in 1840 with three teachers from England but faded after five years. As late as 1875, at the age of 74, she led a campaign against the Navy returning runaway slaves to their home countries. She died virtually penniless in 1887, having used her resources on good works.

### The Shadowy Beginnings of the Women's Suffrage Movement

Rawson was not involved in the mysterious emergence in 1851 in Sheffield of Britain's first organisation for female suffrage.[8] She did not favour female suffrage and the Chartist ladies who took this initiative came from a different social group. This new movement was influenced by Ironside and his Democrats (chapter 4) and by Anne Knight, a 65-year-old abolitionist Quaker from Chelmsford. She was in touch with American anti-slavery feminists[9] and indignant at the treatment of women abolitionists at the 1840 convention. Knight was presumed author of a pamphlet published in 1847, calling for female suffrage. In 1851, Anne Knight wrote to a Mrs Rooke of the National Charter Association in Sheffield to say that her friend, Isaac Ironside, had favoured her with the names of 'seven ladies who waited on him to beg the exercise of his vote' to support revising the first article of the Charter (which would only enfranchise men).

It was on 26 February 1851 that the 'Sheffield Female Political Association'[10] held their first meeting at the *Democratic Temperance Hotel*, 33 Queen Street, Sheffield. They were chaired by Mrs C. Ash, president, and their corresponding secretary, who perhaps corresponded with Anne Knight, was Mrs Abiah Higginbottom, a name which caused Roger Fulford some schoolboyish amusement. The association agreed the following address:

> we are brought to the conclusion that women might, with the strictest propriety, be included in the proclamation of the people's charter; for we are the majority of the nation and it is our birthright, equally with our brothers, to vote for the man who is to sway our political destiny ... Heartily should we rejoice to see the women of England uniting for the purpose of demanding this great right to humanity ... For what would not the patient energetic mind of woman accomplish once resolved? ... Is this oppression to last for ever? Are we always to remain the drudges, the helots of society? We the women of the democracy of Sheffield answer No ... We put forth the earnest appeal to our sisters of England to join hand and heart with us in this noble and just cause. We have commenced an Association designated the 'Sheffield Women's Political Association'. Our special object will be the political enfranchisement of our sex; and we conjure with you, our Sisters of England, to aid us in accomplishing this holy work of liberty and fraternity.

This address is notable for its eloquence and confidence and for anticipating by 20 years the strategy later adopted in Manchester of launching a national movement of women (not men on their behalf) to press for the vote.

The association held regular meetings. They persuaded the 7th Lord Carlisle, former Viceroy of Ireland and progressive nephew of the bachelor Duke of Devonshire, to petition the House of Lords 'to take into their serious consideration the propriety of enacting an Electoral Law which will include adult females'. After this, the association received enquiries from all over the country.

In 1852, the group resolved to set up a National Women's Rights Association, with Anne Knight as president, but all the members apart from Anne Knight were from Sheffield. However, nothing more is heard of this initiative. This group had set themselves a task beyond their capability and their confidence may have been undermined as the Chartist or Democrat movement in Sheffield declined (chapter 4).

## The Moderate Suffragist Movement

Sheffield was quiescent for a while after this, but women's suffrage groups sprang up in the 1860s elsewhere, notably in Manchester and in 1867 theis society brought together various suffrage groups to form the National Society for Women's Suffrage (NSWS). In 1869, single women ratepayers got the vote in local elections and this was extended to married women in 1894.

Sheffield's progressive attitude towards the role of women was illustrated by two developments in the 1870s. First, H.J. Wilson and his wife Charlotte became major allies of Josephine Butler in the fight against the Contagious Diseases Act. Although it was a taboo subject for respectable ladies, Charlotte courageously formed a Sheffield Ladies Association to spearhead opposition in the North of England to 'legalised prostitution'.[11] Secondly, Sheffield's major new civic college and precursor of the University of Sheffield, Firth College, 'admitted women on a par with men from its opening day in 1879'.[12]

Then the campaign for female suffrage spread to Sheffield. In 1882, the National Society for Women's Suffrage organised a meeting chaired by Viscountess Harberson in Sheffield at the Albert Hall, which was so full that an overflow meeting was held at St Paul's School. This led to the launch of the 'Sheffield Women's Suffrage Society' (SWSS). Unlike the Chartist women of the 1850s, the women leading the new society came from the prosperous middle class and were seeking suffrage based on property qualifications. They launched petitions and lobbied MPs.

In 1896, Millicent Fawcett drew the various women's suffrage groups into the National Union of Women's Suffrage Societies (NUWSS), which, in the early 20th century, became a powerful national lobbying group, bringing pressure to bear on all political parties. The SWSS was affiliated to the NUWSS.

## The Rise of the Militant Suffragettes

In 1903, Mrs Emmeline Pankhurst and her eldest daughter Christabel formed the Womens' Political and Social Union (WSPU) or militant suffragettes in Manchester. The Pankhursts embarked on militant tactics quite different from the more genteel lobbying of the NUWSS. Their new movement attracted young women who resented the suffocating restrictions on the role of women in society that Carpenter had bitterly criticised (see opening of this chapter). The WSPU later moved their office to London, where the Pankhursts, disillusioned with the new Liberal Government, sought Conservative support.

In 1906, Herbert Asquith, the Home Secretary, spoke at a public meeting in Sheffield. He was interrupted by women demonstrators, including Mrs Emmeline Pankhurst, who were forcibly removed. Asquith told his audience that female suffrage was 'a sham issue: no good cause could be served in such a way'. In 1908, he became Prime Minister and his scepticism was one of the major obstacles to female suffrage.

In January 1907, a branch of the WSPU was formed in Sheffield and soon organised its first meeting at Montgomery Hall.

## The Sheffield Suffrage Scene

Like the Chartists, the women's suffrage movement was divided. Initially, the main groups collaborated but, as the WSPU became more extreme and unpopular, the other groups distanced themselves from it.

In Sheffield, the moderate suffragists remained organised in the SWSS. In 1908, the SWSS, with Mrs Robert Styring as president, were in the forefront of a march of 2,000 women in Manchester, including the impressive figure of Dr Helen Wilson (chapter 8), resplendent in the scarlet and purple garments of a Doctor of Medicine. In 1909, Dr Helen Wilson became secretary of the SWSS, opposing militant tactics and favouring persuasion. With some justice, she and other moderates feared that militancy would delay rather than accelerate the granting of the franchise.

The WSPU was centrally organised and their Sheffield leaders both came from Manchester to 'make mayhem' in the town. We know less about the Sheffield-born militants, but one Sheffield suffragette was Edith Whitworth[13] of 70 Wath Road, Nether Edge, who was married to a postal telegraphist and had two young children. She became secretary of the new Sheffield WSPU branch.

In February 1907, Edith Whitworth and three other women travelled to London to attend a national convention of the WSPU. Afterwards, they joined a party of suffragettes who tried to force entry into the House of Commons. They were arrested and given sentences of 14 days' imprisonment in Holloway Prison, where they were badly treated with some 'abominable' food. On their release, they were greeted by a brass band and Edith Whitworth told a reporter: 'We are the true daughters of old Chartists and mean to fight, if needs be laying down our lives for the struggle.'[14] The conservative *Sheffield Telegraph* was surprisingly sympathetic, headlining its report 'The Sheffield Martyrs'. Edith Whitworth also supported Adela Pankhurst in her escapades at the 1908 Cutlers' Feast. However, she then left the WSPU and joined a third group, the Women's Freedom League, which formed a branch in Sheffield. The Women's Freedom League represented women who resented the Pankhursts' high-handedness and their opposition to the labour movement. It is not surprising that there should be such a group in Sheffield.

There was a fourth group in Sheffield – the anti-suffragists – whose chairman was the Duke of Norfolk. They held meetings and demonstrations particularly in 1912, but never had much support. Opinion in Sheffield generally supported women's franchise and was critical of the prevarication of Westminster politicians. In 1907, the influential Sheffield Trades and Labour Council resolved in favour of the female franchise. In 1911, Sheffield City Council called on the Government to support the franchise.

We now look at two remarkable young women who led the WSPU suffragettes in Sheffield – Adela Pankhurst and Molly Morris.

## Adela Pankhurst

Adela Pankhurst[15] (1885-1961) was the third daughter of Richard Pankhurst, a radical Manchester barrister who drafted the first female suffrage bill, and his wife Emmeline. Richard's death in 1898 placed the family in financial difficulties. Adela was delicate from birth and did not have as privileged an educational background as her elder sisters, Christabel and Sylvia. She became a pupil teacher in a poor part of Manchester. Adela felt marginalised in this strange family. Later, she called the family attitude, 'Cause first and human relations – nowhere', and said of her mother: 'She had not developed her gift for individual maternity, but merged it into a larger feeling for all homes and all children.'[16]

When her mother and sisters plunged into the maelstrom of the militant suffrage campaign, Adela joined in. She later described the experience as follows:

> From a shy somewhat melancholy girl, I became, before I was nineteen, a self-confident woman who could hold crowds of thousands ...All I wanted was a piece of chalk and a 'lorry' (low flat wagon) because I was too small to speak off a soap box and all by myself I could rouse any district.[17]

VOTES FOR WOMEN.

Miss **ADELA PANKHURST,**

Organiser, National Women's
Social and Political Union,
4, Clement's Inn, Strand, W.C.

63   Adela Pankhurst.

Militant action required courage and endurance. In July 1906, her interruptions to a big Liberal rally in Manchester, featuring both Winston Churchill and Lloyd George, led to imprisonment and subsequently a beating from a gang of young men. Yet she taught in her school the next day. She soon gave up teaching and became a full-time organiser.

In October 1908, Reginald McKenna, First Lord of the Admiralty, came to Sheffield to speak at the Cutlers' Feast at a time when Sheffield steel barons were keen to hear about the expansion of the fleet. Adela, accompanied by Edith Whitworth and a few others, disguised herself as a kitchen maid in order to get into the Cutlers' Hall. A policeman blocked her way, so she went to the town hall where she held forth from the steps to a crowd, which grew to 800-900 people. She cried, 'I am going to the Cutlers' Hall.' The crowd responded, 'And we are going with you.' After a short walk, Adela, followed by the crowd, arrived at a police cordon in the High Street. She declared, 'I want to see Mr McKenna. I am going in. Now, I shall. We want votes for women.' Chief Inspector Hollis replied, 'No, you are not going.' The ensuing struggle lasted for some 90 minutes. There were ugly rushes and Adela and the others were roughly handled. Eventually, they withdrew to the town hall and Adela boarded a tramcar to her hotel where she discarded the maid's uniform. An hour later, she arrived in a cab at the Cutler's Hall and made a dash to get inside but was stopped and escorted away. The police had the good sense not to arrest her.

In Spring 1909, there was a by-election in Attercliffe (chapter 10). All three suffrage organisations intervened in different ways. Helen Wilson and the SWSS focused on non-party propaganda and a petition for the vote. Adela organised numerous outdoor meetings at which the WSPU opposed the Liberal candidate. Her mother arrived and drove round the constituency in an open carriage. The Women's Freedom League also organised meetings and sent postcards with 2,300 pro-suffrage signatures to Asquith.

Arrested during a campaign in Scotland, Adela resorted to the suffragettes' alarming new weapon, the hunger strike. A prison doctor described her as 'a slender under-sized girl five feet in height and (in health) seven stone in weight', and pronounced her unfit for forcible feeding. She was released. In another incident, a young Liberal supporter wound his scarf round her neck until he nearly strangled her.

She fought the 1910 General Election based in Scarborough. But in spring 1910 she returned to Sheffield and she and a colleague, Helen Archdale, made the city their regional headquarters. They lived at 45 Marlborough Road in Broomhill, which initially was also their meeting place and office. Hostility to the WSPU was so great that some of their

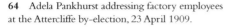

**64**   Adela Pankhurst addressing factory employees at the Attercliffe by-election, 23 April 1909.

**65**   Mrs Emmeline Pankhurst at the Attercliffe by-election, 3 May 1909.

opponents 'tarred and feathered' 43 Marlborough Road, thinking it was their house.[18] Then the WSPU acquired a city centre 'suffrage shop' at 26-8 Chapel Walk. From this Sheffield base, they built up the suffragette movement in Yorkshire, helping to form WSPU branches in Barnsley, Doncaster and Rotherham.

In autumn 1911, she gave up her organiser role and moved to London. There were several reasons. She was upset by the death of her younger brother, Harry. Her health had deteriorated and she had lost her voice. She was increasingly doubtful about militant action. She had fallen out with Christabel, who regarded her 'as a very black sheep among organisers … because of the warmth of her socialism'.[19] Some thought that Adela did not resign but was pushed out by Emmeline and Christabel.

Adela dabbled in horticulture and then in 1914 moved to Australia, where she was in general much happier. She married Thomas Walsh, a militant socialist and trade union organiser, and bore five children. She became a well-known public figure, going through astonishing twists and turns in her opinions, ranging from communism to support for the British Empire. She died in 1961.

### Molly Morris

After the departure of Adela, there was no paid WSPU organiser in Sheffield for over a year. The branch and its Chapel Walk shop were run by Miss Elsa Schuster, hon. secretary and treasurer, who organised 'fund-raising self-denial efforts' and 'At Homes'.

In 1912, they advertised for an organiser in *The Suffragette*. The successful candidate was a 21-year-old woman called Molly Morris[20] from Manchester. Molly was born in Leyland. Her father was an industrial manager whose support for a workers' wage claim had led him to give up his job, plunging the family into poverty in the Salford slums. Her mother became the family breadwinner and her father eventually left home. Molly and her mother joined the WSPU in Manchester and met the movement's leaders. Molly was shocked by the middle-class complacency of some of them.

Molly set off by train across the Pennines and was met at Sheffield Station by Elsa Schuster who, though much older, became her close friend. They joined together in nocturnal expeditions to chalk suffragette slogans on buildings and pavements. They went as far as Doncaster and did not finish until the workers were streaming into the factories at 6 a.m. This chalking eventually was abandoned because 'the people with whom I lived became alarmed lest my "nights out" found me otherwise engaged than in chalking pavement and walls!'

Molly's main duty was to run the shop in Chapel Walk, selling both the literature of the movement and handiwork, needlecraft etc made by members to raise funds. But she was also involved in propaganda work. At the time, the favourite venue for open-air meetings in Sheffield was the statue of Queen Victoria, then outside the town hall, but now in Endcliffe Park. For Molly, Victoria 'typified in her outlook, almost every aspect of womanhood against which we were in revolt'. But it was a good place for a meeting. On Sunday evenings, the Salvation Army appeared first and then the suffragettes competed with other groups to take over from them. The losers went to Barker's Pool.

The most bizarre feature of Molly's job description was firing post boxes. This was centrally organised from London and Elsa Schuster and Molly travelled to London to get 'bombs' (presumably packets containing flammable liquids). Here she describes firing the big letterbox outside the town hall:

66    Molly Morris, militant suffragette organiser in Sheffield, later wife of communist J.T. Murphy.

> I slipped several ('bombs') into this box as if posting letters. Contrary to expectations, in that some time was supposed to elapse before they fired, I had walked only a few yards when smoke belched out of the box. At the same time, a car backfired in the street and the people thought a bomb had exploded. The fire brigade came dashing up and a crowd gathered round. I mixed with the crowd and looked on. Of course, the police and detectives came too. A detective standing beside me remarked most sympathetically: 'We know it's the London lot who do this kind of things, Miss Morris, and not you young ladies. I wish all your people were like you. It would make our job so much easier.' How fortunate I was he thought like that. I had quite a number of these little troublemakers in my handbag ready for posting! The shocked little lady in the teashop opposite us in Chapel Walk said also 'I'm sure my little lady (that's me) wouldn't do anything like that.' Poor dear, little did she know how often I had taken advantage of her kindness and left packets of the damned stuff in her shop lest ours be searched.[21]

When she wrote her autobiography, Molly could not remember how many postboxes she fired. They were not only in the city centre but also in Nether Edge and Abbeydale Road. Most incidents were innocuous but, when a box at the General Post Office was emptied, a packet burst open in a postman's hands and he only narrowly escaped injury.

The shocked moderate suffragists held a big rally at the Albert Hall condemning militancy. The moderates also organised a great national pilgrimage in 1913. It proceeded from Leeds to Wakefield and then through various mining communities to Rotherham. On Saturday 5 July 1913, the procession entered Sheffield, accompanied by the Recreation Prize Band, and held a big peaceful rally of some 5,000 people. The SWSS membership swelled to 200 at this time. After the weekend, the marchers set off for Chesterfield on their way to Hyde Park in London.

**67**   Pilgrimage of the moderate suffragettes (NUWSS) leaving Sheffield via Pinstone Street on their way to London, 7 July 1913.

On Sundays, Molly often joined up with the Clarion Ramblers, led by G.H.B. Ward (chapter 11). On one occasion, they walked to Millthorpe and called on Edward Carpenter, an active speaker for female suffrage in the North.

Molly was an attractive young woman and young men would hang around the shop. The lady members from Fulwood objected and Molly resigned. She took another job but continued campaigning in her spare time. One of her admirers was Jack Murphy[22] (chapter 10), an able young trade union activist from Vickers. In the years up to 1914, he proposed to Molly three times but was turned down. He proposed again in 1920 and was accepted.

### Epilogue

Female suffrage agitation was suspended during the First World War. In 1918 the franchise was granted to nearly all women aged over thirty. In 1928, the voting age for women was lowered to twenty-one. In the great battle for female suffrage, Sheffield had an early pioneering role. Later on Manchester was in the lead, but Sheffield's solid support for the suffrage movement contributed to its ultimate success.

**68**   Ten women Labour councillors elected to the council in 1929 – indicating the progress made in female political representation.

*Chapter 10*

# The Triumph of Labour 1893-1926

WE ARE LOST – The Sorry Wail of Sheffield Liberals.
Headline in the *Sheffield Daily Telegraph*, 2 June 1922

He guided a rather raw party … towards its great achievements until for a time it became a model and an inspiration to struggling labour parties all over the country.
Fred Marshall on Ernest George Rowlinson at the Edward Carpenter Memorial Service
on 6 July 1947[1]

1893 was a significant year in Sheffield and in politics more generally. It was in 1893 that Sheffield became a city, at a time when the Conservatives were in control of the council. Four years later, the aged Queen Victoria, greeted by ecstatic crowds, opened the fine new town hall, though she never left her carriage.

The other event of 1893 was the foundation of the Independent Labour Party in Bradford, harbinger of a new third force in British politics. Only 33 years later in 1926, the Labour Party took control of Sheffield City Council, before it took over in any other major city in the UK. The party has remained in power ever since, except for four periods – 1932-3, 1968-9, 1999-2003 and from 2008.

Sheffield was the largest purely manufacturing city in the country. Lacking the strong commercial sector of Leeds or Manchester, it had a relatively small middle class.[2] Given the extension of the franchise, it might seem inevitable that a working-class political party would take control. But before 1914 that would have seemed highly unlikely, as Labour representation on the council was tiny. For Labour to take over, three conditions had to be met: the emergence of a self-conscious working class, skilled leadership of a highly organised political party and a major tactical failure on the part of the two traditional parties to woo the working class. This chapter describes how these conditions came about in Sheffield.

69  Sheffield's new town hall was opened by Queen Victoria in 1897, but she never left her carriage. This image has a soldier on top rather than the familiar Vulcan.

The triumph of Labour was a collective effort spread over 30 years and it is difficult to pick out any individuals as being primarily responsible. But if one had to pick out one individual, it would be Ernest George Rowlinson, who led Labour to power in 1926.

### Changes in Sheffield 1880-1926

Sheffield, the largest city in Yorkshire in 1911, was slow to acquire the status and grandeur of a great city. Its ablest Liberal politician, Mundella, described it as 'mean, petty and narrow in the extreme' (chapter 5). This was largely due to the prudence of the Liberals who had dominated the town since 1832. After 1880, things changed, mainly thanks to the Conservatives, who were influenced by Joseph Chamberlain's Birmingham. Services like water, the trams, the electrical undertaking and the markets were municipalised. There was extensive suburban house-building as the trams made possible daily commuting to factories and the city centre. But the council was slow to resolve the city's sanitation problems or to improve the housing of working people, apart from replacing the Crofts with new tenements and launching an innovative housing scheme in Upper Wincobank. Far more progress was made with education. Founded in 1870, the school board provided 51 schools and had nine other school projects in progress in 1902 when its work was handed over to the city council. Nor was higher education neglected. In 1905, the University of Sheffield was established from the existing university college and its new buildings were opened by King Edward VII. In 1914, the Anglican Diocese of Sheffield came into being and the old parish church became a cathedral.

Sheffield's iron, steel and engineering base expanded right up to 1914. In 1913, Harry Brearley invented stainless steel. From 1914-18, Sheffield was a vital centre of munitions production. But in the post-war slump, Sheffield's iron and steel industries (and mining, particularly after 1921[3]) were extremely vulnerable. In the 1920s, this over-specialised city faced mass unemployment.

### The Rise of the Conservatives

Paradoxically, Labour's takeover was preceded by a long period during which the Conservatives dominated Sheffield politics. Sheffield followed a strange zig-zag course politically and was not consistently radical. Chapter 5 showed how Roebuck relied on Conservative support for his last electoral victory in 1874. After his death in 1879, his seat was eventually won by Sheffield's first Conservative MP, Charles Stuart-Wortley (1851-1926), younger son of Lord Wharncliffe (chapter 3) and from the influential Conservative family of Wortley Hall. In 1885, the single two-member constituency was replaced by five separate constituencies. This benefited the Conservatives, who thereafter regularly returned three MPs to Westminster. Meanwhile, the Conservatives built up a dominant role on the city council. Between 1893 and 1919, the Conservatives and the Liberals alternated in power, but the Conservatives were in charge for much longer periods than the Liberals.[4]

This Conservative dominance was not typical of Northern towns and needs explanation. One factor was the influence of the newspaper editor and party boss, William Leng (chapter 5). He took advantage of the floods and outrages of the 1860s to discredit the Liberals. Moreover, Gladstonian Liberalism alarmed some middle-class people who saw the Conservatives as safer and more predictable.[5] Another reason for the Conservatives' success was Sheffield's emergence as a centre of armaments manufacture. Leading manufacturers were attracted by the Conservatives' imperialism, rejecting the Liberals who were split on issues like the Boer War. Another issue was trade. By the late Victorian period, most Sheffield manufacturers agreed with Leng and his colleagues in calling for 'fair trade', which meant imperial preference and retaliation against the tariffs imposed by France, Germany and the USA. Finally, the Conservative advance owed much to the relative weakness and disunity of the Liberals.

**70**   Political meeting in Paradise Square. From the 1790s until the early 20th century, Paradise Square was the scene of huge and often intense and dramatic political meetings.

## *The Strange Death of Liberal Sheffield*

George Dangerfield's brilliant book *The Strange Death of Liberal England* described the fatal decline of the apparently powerful Liberal Party in the years leading up to 1914. In Sheffield, this decline began much earlier. The Liberal Party was a coalition between the nonconformist middle class, the manufacturers and Lib-Lab trade unionists and workers. After 1886, Gladstone's policy of Home Rule for Ireland led many manufacturers to follow Chamberlain and the National Liberals into alliance with the Conservatives, while the trade unions began to consider separate Labour representation. It was a divided party.

One faction of Sheffield Liberals was led by H.J. Wilson (chapter 5), who campaigned

for Temperance and against imperialism and church schools. He later became MP for Penistone. But it was the Cleggs, father and son, who took over Robert Leader's role of running the Liberal Party in Sheffield. W.J. Clegg, son of a butler and an Anglican, became a solicitor in his forties and then prominent both on the council and in the Temperance League. After he died in 1895, his son William Edwin Clegg (1852-1932) – knighted in 1906 – also a solicitor and an Anglican, became leader of Sheffield liberalism well into the 1920s. He was an ambitious and domineering local politician, who shared Wilson's zeal for Temperance but differed strongly from Wilson on imperialism, the Boer War, education and the crucial question of Liberal relationships with the trade unions. Wilson accused him of 'dishonesty and double dealing'.[6]

**71**   Sir William Clegg, Liberal leader, whose anti-Labour policies led in 1919 to alliance with the Conservatives to form the Citizens' Party.

Clegg was the principal architect of the strongly anti-Labour policy of the Liberals from 1907 onwards, which led to the formation in 1919 of the Citizens' Party, an alliance with the Conservatives. It was an ill-judged policy, which paved the way for Labour's takeover in 1926 and the virtual demise of Sheffield's Liberal Party.

## *The Emergence of the Labour Party*

In the 1880s various forces were coming together to create the Labour movement in Sheffield, including Carpenter's Socialist Society and the increasingly politically aware trade unions (chapter 6). Following the formation in 1893 of the Independent Labour Party (ILP) in Bradford, ILP branches swiftly appeared in Sheffield, which soon could claim between them some 400 members.

The Attercliffe by-election[7] of 1894 became a test case of the new politics. The trades council proposed that Charles Hobson, a prominent Lib-Lab councillor, should stand for the Liberals. The Liberals were split. H.J. Wilson and his brother, John Wycliffe, favoured Hobson for this overwhelmingly working-class constituency. But Sir Frederic Mappin, one of the few leading manufacturers still in the Liberal Party and not a friend of the trade unions, swung the Liberal Association in favour of Batty Langley, saw-mill owner, Queen Street Congregationalist and former mayor. Hobson withdrew but Keir Hardie and the ILP intervened to put forward their own candidate, Frank Smith. Langley won:

|                     |       |
| ------------------- | ----- |
| Batty Langley (Lib) | 4,486 |
| Hill Smith (Cons)   | 3,495 |
| Frank Smith (ILP)   | 1,249 |

There was much heart-searching about this affair. Mappin and his colleagues miscalculated, for decisions like this were liable to push trade unionists towards separate Labour representation. Indeed, it was this by-election that persuaded James Ramsay Macdonald, future Labour Prime Minister, to join the ILP.

Despite this rebuff, many trade unionists continued to favour Lib-Lab candidates as against Labour candidates. In 1900, Ramsay Macdonald, secretary of the national Labour Representation Committee, came to Sheffield and pressed the case for independent representation, but it was not till 1903 that the Lib-Labs were at last outvoted and the Sheffield Labour Representation Committee (LRC) was formed. Even so, two years later, G.H.B. Ward, famous secretary of the Clarion Ramblers (chapter 11), described Sheffield to Ramsay Macdonald, as 'this benighted city of Liberal Labourism'.[8] Fighting against the Lib-Lab influences were ILP activists, like Alf Barton (1869-1933), a linguist, a remarkably erudite man and 'born agitator', well known for his fiery speeches at the Monolith. Barton was the first editor of the ILP's *Sheffield Guardian*.

72   Joseph Pointer MP. He became Labour's first Sheffield MP in 1909.

In council politics, the Lib-Lab tradition persisted. By November 1906, there were three independent Labour councillors elected, but they were outnumbered by Lib-Lab councillors.[9] In 1909, Labour won its first Parliamentary election in Sheffield, when Joseph Pointer became MP for Attercliffe. His success in 1909 was due to a split vote between two Conservative candidates but he retained his seat, with Liberal support, in the two 1910 elections.

Around 1910-11, there was an important ideological split within Sheffield's Labour ranks. Alf Barton, one of Sheffield's first Labour councillors in 1907, criticised Pointer for excessive support for the Liberal Party's policy of House of Lords reform. In 1911, the new British Socialist Party, the precursor of the British Communist Party, was formed mainly from SDF activists. Barton, George Fletcher (see below) and others soon joined the new group. Barton's successor as editor of the *Sheffield Guardian*, Hawkin, wrote that it was 'more important to feed a dying child than to preach the class war'[10] – a statement that summed up the divergence that was developing between the Labour left and the Labour mainstream.

Right up to 1914, Labour remained weak politically and splits and disputes dissipated its strength. In 1912, Labour had no councillors and in 1914 it only had two. But there were also signs of revival. In particular, the Labour Representation Committee was reconstituted as the Sheffield Trades and Labour Council, which at last gave the Sheffield Labour Party an effective central organisation. The outstanding Ernest George Rowlinson became its chair.

## The First World War

The experience of the First World War was crucial in building up Labour's strength. Sheffield became a massive arsenal, with a huge labour force working long hours producing munitions. In the early years of the war, Sheffield was intensely patriotic, as it had been in the Crimean and Boer Wars. Even left-wingers like Alf Barton supported the war as a struggle against German militarism. But opposition developed. As early as 1914, a branch of the Union of Democratic Control (UDC) was formed in the city and, as time went on, pacifist voices, like that of H.J. Wilson's eldest son Cecil, became stronger. In 1915, a branch of the No Conscription Fellowship was formed. Cecil Wilson eventually joined the ILP at the end of the war – one of a number of Liberal radicals who joined Labour. He became Labour leader in the council until 1922 when he became a Labour MP.

Sheffield's most important challenge to the war effort came from the shop stewards' movement in the great factories of the east end. This was led by a remarkable troublemaker, J.T. Murphy[11] (1888-1965). He grew up in Wincobank and became a lathe-turner at Vickers' Brightside works. Largely self-taught, he repudiated the Primitive Methodism of his teens and became a Marxist analyst and syndicalist, advocating workers' control of industry. During the First World War, he had little time for 'reformist' union leaders or Labour Party leaders who collaborated with the Government. He built up a powerful shop stewards' movement, which campaigned against the under-payment and dilution of skilled labour. The movement was strongly against conscription and, when in November 1916 a skilled fitter called Leonard Hargreaves was conscripted, Murphy organised a strike of 12,000 workers. The Government swiftly capitulated and Hargreaves returned within two days. Murphy brought the city's shop stewards together in a workers' committee, which embraced the heavy and light trades and skilled and unskilled workers. By now, he was a national leader of the shop stewards' movement.

The Bolshevik Revolution in Russia was welcomed in Sheffield's Labour circles. In December 1917 the Sheffield Trades and Labour Council passed, with only one dissentient voice, a resolution congratulating the Russian people. W.C. Anderson, who had succeeded Joseph Pointer as MP for Attercliffe, even proposed a workers and soldiers council for Sheffield, but this was not pursued for fear of police intervention. Nonetheless, Sheffield shop stewards seriously considered calling strikes to bring the war to an end – a form of militancy that was restrained by the final German offensive.[12] Sheffield's shop stewards' leader, Murphy, would soon move onto the world stage as a comrade of Lenin.

**73**   Labour group on the council in 1921-2. The number of councillors is increasing.

*The Politics of Post-War Sheffield*

After the war, some expected politics to revert to its traditional Liberal/Conservative dualism. But this was not to be. For one thing, the franchise was greatly extended by the 1918 Reform Act, so that Labour could extend its support among the poor, while all parties could reach out to women over 30 who had votes for the first time. But the impact of this reform was delayed because of Lloyd George's opportunism in hastily calling the 'coupon election', in which his coalition with the Conservatives won a landslide victory over both the Asquithian Liberals and Labour. In Sheffield, Labour lost its one seat in Attercliffe.

In the municipal elections of 1919, Labour at last made the breakthrough that it had long sought. It now held 12 seats, compared with 18 for the Conservatives and 15 for the Liberals. The *Sheffield Daily Telegraph* called the election the 'most sensational in the history of the City', as 'unknown men and women' took almost all the vacant seats.[13] But Sheffield did not settle down to three-party politics. Instead, Clegg, Sheffield's Liberal leader, together with Cattell, the Conservative leader, formed the Citizens' Party, a coalition designed to keep Labour out of power. The *Sheffield Independent* said that the Citizens 'had no programme – just a few vague generalities'.[14] The old Liberal radicals had disappeared. The Citizens used their control of the council to deny Labour seats as aldermen and to refuse them their proper share of seats on committees. These were flawed tactics that led in 1921 to a two-month Labour boycott of all committees and in 1926 to a Labour cull of Liberal and Conservative aldermen. One of Clegg's leading colleagues, Robert Styring, later wrote that Clegg should have 'endeavoured to guide the rising spirit of Labour, rather than to fiercely combat it on every occasion'.[15]

In this period, the Labour Party became more solid and united. Cecil Wilson was a disarming leader. The *Telegraph* commented that 'Ordinary folk cannot imagine that a party with such a highly respected leader can be working towards Bolshevism.'[16]

In 1920, the two trades councils were united to form the Federated Trade and Labour Council, under the presidency of Mrs Gertrude Wilkinson. The Co-operative Party held three wards and was a valuable ally to Labour. In the 1922 General Election, Labour achieved a parliamentary breakthrough when it won three seats – Attercliffe (with a swing of 33.5 per cent), Brightside and Hillsborough. The Hillsborough seat went to the Co-op Party candidate, A.V. Alexander, who was to serve as First Lord of the Admiralty three times, including during the Second World War.

To the left of the Labour Party was the new and highly disciplined British Communist Party, formed in 1920 from the British Socialist Party and the Socialist Labour Party. The communists followed the party line set by Moscow. Among the party's progenitors was J.T. Murphy who, in 1920, went to the Communist International in Moscow. On his second visit to Moscow in early 1921, he took his young bride, Molly (chapter 9) to meet Lenin. Murphy supported Lenin's idea of a communist vanguard seizing power on behalf of the working class. Lenin and his colleagues trusted Murphy and gave him a high profile throughout the 1920s. In 1921, he helped launch the Red International of Labour Unions. Back in Britain as a leading Communist Party organiser, Murphy was tried at the Old Bailey in 1925 and gaoled for six months for his communist activities. From 1926-8, he served in Moscow on the Executive Committee of the Comintern, where he moved the motion for the expulsion of Trotsky. But he fell out with the party leadership and left the Communist Party in 1932. Molly served as a nurse in the Spanish Civil War. In the late 1930s, Murphy advocated a popular front alliance against Nazism. In his old age, he became disillusioned with communism. But in his early career Murphy had risen higher in the world communist movement than any other Sheffielder.

**74**  J.T. Murphy, formidable shop stewards' leader in the First World War. After the war, he became prominent in the Communist International, meeting Lenin several times. Here he is seen top left with his son Donald at Lenin's tomb in 1927. In the front row (from left to right) are Bukharin, Kalinin, Uglanov, Stalin and Tomsky. Of the Russians, only Kalinin and of course Stalin survived the purges of the 1930s.

Murphy was in Moscow on 18 August 1920 when the Sheffield branch of the Communist Party held its inaugural meeting, with 50 or 60 present. Leonard Royle was treasurer and George Henry Fletcher[17] (1878-1958) was secretary. Fletcher was both a highly successful businessman and an ardent communist. He built up his chain of bakeries from scratch, was generous in pay and conditions and pioneered sliced bread in the hungry 1930s. Another founder member was Alf Barton but he then swiftly withdrew. He was an ethical socialist rather than a Marxist and preferred to devote himself to the libraries committee. Sheffield was prominent in the Hands Off Russia campaign at a time when Britain, under Churchill's influence, was supporting the White Russians against the Bolsheviks.[18]

*Unemployment*

In the acute post-war economic depression, Sheffield was especially vulnerable because of the sharp decline in world demand for steel products. In March 1921, unemployment reached 30,000 and the following winter it was between 40,000 and 50,000. Unemployment became a huge and intractable political issue. The Communists and Labour responded in different ways. Initially, both supported the Sheffield District Council of the Unemployed, but the Labour Trades Council pulled out when the communists encouraged meetings and demonstrations that were banned by the police. To the communists, the unemployed were 'the only fighting element of the working class'. In August 1921, there was a huge meeting of the unemployed outside the town hall. The windows of the *Sheffield Daily Telegraph* were smashed and the police made a baton charge. At a demonstration in Walkley, two left-wing councillors were arrested and subsequently imprisoned for one month. The unemployed also followed the Chartist model of 1839 (chapter 4) and organised visits to churches and the cathedral.

Labour operated through legal demonstrations, through resolutions addressed to Government and the city council calling for public works and other remedies and through serving as Poor Law Guardians, so that they could influence relief policy. The Sheffield Board of Guardians got into heavy deficit. Eventually Labour succeeded in getting it amalgamated with Ecclesall board, but on the proviso that the Ecclesall poor rate continued at 4s. in the pound.

## Ernest George Rowlinson

In 1922, Ernest George Rowlinson (1882-1941) became leader of the Sheffield Labour Party. He was a lapsed Baptist. He had been a railwayman at Midland Station but lost his job in 1911 as he had been leader of a railway strike. He became an agent of the Co-operative Insurance Society and was chair of the Sheffield Trade and Labour Council from 1912 to 1927. Serving in the First World War, he was gassed and as a result was never fully fit. He quickly rose to political prominence after he was elected to the council in 1921. For a time, he was Labour's political agent. He commanded a great deal of trust and respect. A colleague said that 'Under his inspiration the Sheffield Labour Group set the pace and blazed the trail for most of the big Municipalities in the country. His grasp not only of general principles but of a vast mass of details was amazing.'[19] His patience and skill with argumentative colleagues were legendary: 'Never once did the Labour Group go to the Council divided on a big matter of principle.'[20]

**75**   Ernest George Rowlinson, former railwayman, who led Labour to take control of Sheffield Council in 1926.

He was abused by communists because of the disciplinary approach that at times he took towards them, but in this he was following national Labour Party policy. There were good reasons for Labour to be cautious about communist infiltration. Lenin once said that communists should support the leadership of bourgeois socialists 'as a rope supports the hanged'.

Rowlinson's greatest concern was education and in 1926 he and Labour challenged the Citizens' failure to provide enough school capacity on the new Manor estate. Once in power, he made the building of schools a top priority. Later on, Rowlinson played a national role in education as president of the Association of Education Committees. He remained leader of the Labour Group until 1940.

## The Gang Wars

Sheffield was a turbulent place in the early 1920s. Along with mass unemployment and acute unrest in both the engineering and mining industries, there were the gang wars.[21]

Gambling gangs in Sheffield were not new and had flourished during the First World War, but in the 1920s violent gang wars broke out that caught the national headlines. The wars were over control of the lucrative tossing rings on Sky Edge, under Norfolk Bridge and in other locations. There was a tradition in Sheffield of a very simple form of gambling based on bets on tossed coins. Those in charge of the game (the 'tollers') collected a toll on bets made. Just as Sky Edge had been a favoured location for revolutionary meetings back in the early 19th century, so it was also the preferred location for these illegal games, since scouts (called 'pikers' or 'crows') could be stationed all around to watch out for the police and to crow like a rookery if they were on their way. The two main gangs were the Mooney Gang, following George Mooney of West Bar, and the Park Brigade, following Sam Garvin of the Park area, then a warren of courtyard slums.

A series of violent assault cases came to the local magistrates courts and at first were dealt with leniently. Father Ommanney believed that the magistrates themselves were intimidated.[22] Gradually the violence increased. In addition to the two main gangs, there were also 'junior gangs' attacking respectable citizens in the street in broad daylight. The *Sheffield Mail* accused the authorities of complacency. In April 1925, a Scot called Plommer was murdered in Princess Street in Attercliffe by a group of Garvin's men led by two brothers called Fowler. The Fowler brothers were both eventually hanged and their colleagues served long sentences for manslaughter.

Under pressure from the Home Office, the chief constable, Lieut-Col Hall-Dallwood, set up a 'Flying Squad' of policemen of formidable size and fighting skills to intimidate gang members until they gave up or went elsewhere. The squad would follow gang members into a public house and then instruct the licensee not to serve them. If this led to a fight, the gangs would be charged with assaulting the police. On one occasion, the accused appeared in court swathed in bandages from his fight with the police, but the courts supported the police. This pragmatic policy worked and the gang wars subsided.

There are still two mysteries in this story. First, unlike the Sheffield outrages of the 1860s (chapter 5), the gang wars were purely criminal and lacked any industrial or political rationale; however, there were suspicions of a link with the Citizens Party, in that some Labour meetings were broken up by thugs recognised as from the Park Brigade and Sam Garvin was one of the first to get a house in a new estate in Walkley.[23]

The second mystery is stranger still. Lieut-Col Hall-Dallwood, the chief constable, who took early retirement in March 1926, said at his farewell party that he was 'the victim of some insidious influence from outside, which for years has been working against me. At times during the War and since, my anxieties have been seriously increased by this disquieting and horrible element which rendered one's position almost intolerable.'[24]

It has never been revealed what these 'insidious influences' were. His successor, who took office on the first day of the General Strike, was Captain P.J. Sillitoe, the most famous of all Sheffield's chief constables. He

**76**  The General Strike, 1926. Demonstrators and police in Fitzalan Square. The Sheffield labour movement strongly supported the General Strike and there was great disappointment when the strike was called off by the TUC.

later became Head of MI5. In his memoirs,[25] he claimed the credit for ending the gang wars, though arguably this was an achievement of his predecessor.

### The General Strike

The Labour movement in Sheffield was united in its support for the miners in the General Strike of 1926.[26] In part, this reflected solidarity with 10,000 miners in Sheffield and many more elsewhere in South Yorkshire and Derbyshire. But Labour activists also saw it as an opportunity to stand up for the rights of organised labour more generally. The wage cut proposed for the miners raised similar issues to those faced by Sheffield's engineering workers in 1920-2 when the engineers had fought a bitter and unsuccessful struggle against drastic cuts in wages and conditions, culminating in the lock-out of 1922. The engineers had had no pay increase since then and many lived near the poverty line.[27] Only eight weeks before the General Strike, the Sheffield engineers had called for a strike against threats of a further engineering lock-out. The unions and the political wing of the Sheffield labour movement joined in responding positively to the TUC's call for a General Strike.

Leadership in the General Strike in Sheffield rested with the executive of the Trades and Labour Council, which formed a Central Disputes Committee (CDC), chaired by Rowlinson. They first called out the railwaymen and a few days later other transport workers and engineers. Most workers were very ready to strike: indeed, Rowlinson found that the main problem was to keep those at work whom the General Council of the TUC had said should continue working. But most big steel firms still had some non-unionists working and some printing unions refused to strike. As a result, the *Sheffield Daily Telegraph* and the *Independent* continued to appear, though in smaller size. Indeed, the *Telegraph* was the only paper available in London on the first two days of the strike.

In addition to the official committee, there was the Minority Movement Strike Committee, a ginger group formed by the communists to stiffen the official leadership and to put out propaganda in support of the strike. The party judged that revolutionary action was inopportune but argued that a defeat of the miners would put the whole working class at risk. Twelve communists were arrested and fined for producing a special strikes bulletin.

The Citizens supported the Government. They opened a volunteer recruiting centre at the town hall and Clegg became president of the Sheffield Organisation for the Maintenance of Supplies – seen by Labour as strike-breakers.

R. Fearnley, manager of the tram service, held a strike ballot, which was challenged by Rowlinson on the grounds that each voting form contained the worker's work number. The trams largely closed down.

On 12 May, the TUC called off the strike after nine days and just after the Sheffield engineers had come out. Both Labour and communist politicians in Sheffield were shocked and angered by the TUC's decision. The next day, the CDC sent a resolution to the TUC calling the TUC's action 'altogether unwarranted' and liable to leave the strikers 'exposed to the attacks of the employers'.

The CDC continued to support the miners. As a resumption of strike action was clearly ruled out, they urged the TUC to impose a general ban on overtime and called for an embargo on imported coal. By contrast, the council brought in Silesian coal. The CDC supported a Women's Committee for the Relief of Miners' Wives and Children, which held collections at cinemas, but were barred by the council from holding collections at football matches.

## Labour's Electoral Victory

In November 1926, municipal elections were held, only six months after the traumatic events of the General Strike. Workers in Sheffield must have felt that, even if they had been let down by the TUC in London, they at least had been united and determined. Alf Barton described the strike as 'a magnificent example of working class solidarity'. But he and others now doubted whether the Labour movement could achieve its goals through strike action against a determined and well-resourced Government. The ballot box was a more promising option. So they redoubled their efforts in the local elections.

Labour bitterly attacked the Citizens' low-rates policy and the council's consequent failure to undertake public investment, such as new schools on the Manor. In September 1926, it had emerged that only one-third of the children on the Manor were attending school.[28] They also criticised the Citizens' housing record, where the only achievement was the building of the Manor estate in which the houses had been badly constructed by private building firms.

There was a turnout of 51 per cent in the election. Fifty years later, a local Labour supporter in Handsworth still recalled the excitement on the night of 1 November 1926 when a cyclist came from the city centre, waving his arms and calling out 'We've done

**77**  The Labour group in the council after Labour took control following the local elections of November 1926.

it!'[29] This victory was achieved despite the opposition of all the local press – the *Telegraph, Independent* and *Star*.

Labour had made seven gains, giving the party a majority of three seats. But Labour removed eight Citizen aldermen (still leaving seven in place) and appointed seven of their own, alongside the two former Lib-Lab aldermen who belonged to the Labour group. This gave Rowlinson's Labour group 38 seats on the council as against 25 for the Citizens. It was a healthy majority, which enabled a complete change of council policy.

Labour's triumph had three main causes. The first was the increased self-consciousness of the city's huge working class in the First World War and their resentment at post-war unemployment and worsening wages and conditions. The second was the development of the Labour Party as a highly effective political force, so that, under Rowlinson's inspired leadership, it could seize the opportunities open to it. The third was the ineptitude and negativity of the Citizens' Party and their failure to appeal to the working-class majority. Clegg, Cattell and their colleagues had not learned, from predecessors like Mundella on the Liberal side and Leng on the Conservative side, that successful politics in Sheffield had to reach out to the masses. Instead, their watchword was 'economy' and one historian argues that it was the 'passionate revulsion' against this policy that 'was the cause, as much as anything, of the landslide of 1926'.[30]

Labour in power proved to be highly competent. An historian writes:

> insofar as Labour was able to shape its own destiny for the city, it did so in a very positive way. Its achievements in housing … education, public health and general management were ones of which it was justly proud and for which it gained the respect and support of large numbers of Sheffielders.[31]

The 'revolution' was put on hold. Instead, Labour activists devoted themselves to a serious-minded Labour version of municipal socialism. Sheffield's Labour politicians had ceased to be troublemakers.

# Struggle for the Countryside

1. Longshaw Estate
2. Blacka Moor
3. Lose Hill/Ward's Piece
4. Jacob's Ladder
5. Snake Inn
6. Doctor's Gate
7. Kinder Scout
8. Winnat's Pass
9. Bar Dike
10. Duke's Road
11. Derwent Reservoir
12. Stanage Edge
13. Bamford Moor
14. Ladybower Reservoir

-·-·- Clarion Ramblers Inaugural Walk 1900

···· Trespass Routes

━ ━ ━ Peak District National Park Boundary — estab. 1951

**78** *The Struggle for the Countryside* by David Bradley (including material published by the Peak District National Park Authority).

*Chapter 11*

# The Struggle for the Countryside

A dirty picture in a beautiful frame.

Comment on Sheffield attributed to John Ruskin

What is now the Peak District and South Yorkshire Branch of the Campaign to Protect Rural England was from the very start the pace setter and model for local environmental organisations in every part of the country to follow

Sir Chris Bonington[1]

Fourteen Sheffielders responded to an advertisement I inserted in the Clarion and, on the first Sunday in September 1900, walked the usual round of Kinderscout, from Edale station. And this, to my knowledge, the first workers' Sunday Rambling Club in the North of England, was formed. Those present were TW Handley, his son and daughter, Joseph and Fanny, Sam and Herbert Hodgson, Frank Johnson, John Jordan, Mr King (manager at Christopher Johnson's works, Portobello St), and his daughters, Isa and Carrie (now Wilford), John Murray, Herbert Stansfield, Fred Watson, and G.H.B.W.

G.B.H. Ward's recollection 50 years later[2]

Sheffielders are deeply attached to the glorious countryside near their city. This goes back a long way. Sheffield's riot in 1791 was over the enclosure of 6,000 acres of common land to the west of the town (chapter 2). Working-class radicals plotting against the authorities met secretly in the surrounding hills (chapters 3 and 4). Thomas Asline Ward, Ebenezer Elliott and Edward Carpenter all enjoyed walking in the countryside. Early in the 20th century, Sheffielders rediscovered the story of the enclosures and how landowners had used their control of Parliament to appropriate vast acreages of common land around Sheffield in a succession of private bills between 1760 and 1840.

The enclosures could not be reversed. But in the 20th century, there emerged two influential Sheffield movements concerned with the countryside. The first was a mainly middle-class conservation movement, led by a dynamic young woman, Ethel Gallimore (née Ward and later Ethel Haythornthwaite). Her group, founded in 1924, later became a branch of CPRE (the Council for the Protection of Rural England, now renamed the Campaign to Protect Rural England). Through this group, she and latterly her husband, Gerald Haythornthwaite, persuaded, pressurised and cajoled the authorities into preserving Sheffield's 'beautiful frame'. The efforts of the Haythornthwaites and their allies led to the acquisition for the nation of large areas of land, to the designation of a Green Belt to the west of Sheffield and to the designation in 1951 of the Peak District National Park.

The second movement was a mainly working-class and lower-middle-class struggle for free access to the countryside. The number of Sheffield ramblers greatly increased with the opening of the Hope Valley railway line in 1894. In 1900, G.B.H. Ward, a young socialist, founded the Sheffield Clarion Ramblers. But ramblers were debarred by landowners from much of the most attractive moorland. Sheffield and Manchester ramblers took the lead in challenging landlords, culminating in two mass trespasses in 1932. New legislation in 1939 and 1949 failed to resolve the issue. In 1982, SCAM (the Sheffield Campaign for Access to Moorland) revived trespasses in the Sheffield area. Eventually in 2000 the Countryside and Rights of Way Act conceded the right to roam in most uncultivated land.

This chapter tells the story of Sheffield's part in these campaigns for the countryside.

### Ethel Gallimore and the Council for the Protection of Rural England

The leading personality in the struggle to protect the countryside around Sheffield was Ethel Gallimore,[3] the daughter of T.W. Ward, Master Cutler in 1913, from a wealthy Methodist family of coal, metal and machinery merchants. Ethel had lost her husband in the First World War. She was very socially aware and, with her sister Gertrude, supported ventures like the Sheffield Educational Settlement (chapter 8). But her passion was the conservation of the countryside and it was to this that she dedicated her life. She later explained her motivation as follows:

**79**   Ethel Gallimore (later Haythornthwaite) came from a wealthy family and founded and led the local branch of the Council for the Protection of Rural England, which campaigned to protect Sheffield's 'beautiful frame'.

My childhood impressions of the city were – a gloomy noisy shapeless phenomenon: but outside the city – there one began to live. To escape into clean air, the gradual return to nature; with these came satisfaction and peace … Along with this came the sickening realisation, as the ugly suburbs straggled out and the farms disappeared, that it was all going. But a helpless uneasiness may be replaced by action, and now some who comprehended the significance of Sheffield's surroundings to her citizens, spend a large part of their lives trying to save them.[4]

On 7 May 1924, the founder members of Ethel's new conservation group met at Endcliffe Vale House, the substantial home of Ethel's mother in Broomhill. They included G.H.B. Ward (who had persuaded Ethel to call the meeting[5]), several members of Ethel's family, the Rev. Martin Pope, H.B.G. Gibbs, architect and Dr W.S. Porter, physician and local historian, who was elected chair. Ethel was elected hon. secretary. The group called themselves The Sheffield Association for the Protection of Local Scenery, but in 1927 they became a branch of the CPRE, which had been formed nationally in 1926.

With her colleagues, Ethel embarked on one of the most skilled and effective lobbying operations in Sheffield's history. The group kept closely in touch with potential developments, investigated the legal position, brought influential weight to bear on the authorities and even acquired land themselves to prevent development. It was time-consuming and difficult work but was facilitated by their social position, contacts and wealth. They engaged in 'propaganda' about the countryside, organising major exhibitions, one of which included an exhibit showing 'What Sheffield left at Stanage last Bank Holiday' – an 'indescribable heap of filth'.

They could not win every battle. For example, they could not prevent the opening of Hope Valley Cement Works in 1927. But they achieved an astonishing early coup in acquiring the Longshaw estate. In 1927, the Duke of Rutland put Longshaw Lodge and 11,500 acres up for auction. Sheffield and Chesterfield Councils bought much of the high moorland for water catchment. Sheffield City Council also purchased Longshaw Lodge and the 747 surrounding acres and conveyed the property to a joint committee of the CPRE and Sheffield Council of Social Service. The CPRE raised £13,000 on a bank overdraft and then paid it off with money from the public, the Town Trust and the National Trust, who took over the property in 1931.

In 1933, Ethel and a colleague called F.W. Scorah approached Alderman Graves, a successful entrepreneur in the mail-order business, who had been on Clarion rambles. They asked him to purchase Blackamoor and present it to the city of Sheffield as an open space for public enjoyment in perpetuity. Ethel later recalled her conversation with Graves after the opening ceremony. Graves said:

> 'Now after we've done all this … will you promise never to trouble us again?' I took a deep breath, thought I'd better be truthful and said 'Whenever the countryside around Sheffield is in danger, I shall appeal to you.' He looked at me, severely but not unkindly, 'Well,' he said, 'now we know.'[6]

In 1936, Ethel recruited a recently qualified architect, Gerald Haythornthwaite, as salaried assistant secretary to the branch. They fell in love and got married in December 1937. Gerald moved to the council's architect department, but the couple now fought their conservation campaigns together, combining Ethel's ability to persuade and influence with Gerald's 'mastery of technical detail over a wide range of disciplines'. They were 'formidable opponents and splendid allies'.[7]

**80**   Alderman J.G. Graves in the office of his mail order firm. Ethel Gallimore persuaded Graves, a great philanthropist, to buy Blackamoor for the city.

In their anxiety to curtail development on the west of the city, the Haythornthwaites consulted a leading Sheffield Labour figure, Alderman Fred Marshall, whose response was 'We must save it all'. He gave invaluable support when, in 1936-7, they submitted detailed plans to the city council for an extensive Green Belt. In 1938 these were largely accepted in the council's published plans.[8] It was a pioneering achievement. At about the same time, Ethel and her family and friends acquired 250 acres below Froggatt Edge, Whin Plantation and Harpur Lees Farm and 75 acres at Shatton.

Before and during Second World War, Ethel was heavily involved in developing proposals for a Peak District National Park, while Gerald served in the forces. She was secretary of the voluntary committee on national parks. In 1944, the booklet *The Peak District – a National Park* was produced – 'a brilliant piece of advocacy and propaganda'.[9] In 1945, she was appointed by the new Labour Government to serve on the Committee on National Parks under Sir Arthur Hobhouse. Few contributed as much as Ethel to the ultimate designation of the Peak District as Britain's first national park in 1951.

**81**   Ethel and Gerald Haythornthwaite. In 1937, Ethel married Gerald, a young architect, and from then on they were a formidable team. The designation of the Peak District National Park in 1951 owed much to them.

## G.H.B. Ward

Behind the scenes, the instigator of Ethel's inaugural meeting in 1924 was George Herbert Bridges Ward[10] (1876-1957) – leading figure among Sheffield ramblers for 50 years, an expert on access to the countryside, local historian, antiquarian and topographer.

Bert Ward was no relation to Ethel but was the grandson of William Ward, founder of Ward and Son, an engineering company eventually based at Centenary Works, Archer Road, Woodseats. Despite his grandfather's success, Bert Ward did not have a privileged upbringing. He lost his mother when he was nine and left school at 12 or thirteen. He

**82**   G.H.B. Ward founded the Sheffield Clarion Ramblers in 1900. He became leader of Sheffield's ramblers and of the movement for access to the countryside for more than 50 years.

became an apprentice fitter at James Jackson, a stay busk manufacturer. He grew up in the Park area and followed his father as a Sunday School teacher at St John Park. But from 1896 he became a socialist and was driven out of the church by the vicar, Canon H.F. Greenwood. Ward became an active trade unionist in the Amalgamated Society of Engineers. In 1900, as a young man of 24, he founded the Sheffield Clarion Ramblers and married Fanny Platts of Dronfield. From 1903-11, he was the first secretary of the Sheffield branch of the Labour Representation Committee, working resolutely for separate Labour Party representation (chapter 10). He campaigned in 1905 about Sheffield's high infant mortality figures and called for council control of the milk supply.

In 1911, he began a long civil service career, starting in the new Sheffield and Brightside Labour Exchange. During the First World War, he served in the Ministry of Munitions and thereafter he was a conciliation officer in the Ministry of Labour until 1941. As a civil servant, he could no longer fight for socialism and was inhibited in campaigning for the right to roam, but continued to lead his Clarion Ramblers and edit their fascinating pocket-size annual handbooks. His home was in Moorwoods Lane near Owler Bar. On retirement, he turned down an OBE but later accepted a much more unusual honour. In 1945, the Sheffield rambling community collected enough money to buy and present to Ward the summit of Lose Hill, to be known as 'Ward's Piece', which he presented to the National Trust.

### The Sheffield Clarion Ramblers

The *Clarion* was a popular weekly newspaper founded in 1891 by Robert Blatchford in Manchester, which promoted socialism but was also entertaining, offering stories, jokes and verses and encouraging outdoor activities like rambling and cycling.[11] Many new cycle clubs and rambling clubs adopted the label 'Clarion'. Most of the original Sheffield Clarion Ramblers already knew each other through the Clarion Glee Club. In Sheffield, rambling was increasingly popular, with John Derry, editor of the *Independent,* publicising walks in his newspaper and later producing a book, *Across the Derbyshire Moors*.[12]

The Clarion Ramblers' inaugural ramble in September 1900 was a formidable 20-mile hike, which John Derry's book recommended as 'absolutely the best walk available from Sheffield'.[13] It ran from Edale via Jacob's Ladder to Hayfield, then via William Clough to the head of Ashop Clough. Here 'after persuading the ladies to go on ahead, several of the men indulged in a bathe in one of the deeper pools'. They then descended Ashop Clough, had tea at the *Snake Inn* and then walked all the way to Hope station. During the walk, the ramblers agreed to form the Sheffield Clarion Ramblers.[14]

This new association 'combined in a way that no other club appears to have done, the need to re-establish the sense of fellowship between men amid the objects of nature'.[15] Ward's annual handbooks were packed with routes, historical and literary information and homely wisdom, like Ward's slogan, 'A rambler made is a man improved.' Despite Ward's politically incorrect language, from the start his ramblers included women as well as men.

SHEFFIELD
# CLARION RAMBLERS
1951-52          Fifty-first Year
### Price 2/-

A Rambler made is a man improved!

Bakewell Church, Cottages, and Electric Standard, or, Ancient and Modern.
Photo by Miss B. Dyson.

*The man who never was lost, never went very far*

**83**   Clarion Ramblers Handbook 1951-2 – Ward's classic pocket publication.

In his intense love of the hills and topographical knowledge, Ward resembled Alfred Wainwright but, whereas Wainwright was a loner, Ward was gregarious and a born organiser of other people. He listed the duties of a leader: to proceed with the ramble wet or fine, to follow the printed route, to make provision for tea, to provide information about landmarks on the route and to see that a song was sung.[16]

*The Struggle for Access*

Today's Peak District ramblers would be astonished at the areas from which the early Clarion Ramblers were debarred. Even the route from Hayfield to *Snake Inn* in their inaugural walk had only been opened to ramblers in 1897 following 21 years of campaigning. In 1876, this route had been closed for grouse shooting by the Duke of Devonshire and two other landowners, despite its famed use by Methodists for their annual 'Love Feast'[17] in a barn at Alport Woodlands. While this path had reluctantly been opened up, many of the best walking areas in north Derbyshire remained closed to ramblers, including the Kinder Scout plateau, Bleaklow, the Broomhead, Howden and Derwent moorlands to the east of the reservoirs, the lovely Baslow, Curbar, Froggatt and Stanage Edges and the summit of Win Hill.

These restrictions on access were a direct result of the enclosures of the late 18th and early 19th centuries. Chapter 2 described the riot in Sheffield prompted by the enclosure of 1791. But most enclosures took place quietly and there was little public awareness of their huge implications until the 20th century. In 1907, Sheffield Independent Press published a book by Carolus Paulus (Charles Paul, a clerk in Cleggs' Solicitors firm for 58 years), giving a detailed account of the enclosures around Sheffield, showing how landowners, including great lords like the Duke of Norfolk, benefited, while 'Parliament omitted to take account of the customary rights and interests of the general community'.[18] Reports appeared in the press with headlines like: 'How Sheffield was robbed,' and 'Noble Lords Seize People's Land.'

G.H.B. Ward contributed to this process of exposure. Much later, in his handbook for 1941-2 he revealed that altogether the enclosures in South Yorkshire and the Peak District had transferred to private ownership 98,314 acres (or 153.5 square miles). Ward noted that, while the rich stole the people's land, a child was sentenced to death in the 1830s for breaking a shop window and stealing some sweets.[19]

Ward pointed out that large tracts of moorland, for instance around Edale and Kinder Scout, had simply been regarded as 'waste' prior to enclosure. Enclosure gave the new landlords exclusive control of game – an asset worth exploiting given the craze for shooting grouse from 1870 onwards. Wealthy sportsmen took absurd pride in record bags, with Lord Walsingham claiming he had killed 1,070 grouse in one day near Harrogate in 1888. By 1910, 1.5 million grouse were being slaughtered for sport across the country in a season. Landlords restricted public access because they believed that ramblers would disturb grouse and prevent them from breeding, a proposition disputed by ramblers and contradicted by a scientific study in 1967.[20]

In 1934, it was found that the Peakland grouse moors were owned by 17 private owners, including three dukes, one earl, two knights, two army officers, eight industrialists and one local authority. These landowners employed dozens of gamekeepers equipped with heavy sticks, and sometimes with guns, who saw ramblers as the enemy.

The Sheffield Clarion Ramblers' first great struggle was to reopen Doctor's Gate, an ancient right of way along an impressive Roman road from Glossop to Woodlands and Ashopton. This route avoided the growing motor traffic on the Snake Road. Soon after the opening of the new Snake Pass turnpike in 1818, Lord Howard had closed Doctor's Gate. From 1898 to 1909, the Peak District and Northern Counties Footpath Preservation

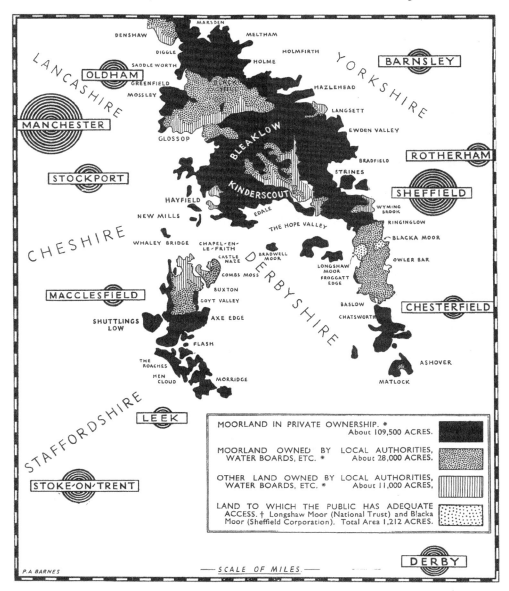

**84**   The Peak District Moorlands. Phil Barnes, formerly an employee in CPRE, produced this map in 1934 to show the restrictions on access.

Society tried unsuccessfully to negotiate access with Lord Howard. Then, in 1909, Ward and the Clarion Ramblers intervened, walking the full length of the track. They and the Manchester ramblers did a series of 'joint raids' and in 1911 an agreement was reached with Howard. But the ramblers felt that Howard then broke the agreement by wiring up the Mossylee (Glossop) end of the path. From August 1912 to 1920 there was a special annual celebration ramble of the Clarion Ramblers along the route. In the 1920s, the Clarion Ramblers were joined by Manchester ramblers and others in groups of up to 100 strong and, on one occasion, Ward smashed the Mossylee padlock. At last, the right of way was established on a slightly altered route and Derbyshire County Council agreed to the erection of notice boards.

In the 1920s, Kinder Scout became the focus of the struggle. Part of Kinder Scout was purchased as a grouse moor by a Mr Watt, a Manchester warehouse merchant, who guarded his land zealously. According to Ward, in 1923-4 about six gamekeepers were employed on the top during summer and autumn weekends to chase off ramblers. Ward was their bête noire. One of the gamekeepers brandished a stick at him, crying 'This is the way to deal with ******* socialists.' Watt served a writ on Ward, restraining him from going on to Kinder Scout. As a civil servant, Ward 'had to apologise and promise not to trespass again on that holy land'. Officially he did not step on that moor for 10 years until the owner died in the early 1930s.[21]

The Clarion Ramblers were not alone. In 1926, Ward managed to create a Sheffield federation of 18 affiliated rambling clubs, which called for access and was backed up by Ward's research. When C.P. Trevelyan produced an Access Bill, the Manchester and Sheffield federations organised a joint mass demonstration at Winnat's Pass, Castleton, on 12 June 1926 in support of this. Demonstrations here or in Cave Dale became annual events, with 8,000 at the 1929 demonstration. Both Ramsay Macdonald and Lloyd George sent letters of support but did nothing in Parliament to help the cause.

*Mass Trespass*

'Trespassing' through grouse moors was something that the Clarion Ramblers did almost throughout their history, though Ward sought routes where he believed there was an historic right of way. But the famous mass trespasses of 1932[22] were a novelty in their scale and the degree of public interest they aroused. The first mass trespass on 24 April 1932 was mainly a Manchester affair, led by Benny Rothman, a young motor mechanic, and the British Workers Sports Federation – which had Communist affiliations. There was an important Sheffield contingent. The Sheffield and Manchester ramblers' federations opposed this mass trespass, arguing that it set back negotiations with the landowners.

Rothman led 400-500 trespassers,[23] pitched against a large force of gamekeepers and police – making it like a bizarre military campaign. Rothman's party took the police by surprise by proceeding swiftly along William Clough. From there, they dashed up the steep side of Kinder while gamekeepers attacked them with sticks. The trespassers greatly outnumbered the gamekeepers and carried on their way, but probably did not scale the plateau.[24]

Meanwhile, a party of about thirty Sheffield ramblers had set off unchallenged from Hope, up Jacob's Ladder to a vantage point from where they watched the battle with the keepers. They then met up with the Manchester ramblers on the Snake Path. The main body of ramblers returned in triumph to Hayfield, only to be met by a combined force of police and gamekeepers, who picked out six 'ringleaders'. They were tried at Derby on 7 and 8 July, before a jury including two brigadier generals, three colonels, two majors and three captains. All but one were found guilty and were sentenced between them to 17 months' imprisonment. These harsh penalties caused a shocked reaction in the rambling world.

The Sheffield-based second mass trespass five months later was a response to these penalties. It was proposed at a meeting of the Sheffield Ramblers' Federation, chaired by G.B.H. Ward, who was in a very difficult position. He was very sympathetic, but could not support the trespass openly for fear of losing his civil service job. At the same time, he did not want the trespass hijacked by the communists. Eventually nine clubs, mostly left-wing, participated. Ward encouraged them to meet separately to organise the trespass. He later met up with the overall leader, Hardy of the Sheffield Educational Settlement (chapter 8), and the other leaders, briefed them on the legal position and wished them well.

Ward influenced the choice of route – from Bar Dike, south of Wigtwizzle, along the Duke of Norfolk's Road, across Howden Moor to Abbey Brook and Derwent Reservoir. Ward's research satisfied him that the Duke of Norfolk's Road had been recognised as a right of way during the enclosure process between 1811 and 1826.

On Sunday 18 September 1932, around two hundred ramblers came by tramcars to Malin Bridge and Middlewood and then walked to Bar Dike, a prehistoric defensive earthwork. Waiting there was just one gamekeeper, who shouted 'Keep off' to them and then bicycled quickly away to warn his colleagues.[25] The rest of the gamekeepers were at the Derwent end of the track, thinking the trespass would start from there. The ramblers proceeded unmolested for several miles until they got to Peter's Rock, a strange, beautiful and normally secluded spot. Here they were faced by a force of around one hundred gamekeepers[26] armed with pit shafts, plus police led by an inspector. The keepers assaulted the ramblers on their heads and shoulders, causing the police to advise them to go for their legs to avoid serious injury. The keepers then withdrew.

The ramblers' leaders were so concerned about possible violence if they proceeded further that they got their people to sit down to discuss the situation. Eventually it was agreed to turn back. A dozen militants, including the young Howard Hill,[27] split off and trespassed across the moors to Bradfield Gate Head and Foulstone Delph. Meanwhile, during the three-mile return journey along the Duke of Norfolk Road, the Duke of Devonshire's chief gamekeeper and his colleagues, frustrated that the ramblers had walked so far along the disputed path, urged the police to make arrests. But the Sheffield police, more subtle than their Derbyshire colleagues, exercised restraint as they had done over the General Strike (chapter 10). They were aware of public indignation at the sentences for the first trespass and also of Ward's claim of a right of way.

The ramblers wanted to follow this up by a walk along Stanage Edge on 16 October 1932, but were prevented by mounted and foot police with alsatians.

*Negotiations and Legislation*

The campaign bore some fruit in the Labour-dominated Sheffield area. In the mid-1930s Sheffield City Council, which had collaborated with CPRE over land purchases, terminated the shooting of grouse on Burbage Moor and secured increased access there and on Houndkirk Moor. About the same time, a 'sufferance path' over Win Hill and the right of way on Derwent Edge (near the scene of the Abbey Brook Mass Trespass) were conceded.[28]

But national recognition of a right to roam on uncultivated moorland was as far away as ever. The ramblers' campaign resembled the suffragettes in that the wishes of large numbers of people were frustrated, direct action was suppressed by the forces of law and order and tensions arose between moderates and militants, with each group blaming the other for lack of progress. There were half a million ramblers across the country and 10,000 attended the Winnats Pass demonstration in 1932. Yet their efforts failed to persuade Parliament to concede the right to roam. The small numbers of landowners and grouse shooters had more influence than the ramblers.

In 1939 Parliament approved Arthur Creech Jones's Access to Mountains Act but this had been emasculated during 'negotiations' and included a much-resented trespass clause that criminalised ramblers who deviated from well-established routes. The Sheffield Federation's protests against it were to no avail. Ramblers condemned the Act and did not bother with the costly and cumbersome process it offered for gaining access.

The National Parks and Access to the Countryside Act 1949, like the 1939 Act, relied on piecemeal local negotiations on access, but entrusted the responsibility for these negotiations to local authorities, except in the Lake District and the Peak District. The Peak Park Planning Board negotiated additional access, for instance in the Kinder Scout plateau in the 1950s, but Conservative Governments after 1951 set back further progress on access.

## SCAM and the Revival of Militancy

GHB Ward died in 1957. In his last years, militancy on access had died away.[29] But it revived in 1981-2 at the time of the 50th anniversary of the 1932 mass trespasses. It was the age of the 'Socialist Republic of South Yorkshire' and of resistance to Mrs Thatcher (chapter 13). Access to private land was an attractive socialist cause. On 21 October 1981, Roy Bullen wrote in the *Sheffield Morning Telegraph*: 'As Howard Hill had shown in his book *Freedom to Roam* ... there are still some 27 moors in the Peak and southern Pennines alone for which access agreement (or access orders) have yet to be made ... the public must not believe that the ramblers' campaign is over'.

The initiative for direct action came from Jon Cowley and Dick Williams, who belonged to the Socialist Workers Party,[30] and the socialist walkers and climbing club, Red Rope. In January 1982 they held an open planning meeting at the Bow Centre in Holly Street, Sheffield, to plan support for the celebrations in Hayfield of the anniversary of the mass trespass. About thirty people attended. It was decided that celebration was not enough and that a new trespass should be organised on Bamford Moor, which stretches from Stanage Edge to Ladybower Reservoir. On 28 March 1982, this took place with about three hundred participants, and the media gave it good coverage. The trespassers included green-shirted woodcraft folk, led by Terry Howard. They met no opposition from the landlord and his gamekeeper, who prudently made no appearance. On 24 April, the 50th anniversary celebrations took place at Hayfield. On 17 May, the Sheffield campaigners met again and decided to form a new body called the Sheffield Campaign for Access to Moorland, with the acronym SCAM.

In the subsequent 25 years, SCAM organised a succession of trespasses. Dave Sissons writes that SCAM also

> acted as a ginger group on the Ramblers' Association, which in turn lobbied the Labour Party, especially during the latter decade or so of its 18 years of opposition (1979-97), urging it to include in its party manifesto a commitment to the passing through Parliament of a new Right to Roam Act.[31]

**85**  The 11th Duke of Devonshire in April 2002, apologising for his family's restrictive attitude to access.

This lobbying paid off. In 2000, the Countryside and Right of Access (CroW) Act was passed, opening up new rights of access to mapped areas of mountain, moorland, down land, heathland and registered common land. For the first time, it gave the public the chance to legally explore away from the beaten track.

The trespassers were no longer irresponsible troublemakers. They had become far-sighted heroes. In April 2002, the 11th Duke of Devonshire spoke as follows at the Kinder mass trespass 70th-anniversary celebrations: 'They [the ramblers] were entirely in the right … My grandfather, I think, took the wrong attitude and I'd like to think that the attitude of my family to ramblers has changed. I'm a great believer in the right to roam.'[32]

G.H.B. Ward was vindicated.

## Chapter 12

# Provocative Parsons:
# Alan Ecclestone and Ted Wickham

The Church of England must prepare … to undertake a powerful and sustained evangelism; and, to begin with, every member of the Church must have it burnt into his mind that the Church is set in the world to redeem it – never for a moment to be a pious clique keeping itself to itself, but a saving, serving apostolic society … the new evangelism will look forward to a new order in both church and society.

Bishop Leslie Hunter's letter on evangelism of 15 November 1941

The weakness and collapse of the churches in the urbanized and industrialised areas of the country should be transparently clear to any who are not wilfully blind, as also the chronic and intractable nature of the missionary problem facing the Church in our modern society.

Ted Wickham[1]

A man who preaches both Christianity and Communism suffers from a fundamental inconsistency of mind.

Cyril Garbett, Archbishop of York[2]

In 1941, Sheffield was a mighty armaments centre, working flat out for the war effort. It may seem a surprising time for Bishop Leslie Hunter to call the churches to mission. But embattled Britain was experiencing religious renewal[3] and Hunter knew that the Church was unusually weak among the working classes in his own diocese. Moreover, his vision of Christianity, like that of his close friend Archbishop William Temple, extended to the whole of life and he believed that Christianity was relevant to post-war reconstruction.

Hunter has been described as a 'strategist for the Spirit',[4] a bishop who took strategic initiatives. One such initiative was to foster the parish meeting, which was designed to involve lay people much more deeply in their local churches. Having heard Alan Ecclestone, a young Anglo-Catholic vicar from Cumbria, talk about this, Hunter invited him to come to the poor working-class parish of Darnall and introduce parish meetings there. What Hunter did not then realise was that for Ecclestone parish meetings reflected socialist convictions

**86** Leslie Hunter, Bishop of Sheffield 1939-62, wanted to reach out to Sheffield's working classes and brought in able and innovative priests like Alan Ecclestone and Ted Wickham. Portrait by Robert Lyon.

so strong that he would join the Communist Party in 1948 and stick with it through thick and thin, despite notoriety and controversy in the divisive days of the Cold War.

Another of Hunter's ideas cut right across the traditional parish system. This was the notion of a mission to workers in industry. In 1944, Hunter asked Ted Wickham to come to Sheffield to lead such a mission. Wickham, 'old Labour' to his fingertips, took readily to Sheffield and, with extraordinary verve, set up 'Industrial Mission' in the great steelworks. This 'para-church' stimulated similar ventures across the world, but was never popular among Sheffield clergy. In the 1960s, after Hunter and Wickham had departed, it nearly perished in a purge by their successors.

This chapter discusses these two able and unorthodox churchmen and their stormy relationship with church, culture and politics in Sheffield.

## Alan Ecclestone's Origins

Ecclestone[5] (1904-92) was the son of a poorly paid pottery designer in Stoke-on-Trent. His mother was radical, with Chartist antecedents, and the home was full of debate on politics, literature and art. Ecclestone attended the high school at Newcastle-under-Lyme and then St Catherine's College, Cambridge, where he first studied history, achieving first-class honours, followed by English literature, with which he was fascinated.

He was greatly influenced by Holy Trinity Church at Sneyd in Burslem, an Anglo-Catholic and christian socialist church, similar to Conrad Noel's famous church at Thaxted. The vicar was Jim Wilson and the curate Harold Mason, who had helped Conrad Noel to draft the Catholic Crusade manifesto calling for a 'democratic commonwealth in which the community shall own the land and capital collectively'. Tim Gorringe writes:

> From this church and its clergy stemmed much of Alan's later vision. He was taken by it, and it held him, and both the piety and the theology of the Catholic Crusade remained central to him. The church life of this parish, he used to say, was the making of him and the reason why he got ordained … although Alan never joined the Crusade, he accepted the imperative. For the church to be effective it needed to meet in order to talk out, decide, plan, and educate its members on what they stood for.[6]

After Cambridge he became a teacher and lecturer. In 1930, he decided to seek ordination. At Wells Theological College, he was known as the college Bolshevik after calling for 'a little less of St Mark and a little more of Marx'.

Ecclestone was a curate in Carlisle and Barrow and then Vicar of Frizington, a village near Whitehaven, which suffered from mass unemployment. He married Delia Abraham, tenth daughter of the former Suffragan Bishop of Derby. Gorringe writes: 'marriage was the single most important experience of Alan's life.' Both were strong personalities, who had their battles but shared values. Their vicarage became a centre of Christian hospitality. He held regular parish meetings and periodic parish conventions.

## Ecclestone as Vicar of Darnall

In 1941 Bishop Hunter heard Ecclestone describe his parish meetings at the Malvern Church Conference and invited him to become Vicar of Darnall, a working-class parish in the east end of Sheffield and to introduce parish meetings there. Early in 1942, Ecclestone accepted and stayed there for 27 years.

Darnall in those days was a large working-class parish with a population of 10,000 people, close to the massive Tinsley and Darnall steel works. It was not multi-ethnic, as it is today. It was smoky and grimy, with men and women working long hours. The vicarage, initially in Industry Road and later in Mather Road, became a parish centre.

Ecclestone was an engaging, humorous, yet deeply serious person and an extraordinarily dedicated vicar. He spent the morning studying, keeping abreast of the latest books and publications and preparing for sermons, WEA classes, parish meetings and so on. From 1.30 p.m. to 6 p.m. each day, he visited some of the 5,600 houses in the parish. It took seven years to get round them. Only once was he turned away. He had no small talk. Asked why he had come, he said 'Because I want to get to know you.' Through his visiting, he found 'the whole texture of human life'. In the evening, he might have a parish meeting, a party meeting or a WEA class. One of his WEA students was Arthur Scargill.

*The Parish Meeting*

Ecclestone was very different from Ommanney (chapter 7). Ommanney was a man of authority, whereas Ecclestone disliked clericalism and wanted his congregation to share in decisions. In his first week, he announced that he had been called to Sheffield to introduce the parish meeting and that these meetings would continue indefinitely. The senior churchwarden resigned in protest. Others reacted positively. Numbers attending ranged from 15 to eighty. It was held in the vicarage sitting room, with Ecclestone, sitting on a low chair near the fire, leading from behind. He would say: 'I need you to become myself.' In other words, one cannot be complete without the depth of encounters with other people.[7]

The object of the parish meeting was to help people to understand the implications of Christian discipleship in an industrial city and a changing world. They discussed theology and political and cultural issues, like the Beveridge Report on the welfare state, the ordination of women, preparation for a play they were to see at the Playhouse, an art exhibition at the City Art Gallery or a book they were reading. Distinguished visiting speakers came, like Albie Sachs, South African treason trial lawyer. The parish meeting often led to action, like welcoming German prisoners of war into homes at Christmas. A 'thank you' candelabra was sent from the camp made from cocoa tins and was promptly painted red and hung in the sanctuary.

Ecclestone's parish meeting had resemblances to the 'base communities' later developed in Latin America, with similar radical ideas of community and democracy. Ecclestone would say outrageous things to provoke debate. Even so, the meetings were not all plain sailing. There were times of perplexity, frozen silence or anger. In the late 1950s, Ecclestone apparently stopped other church meetings to bolster the flagging parish meeting. For Ecclestone, the parish meeting was not optional. He apparently told the congregation that 'If you don't come to the parish meeting, I don't want to see you at Holy Communion.'[8] He saw the meeting 'not as a means but as an end in itself – the assembling of the Church that it may be used by God'. The priest who looked after the parish after Alan's retirement found the congregation 'though not large … amazing for their depth of conversation and awareness'. When the archdeacon was leading a Bible study on Genesis at the parish meeting, one of the parishioners politely interrupted him: 'Excuse me, Archdeacon, haven't you heard of demythologising?'[9]

*Ecclestone and the Communist Party*

Ecclestone was now living in a Labour city and, from 1945 onwards, under a Labour Government with a formidable reform programme. Other clergy like Leslie Hunter and Ted Wickham supported Labour more or less openly. But Ecclestone was idealistic and uncompromising. His communism was rooted in his experience of the Catholic Crusade at Sneyd, and in his subsequent reading of Marx (notably his early writings) and other writers. He admired Marx's understanding of history and saw Marx as 'the greatest of all humanists'.

**87** Alan and Delia Ecclestone in 1969 at the end of Alan's ministry in Darnall. Both joined the Communist Party in 1948, causing decades of controversy.

In 1948 he and Delia joined the Communist Party. The trigger was probably disillusionment at the Attlee Government's alliance with the USA against the USSR in the Cold War.

The party looked like a lost cause. Labour's strength in Sheffield was overwhelming. It had ruled the city successfully for 20 years, with only one brief intermission, and was popular and well organised. The Communist Party was puny as an electoral force. For example, in the 1950 General Election, Labour won five seats out of seven, with 182,278 votes, whereas the two Communist Party candidates won only 1,840 votes between them. In the 1960s, Ecclestone stood unsuccessfully six times as a party candidate for Darnall Ward for the council. He received much hate mail and some letters in support.

The Communist Party was small but disciplined. Its strength was mainly in the engineering unions, with George Caborn (father of Richard Caborn MP) a formidable figure, married to a Methodist. The communists had some influence on the council through their membership of the Trades and Labour Council, until this split into two in the 1970s. Outstanding characters in the party included the baker George Henry Fletcher (chapter 10).

Being a communist brought obligations that the Ecclestones carried out conscientiously. Every Monday night, they attended a branch meeting, which increasingly was held in the vicarage. Leading figures in the party, like Harry Pollitt, Willie Gallagher and James Klugman, were guests, as was the Soviet Deputy Minister of Education. They sold the *Daily Worker* on the streets, took part in public demonstrations and spoke at public meetings.

### The Peace Movement

On one subject – peace – the party could rally substantial support. Ecclestone was particularly drawn to peace campaigns. In April 1949, he and Delia attended the first World Peace Congress in Paris, at which Sartre spoke. The security service followed the Ecclestones' activities closely and the couple received constant anonymous telephone calls in their hotel room. This congress led to the Stockholm Peace Petition, the World Council for Peace and a proliferation of peace committees. Ecclestone became chair of the Sheffield Peace Committee, which collected 50,000 signatures towards the 473 million signatures worldwide for the Peace Petition. As a result, it was agreed that the second World Peace

Conference should be held in Sheffield, beginning on 16 November 1950. Initially, the local Labour Party supported it. Attlee promised that only delegates with a specific charge against them would be excluded. The city hall was booked.

But the authorities in both Church and state then changed their minds. Britain was fighting the Korean War and the threat of world communism seemed very real. Bishop Bell denounced the Peace Movement as an instrument of communist propaganda. The British Council of Churches refused to send delegates. On 1 November, Attlee denounced the conference as bogus. On 10 November, Chuter Ede, the Home Secretary, refused visas for two-thirds of the 2,000 delegates, including Paul Robeson, Dmitri Shostakovitch and Frederic Joliot Curie, president of the Peace Movement.

Nonetheless, 4,500 people turned up in Sheffield on the opening day. The veteran socialist Lady Mabel Smith was among those welcoming the delegates.[10] Alan Ecclestone chaired the first day's proceedings, at which the speakers included Dr Hewlett Johnson, the Red Dean of Canterbury, and Pablo Picasso, who drew a dove, which was auctioned for £21. On 19 November, the whole conference, including Ecclestone, decamped to Warsaw.

In 1952, he attended the third World Peace Conference at Vienna. He missed the fourth conference in Helsinki, but he continued peace campaigning in Sheffield. Following a conference on nuclear weapons with Konni Zilliacus, a protest march was held in April 1958, leading to Ecclestone's arrest by the police. He had failed to notify them in advance. The police did not press charges. The *Sheffield Telegraph* asked in whose name they signed the petition. Ecclestone replied: 'In the name of Him to whose crucifixion you devoted half of page four and forgot on page six …'

## Are Communism and Christianity Incompatible?

Alan's communist activities led to him being cut off by the church authorities. He was not formally disciplined as Ommanney was, but Garbett, the Archbishop of York, made clear his view that communism was incompatible with Christianity. Leslie Hunter was under pressure from his Diocesan Committee and elsewhere to 'deal' with Ecclestone. Hunter resisted these pressures, not only because of 'parson's freehold', but also because Ecclestone was 'the best priest in my Diocese'.[11] But Hunter kept his distance, until he thawed in his later years and told Ecclestone reassuringly that 'I don't get any complaints from *inside* the Parish.' Ecclestone did not promote the Communist Party as such in his parish, but he did advocate communism as a pure way of life.[12] His continued party membership after the suppression of the Hungarian uprising of 1956 imposed strains on his congregation, some of whom left.[13]

What are we to make of Ecclestone's communism? There are strong scriptural foundations for Christian Socialism in the many texts in which the rich are scorned and the poor exalted. Garbett's complaint that the party's ideology was inherently anti-Christian was questionable, as its UK party programme called for respect for 'all religions, creeds and beliefs'.

No doubt Garbett's real concern was Ecclestone's acceptance of the party's subservience to the USSR. Ecclestone said that he stood by the party because, despite its many weaknesses, it stood for the under-privileged, just as he stood by the Church despite its involvement in religious persecution, witch-hunting and anti-semitism. But the churches had largely given up these crimes, whereas in 1948 the USSR was enforcing its grip on Eastern Europe regardless of the wishes of the population. Moreover, the Peace Movement, to which Ecclestone was so committed, was indeed, as Bell argued, an instrument of communist propaganda. In 1985, a Soviet defector, formerly a high-ranking diplomat, said that 'the Soviet-controlled World Peace Council … swarmed with KGB officers'.[14]

Ecclestone knew what communist rule was really like. He visited Czechoslovakia in 1950 and the USSR and Tadikistan in 1955. Like the Webbs 20 years earlier, he gave communist rulers the benefit of the doubt. Unlike many communist intellectuals, he did not leave the party over Kruschev's attack on Stalin or over Hungary or Czechoslovakia. Maybe, he accepted ruthlessness as a prerequisite for revolution. An observer who watched him chair the first session of the Sheffield Peace Conference commented: 'I have no doubt that had it come to the point he would have put us all against the wall and had us shot.'[15] When the Cold War thawed in the 1960s, Ecclestone became involved in Christian Marxist dialogue, writing articles in *Marxism Today*. He left the party much later.

Despite the many paradoxes of the situation, both Church and city benefited from Ecclestone's unusual ministry. As Adrian Hastings wrote: 'It is the strength of the Church of England, at its best, that it is so unable to control its prophetic mavericks.'[16] Not only did he have outstanding pastoral and inspirational gifts. His communism made people question the assumptions of the Cold War, which so dominated thinking at the time. He was one of the first churchmen to challenge the UK's reliance on nuclear weapons, a concern that later spread widely.

## Ted Wickham's Origins

Like Ecclestone, Ted Wickham[17] (1911–94) came from a modest background, was Anglo-Catholic, left of centre and very widely read. But Wickham was less idealistic and more pragmatic than Ecclestone. They were physically contrasting – Ecclestone, slim and of medium height, from the Potteries and Cambridge, Wickham, a short and irrepressible Londoner from Tottenham. They knew each other well from a discussion group of lively young Sheffield clergy who met in the 1940s.

Wickham's education was much less privileged than Ecclestone's. Leaving school at 15, he worked for nine years in local plastics factories. Drawn in his teens into his local Anglo-Catholic church, St Philip's, Tottenham, he developed a vocation for the priesthood. With restless intellectual energy, he obtained a degree in divinity at London University through external study. He then spent a year at St Stephen's House, Oxford, before being ordained in Newcastle, where he was curate in Shieldfield. In 1941 he moved to Swynnerton, Staffordshire, as chaplain to a huge explosives factory. There he met his future wife, Helen Moss, a labour officer. He also pioneered his techniques of talking to people about Christianity.

## Wickham's Move to Sheffield

Bishop Hunter talent-spotted Wickham as the man to undertake a mission to industry, but funding was needed. Hunter was an opportunist as well as a strategist. In Trollopian fashion, he persuaded the trustees of the Duke of Norfolk's Shrewsbury Hospital almshouses to take Wickham to work both for the hospital and for industry. So it was at the hospital in Norfolk Road that Wickham, and soon his wife Helen, lived when they moved to Sheffield in 1944. By 1949, the duke and the hospital trustees were

**88**  Shrewsbury Hospital. Under a Trollopian arrangement engineered by Hunter, Wickham came to Sheffield in 1944 technically as chaplain and governor and lived at the hospital.

**89**   Ted Wickham (centre) and Bishop Hunter (third from right) talk to Sheffield workers, soon after they established Industrial Mission in Sheffield.

'restive' that 'their chaplain should be chiefly distinguished by the work he does outside the Hospital'.[18] Hunter eventually found alternative funding.

Hunter gave Wickham this brief: 'to find out by trial in the next two years whether there might be a full-time job for a man with his experience on the shop-floors of the big steel works if managers and men invited them.' It was a daunting assignment. The steel works were huge, busy and secular places and the workers reputedly had little time for religion. But Hunter gave Wickham an introduction to Eric Holmstrom, managing director of Firth Vickers Stainless and a sympathetic church burgess. Holmstrom sent round a memorandum to say that a clergyman would be coming around with the sole aim of trying to relate Christianity to industry. As was his invariable practice, Wickham's first move after meeting management was to meet trades union officials. He then began to visit all parts of the works. He developed the 'Sheffield model' of factory visiting in four stages: negotiating access, visiting, 'snap-break' (sandwich or lunch break) meetings, and taking debate further. This model was at the heart of what he now called 'Sheffield Industrial Mission'.

*The Consolidation of Industrial Mission*

Wickham soon reported to Hunter that there was a role for an industrial chaplain. He negotiated entry into several of the other great steelworks. In 1948, an assistant chaplain was appointed.

Particularly important in Wickham's model were the third and fourth stages. For him, the third stage – the 'snap-break' meeting – was just as crucial as the parish meeting was to Ecclestone. Wickham would arrange the meeting a few days in advance through a sympathetic individual, who would 'round up the lads'. It would be held openly, not behind closed doors. He would trigger an animated debate with some topical reference. Like Hunter and Ecclestone, he saw Christianity as about the whole of life, so topics would include politics, economics, culture and society. He had great verbal fluency and was witty, well-informed and more than a match for shop-floor debaters. He only had 15–20 minutes, but could arouse interest and, if possible, encourage further exploration of Christianity.

The fourth stage of the model – taking debate further – raised difficulties. Hunter had originally assumed that workers might be drawn into their local church. But Wickham found that workers were deeply alienated from traditional church structures. Instead, he encouraged workers associated with the mission to form groups that would remain outside the parochial structure, at least for the foreseeable future. They became a 'para-church' or a 'church outside the Church', meeting together on Sunday evening or Thursday evening.

Explaining Industrial Mission, Wickham used the homely metaphor of churches fishing in muddy waters: their task was not to draw people out into the clean waters of the Church, but to clean up the water. Like Thomas Arnold and F.D. Maurice, Wickham wanted to Christianise society.

Wickham criticised parish churches as imprisoned by the middle class, complacent, introspective and unable to relate to industry. Much later, Hunter commented that Wickham 'did not get on well with the parish clergy and wasted a lot of venom criticising them. Perhaps he had rather a chip on his shoulder.'[19] Unfortunately, this was reciprocated. Indeed, on coming out of a diocesan meeting in the late 1950s, Wickham remarked to a colleague: 'You realise that our only friend amongst them is the Bishop?'[20] The failure to win friends in the diocese made the mission vulnerable once Hunter was no longer there as patron.

In 1949, Hunter formally reviewed the mission and confirmed its success. He then persuaded the Master Cutler to convene a meeting of 142 industrialists, who agreed on the need for expansion and committed themselves to support it, financially and in other ways. In 1950, the mission took on a more structured form. Wickham left Shrewsbury Hospital and became a residentiary canon of the cathedral. Hunter set up an advisory

**90**   Ted Wickham, a master of repartee, addressing the workers.

committee under his chairmanship, with employers, trades unionists and clergy. Employers and workers contributed money. At Samuel Fox, workers accepted voluntary deductions from their wages.

The employers' support for the mission came partly from a sense of the importance of Christianity in English society and from the church allegiances of individual senior managers. But employers were also fearful of the powerful communist influences in the trades unions and hoped that the mission could form a bulwark against it. Wickham established friendly relationships with communist shop stewards, but he also strongly advocated reconciliation between employers and workers – very different from the communist belief in class war.

Some of Wickham's work was adult education and some 'outward bound', but the religious aspect was central. In 1950, he issued a leaflet urging people influenced by the mission to 'cross the line' – 'to join the movement' of the Christian Church. The Church was not about attending services, but about joining a movement. The Thursday evening group became a lay leaders' group, with Holy Communion at the cathedral once a month. In the 1950s, he sought to build up lay leaders of groups, with only occasional participation by chaplains.

### Wickham's Grand Plan

The years 1957–9 were critical in Wickham's life. By now, he was running a substantial and unprecedented Christian mission in 20 of the largest steelworks and in the railways. There were eight full-time chaplains and 270 discussion groups, involving 3,000 people, mostly with no church background.

Visitors came from all over the world and Industrial Mission spread abroad. Wickham had strong contacts with worker priests in France. He was also in touch with leading theologians like Tillich, Bultman and Reinhold Niebuhr. Bultman even corresponded with some Sheffield steelworkers. Wickham met Tillich and Niebuhr on visits to the USA and Tillich visited him in Sheffield, later writing: 'I remember every moment in which you were kind enough to drive me through Sheffield and tell me about your work in the factories … I have never forgotten that day and the most impressive drive between the walls of the large Sheffield iron works.'[21]

Wickham took two crucial initiatives. First, in 1957, he produced his seminal book *Church and People in an Industrial City*,[22] drawing on the religious history of Sheffield to explain working-class alienation from the Church and recommending a new missionary structure. It was a profoundly influential book and, despite subsequent criticisms,[23] remains compelling.

Second, he became secretary to a working party of the Church Assembly, which produced a report entitled *The Task of the Church in relation to Industry* (CA 1288), again advocating a new missionary structure to bring together coherently all the Church's ventures in industry.

Wickham hoped to lead this new missionary structure but it was not to be. It would have cut across the autonomy of diocesan bishops. He was seen as altogether too dominant a figure to be let loose in this way. Instead, a much weaker structure was established and Wickham was offered the consolation prize of becoming Bishop of Middleton in the Diocese of Manchester.

In 1959, after much agonising and after both archbishops had urged him to accept, Wickham agreed to cross the Pennines and become a bishop. But he later told his friends that he had been 'blackballed into the episcopacy'.

## *The Crisis in Sheffield Industrial Mission*

The 1960s exposed the excessive dependence of Sheffield Industrial Mission on Hunter and Wickham.[24] The new senior chaplain was Michael Jackson, an intense and intellectual young man, who had worked in steelworks. Trained by Wickham, he appeared to share his predecessor's theology and approach, though he lacked his communication skills.

For several years the mission continued largely unchanged. In 1963, Jackson and his colleagues compiled a book called *Christian Mission in Industry*, which, like other writings of the time, reflected radical secular theology. At the last minute, Jackson withdrew it from publication.

In 1965, Jackson had a crisis of conscience and abandoned the mission's liberal theology. Two factors may have contributed. First, in 1962, Hunter had retired, to be succeeded by Bishop John Taylor, who was struck down by a cerebral thrombosis before his enthronement. When he eventually took up his duties, it became clear that he was much less liberal and much more parish-orientated than Hunter. Jackson probably discussed the future of the mission with Taylor. The second factor was the great furore that followed the publication of Bishop Robinson's *Honest to God*, which mentioned Wickham by name. Jackson's reaction was to revert to traditionalist orthodoxy, but he was not straightforward about this and did not allow scope for debate, let alone dissent.

In September 1965, Jackson gave two chaplains notice, apparently on the grounds that they had gone native in industry and ceased to convey the Christian gospel. Bishop Taylor endorsed his action. Jackson's colleagues were deeply unhappy. Some consulted Wickham in Manchester and others consulted friends in Sheffield. It took time before the affair turned into a public furore but, by March 1966, it was widely featured in the national press. One of the chaplains, Michael Atkinson, contacted the *Guardian*, whose eminent

**91**   Leaders of Industrial Mission say farewell to Bishop Hunter in 1962. From left to right: Ted Wickham, Leslie Hunter, Tom Kilpatrick (Steel, Peech and Tozer), Michael Jackson and Ron Hogg (Firth Vickers). In 1959, Jackson had taken over as senior chaplain from Ted Wickham, who became Bishop of Middleton. In 1965, Jackson repudiated Wickham's theology, triggering a major crisis.

columnist Geoffrey Moorhouse wrote extensively about the dispute.[25] The *Times* also
reported it. Supporters of the mission in industry and the trade unions became involved
and there were strong complaints at the mission's advisory committee and at Rotherham
Deanery Synod. In April 1966, members of the works council at Steel, Peech and Tozer
suddenly decided to set off in private cars for York. They called at Archbishop Coggan's
palace. Coggan was there and listened to their call for an inquiry and for the recall of
Wickham. But Wickham's return was the last thing Coggan and Taylor wanted.

Two inquiries were held. The first, set up by Bishop Taylor, was a diocesan inquiry into
the past and future of the mission and formed the basis for the Mission's later rebuilding.
However, as it included Jackson in its membership, it was not independent. So Archbishop
Coggan set up a second inquiry, chaired by Edwin Barker, secretary of the Board for Social
Responsibility, with members from outside the diocese. They came down strongly on
Jackson's side of the dispute and criticised Wickham for meddling.

The dispute had a devastating effect on the mission. Many staff left, so that by September
1966 only three were left, one of whom was working out his notice. Some firms withdrew
their support. It took years before the mission was fully restored.

*Aftermath*

Neither of Hunter's initiatives had run smoothly. Ecclestone remained in Sheffield for 27
years, but Hunter's original idea of using his example to spread parish meetings through
the diocese foundered because of the notoriety of his communism and because parish
meetings demanded unusual skills of facilitation. Nonetheless, Ecclestone was a fine parish
priest for Darnall and played a wider role in the city in making people think. In his
retirement, Ecclestone found a new fame as a writer and speaker on prayer. His book *Yes
to God* won the Collins Religious Book Award for 1974-6.

Hunter's choice of Wickham for his mission to industry led to the greatest effort
ever made by Sheffield churches to reach out to the working classes, even if it proved
unsustainable after its creators had departed. The diocese reverted to its default position of
low-church orthodoxy. The diocese's able historian, Mary Walton, could not understand the
'extraordinary fuss and publicity' that followed the decision to dismiss the two chaplains.[26]
But another observer, Alan Webster, Dean of St Paul's, wrote: 'It was tragic that lack of
continuity in the Sheffield Diocese led to troubles which inhibited the growth of this
courageous and far-sighted venture.'[27]

As Bishop of Middleton, Wickham did much constructive work but did not find the
same fulfilment as he had as senior chaplain in Sheffield. He was disappointed at not being
promoted to diocesan bishop. He found the events in Sheffield of 1965-6 'shameful'.[28]
He was also hurt by an extraordinary article that Jackson wrote for *Theology*, accusing
Wickham (though not by name) of numerous heresies.[29] It is unusual for a bishop to
be pilloried in this way by a former colleague. Constrained by his position, he declined
to publish a thoughtful book he had written in the early 1960s called *Christianity in a
Secular Age.* 'He did not have the time to deal with the aftermath of argument that might
take place.'[30]

In its heyday, Sheffield Industrial Mission was a remarkable movement, touching many
people's lives. Workplace chaplaincy still operates in Sheffield. Wickham's 'para-church'
concept became official Church policy in the *Mission Shaped Church* report in 2004.[31]

## Chapter 13

# Blunkett and the Socialist Republic of South Yorkshire

We were extraordinarily proud of the title 'Socialist Republic of South Yorkshire' and at least a dozen councillors and journalists will swear blind that they were the first to use the name. However, in the Eighties ... we were surprised to be told by the chief officer charged with industrial development that the name Socialist Republic was not the best slogan with which to attract new investment ...

John Cornwell, *Tomb of the Unknown Alderman*[1]

There he was, this Christ-like bearded blind man, standing on the rostrum appealing to Derek Hatton to withdraw his Liverpool resolution asking for industrial action in support of councillors 'not prepared to carry out Tory cuts'. 'Will you do that? Will you do that, Derek?' He stood there waving his hand into the darkness. So Hatton, who is a bit of a smart alec, ran towards the rostrum and said 'Yes, in the interests of unity, Liverpool will withdraw its resolution.' There was an explosion of applause. I believe the right wing were angry with Blunkett for having done this.

Tony Benn's Diary for 2 October 1985[2]

I am making a lot of judgements by instinct, just by feeling in my guts whether the information being given to me stands up. Much of politics is like this. People expect it to be scientific and clinical – but it isn't.

David Blunkett, November 2002[3]

Once Labour became the dominant political party in Sheffield in 1926, its leaders ceased to be troublemakers and instead became the Labour establishment, which ran the city. They sought constructive relationships with central Government, even when it was Conservative. This worked well. For example, it was largely a Conservative Government that paid for Labour's iconic Park Hill Flats, built around 1960, when Roy Hattersley was chairman of housing. All this changed in the confrontational period of the 1980s. Labour in Sheffield had swung to the left, while the Conservative Government under Mrs Thatcher had swung to the right. The stage was set for conflict.

In the early 1980s, Sheffield's Labour Council appeared more left wing than at any other time in its history. It was led by David Blunkett who, in the eyes of the then Prime Minister, must have seemed a dangerous troublemaker, even if she sent him a handwritten note of condolence in 1988 when his dog Teddy died. Blunkett combined populist gut instincts with a sophisticated understanding of politics and society. In 1983, he joined the Labour Party National Executive at a time of unparalleled party strife and became a pivotal figure, bridging the left and the leadership.

In 1987, he became MP for Brightside and went on to climb higher up the 'greasy pole' of politics than any other Sheffielder, being successively Secretary of State for Education and Employment, Home Secretary and Secretary of State for Work and Pensions. His fame as a Minister, however, was not for left-wing extremism but rather for his energy and outspokenness as one of Tony Blair's closest allies in pushing through New Labour policies.

This chapter looks at Blunkett's role in left-wing politics in Sheffield in the 1970s and 1980s and his struggle with Thatcherism before he went to Westminster. It does not assess his tumultuous career in Westminster, which is national rather than local history.

### David Blunkett's Origins

Blunkett is a true son of working-class Sheffield, born in 1947 of middle-aged parents.[4] His father was a foreman for the East Midlands Gas Board. The family was squashed into a two-bedroom house in Longley, later moving to a better three-bedroom house in Pollard Crescent on the Parson Cross Estate. David was born blind: 'the optic nerve behind each eye had failed to develop properly owing to the fact that my mother's and father's genes were not compatible – a one in a million failure.'[5] The shocked parents handled the situation with fortitude and trained their son to be self-reliant. His father passed on a 'vast fund of general knowledge', while his mother's expectations influenced her son profoundly.

Under Sheffield's policy at the time for handicapped children, David was sent at the age of four to board at the Manchester Road School for the Blind (later Tapton Mount and now closed). The parents had to bring the child and then quickly depart. Blunkett comments: 'Obviously this has a profound effect on an infant, who feels totally abandoned and terrified, particularly when he cannot see who or what is around him.'[6]

He was allowed home for the holidays and for one weekend in four in term time.

The school trained its pupils in Braille, reading, writing and arithmetic. Like the boarding schools of the well-to-do, the school inculcated toughness and self-reliance.

In 1959, 12-year-old Blunkett suffered a terrible shock. His father fell into a giant vat of boiling water and died a month later. The gas board tried to evade responsibility. Eventually meagre compensation was awarded, but his mother was 'desperately poor'. Blunkett later commented:

> Those who have never experienced real poverty are all too often very sentimental about it and about poor people in general. I have to smile at this and think: if only you knew what it was like, you would know all about aspirations and expectations, and why it was that, in the community in which I grew up, escaping the poverty trap and achieving success were the key aims. That is why I am so keen to give people ladders out of poverty: to give them a hand up rather than a hand out.[7]

His mother later developed cancer and his grandfather had to move into the geriatric ward of Northern General Hospital. Visiting this ward was 'a heart-breaking experience' and motivated Blunkett to try to lift people out of such conditions.[8]

Blunkett's secondary boarding school – the Royal Normal School for the Blind at Rowton Castle near Shrewsbury – was educationally unambitious. When he was 16, he was moved to the further education branch of the college at Albrighton for a commercial course. But Blunkett's self-reliant personality asserted itself. He joined the Labour Party and, with five classmates, enrolled in evening classes at the local technical college three miles away. Blunkett obtained a good batch of 'O' levels and 'A'-level Economics.

Returning to Sheffield, the 19-year-old Blunkett obtained a clerical job at the East Midlands Gas Board, but he soon took charge of his own destiny. He became a Methodist local preacher. At the Methodist youth club, he met Ruth Mitchell, whom he later married against his mother's instincts. They had three sons, but finally separated in 1987.[9]

He continued part-time study to gain further 'A' levels and a National Certificate in Business Studies. He decided to become a teacher and was accepted by Sheffield University to study Politics and Modern History. The then Professor of Politics, Bernard Crick, became a friend who three decades later assisted Blunkett in introducing citizenship into Britain's schools. To help in finding his way around the university, Blunkett acquired his first guide dog, Ruby, whom he describes as 'lively, mischievous and in many ways outrageous'. Crick maintained that, whenever he mentioned Marx, Ruby barked. Despite political distractions, Blunkett secured a 2:1 in his final degree and went on, via a teachers' training course in Huddersfield, to become a lecturer at Barnsley College of Technology in September 1973. From Crick and others at Sheffield University, Blunkett acquired a reflective and analytical approach to politics, which could be at odds with his gut instincts.

**92**   David Blunkett and his wife, Ruth Mitchell, in 1973 in the General Cemetery. Are they looking for Holberry's grave?

## Sheffield Labour Politics in the 1970s

For Blunkett, politics came first.[10] While still a student, he immersed himself ever more deeply in the Labour Party. Unlike other students who theorised about Marxism, Blunkett joined his local Labour Party in Parson Cross and took up canvassing with Ruby's help. In 1970, a safe seat for a councillor became vacant and the local party, sensing a need for 'new blood', encouraged him to stand. Thus he became a councillor at the age of twenty-two.

A predecessor of Blunkett in Sheffield Labour politics, Roy Hattersley, describes the Labour Group at the time he joined the city council in 1957:

> Ernest George Rowlinson was a legend and a name engraved on the brass remembrance of past Lord Mayors. The Labour Group he had fashioned and formed was still in absolute control, able to increase the rates with the impunity enjoyed only by the truly invincible … We ran the City with fists of stainless steel, a metal no decent Sheffielder would cover with a velvet glove.[11]

Thirteen years later, the Labour Group that Blunkett joined no longer felt invincible. In 1968 it had lost power to the Conservatives, partly because of the Wilson Government's unpopularity and partly as a result of a Labour split over a rent rebate scheme for council housing. In 1970 Labour was back in office and was still led by Sir Ron Ironmonger, from whom Blunkett learned much. He was also helped by two older women councillors – Winifred Golding and Enid Hattersley, mother of Roy and herself a legend in Sheffield. But the older generation of councillors was gradually making way for some very different younger ones. Blunkett was part of the 'Brightside mafia,' – young councillors from Brightside constituency, including Bill Michie, Roger Barton and Peter Price, joined a little later by Joan Barton and Clive Betts.[12] Others from outside Brightside also became prominent, such as Rev. Alan Billings, who was vicar both in Broomhall and Walkley.

Members of the Brightside mafia were not far-left Marxists but were mostly well to the left of traditional Sheffield Labour and the national party. The label 'left' may be too simplistic for a group of varied backgrounds and views. Roger Barton and Bill Michie came from the trade union left and would 'fight to maintain working class living standards and bargaining powers'.[13] Blunkett, influenced by his puritanical Methodist background and his political studies, emphasised values rather than ideology and sought efficient delivery of services that people actually wanted.

The Brightside mafia joined together in the campaign to oust Eddie Griffiths as MP for Brightside for failing to fight the Conservative Government with sufficient vigour.[14] In 1974, he was replaced by Joan Maynard, known as 'Stalin's granny'. They deplored the compromising tendencies of the Labour Governments led by Wilson and later Callaghan.

## South Yorkshire County Council and Cheap Fares

In April 1974, a new two-tier local government structure was introduced.[15] In addition to Sheffield Metropolitan District Council (with enlarged boundaries), there was the entirely new South Yorkshire Metropolitan County Council, with responsibility for police, fire services, transport and structural planning. Ironmonger became leader of the new county council, handing over the leadership in Sheffield City Council to George Wilson, seen as on the left but in reality a maverick. Relations between the two councils were often acrimonious. Initially, the energetic Blunkett belonged to both the city and county councils but he left the county council in 1977.

Blunkett was one of a group of four who, in December 1972, 'on a cold wet evening in Rotherham', devised a public transport policy for the new county council. For him, the policy was driven not by ideology but by the need for economic and social mobility. It was already policy for Sheffield Labour Party. Sir Ron Ironmonger had initially been sceptical but his support was crucial in convincing non-Sheffield colleagues.[16] The new county council's cheap fare policy on South Yorkshire buses had the ultimate goal of free transport. In 1977 the fare for a 2.5 mile journey was 7p, compared with 36p in West Yorkshire. By 1983, the subsidy had risen to 85 per cent of operating costs, but, according to Blunkett, this was the lowest subsidy *per passenger mile travelled* in the UK, because of the increase in passengers. There were benefits for personal income (lower living expenses), manufacturing (giving a strong base for an export trade in buses) and commerce (reducing congestion).[17] The policy was very popular in South Yorkshire. According to Blunkett: 'While passenger mileage fell around the country – a 30% decline in urban areas between 1974 and 1984 – bus travel in South Yorkshire increased by 7% in the same period. During 1982-3 more passengers boarded per mile in South Yorkshire than anywhere else in the country.'[18]

## Community Politics

Labour's power in Sheffield was built on tight discipline and centralisation but could be insensitive to local opinion. Blunkett was sympathetic to the new community politics. In a 1983 Fabian pamphlet called *Building from the Bottom,* he and Geoff Green pointed out that ordinary people would not support Labour's efforts to protect public services if they found these services unresponsive and bureaucratic:

> local councillors and council officers alone could not sustain the vitality of each community. Helping the residents themselves to give expression to complex needs is an essential part in regenerating our city. It is not primarily a question of responding to individual grievances but of supporting their collective contribution to the life and well-being of their neighbourhood.[19]

In 1976, Blunkett became chair of the Family and Community Services Committee (known elsewhere as Social Services). Recalling his grandfather's unhappy experience in the Fir Vale geriatric unit, he 'put pressure on the local health authority' to close this and other similar units. They were replaced by new and attractive homes run by the local authority.[20]

Blunkett also supported democracy within the Labour Party, at a time when the district Labour Party was increasing its influence. His enthusiasm for community politics and decentralisation is reminiscent of Ironside (chapter 4), but Blunkett had a single-minded ambition, which Ironside conspicuously lacked. As a Minister, Blunkett gained a reputation as someone who confidently wielded state power, rather than someone who devolved it to others.

### Leader of the Labour Group

George Wilson became increasingly unpopular as leader of the Labour Group and the council and eventually resigned in 1980.[21] Blunkett was elected to take his place – an extraordinary achievement for a blind young man of 33, reflecting in part his self-confidence, political adroitness, hard work and debating skills and in part his left wing credentials as the Labour Group moved to the left. His colleagues were in awe of his ability. Thus, when a councillor from another authority suggested that it 'must be impossible for (Blunkett) to do the job properly with a handicap', Alan Billings retorted, 'Oh that, that isn't a handicap, just a leveller.'[22]

Blunkett and Billings stood for leader and deputy leader together as a 'dream ticket' with Blunkett seen as left wing and Billing as right wing in local party terms.[23] This was part of a wider takeover by younger councillors, some but not all on the left of the party. It would be misleading to see the council as dominated by Blunkett at this time. He was working with an unusually able team, which was nationally influential in the Association of Municipal Authorities.[24] In a period when Labour authorities were divided and felt under siege, the Sheffield team provided national leadership because of their competence and their skill in reconciling rival factions.

Blunkett's new leadership role was a poisoned chalice. He faced two unprecedented challenges – meltdown in Sheffield's traditional industries and the Thatcher Government's hostility towards big Labour local authorities. He was not a man to retreat under fire. Nor would this have suited the mood of the party. For this was the classic period of the 'Socialist Republic of South Yorkshire' – a phrase that many claimed to have coined (see the opening of this chapter) but probably originated as abuse from Sir Irvine Patnick, leader of the South Yorkshire Conservatives and later MP for Hallam. The phrase was relished by the Labour left as suggesting that, regardless of Westminster, South Yorkshire would maintain its socialist policies. This proved an illusion. Like many others, Sheffield's left underestimated Mrs Thatcher's ruthlessness in seeing off any troublemaker who stood in her way.

**93** Demonstration against public sector cuts. In the 1980s, the council and the unions were united in protesting at Government cuts.

The early 1980s was a period of unusual left-wing fervour in Sheffield. It was at this time that the Holberry Society (formed in 1978 to 'involve the Sheffield Labour movement in an independent investigation of its own history') persuaded the council to commemorate Samuel Holberry in the Peace Gardens. In 1981, it was decided to hang the Red Flag on the town hall on May Day.[25] When the town hall attendants proved unwilling to erect the flag, the deed was done by Councillor Bill Michie (later MP for Heeley). This custom continued for several years. Blunkett, a keen unilateralist, and his colleagues declared the city a nuclear free zone.

Blunkett inaugurated a series of Marx memorial lectures, the first being given appropriately by E.P. Thompson, but the second on Orwell was given by his old mentor Bernard Crick. Here, perhaps, Blunkett was playing a subtle game, for Crick, Orwell and Blunkett himself were not Marxists. Indeed, when Blunkett and Crick sought in 1988 to define Labour Party 'aims and values' they acknowledged their debt to William Morris, Tawney and others, but not to Marx.[26] Sheffield Labour still owed less to Marx than to Methodism (see chapter 10). Blunkett's attitudes were affected by his Methodist roots, and Methodists like Rev. John Vincent influenced the party.[27]

Blunkett's acceptance of left-wing gestures was in part a way of securing his power base at a time when hard decisions had to be made. For example, he persuaded his party to reject non-co-operation with Thatcher's popular 'right to buy' policy for council homes, but instead reduced the attractions of the policy for Sheffield tenants.

But at the same time Blunkett wanted local authorities to act as 'a focus of socialist resistance' to Thatcherism. Labour should be prepared to challenge capitalism. This approach was evident in his and Geoff Green's Fabian pamphlet *Building from the Bottom*. Referring to the 'idiocy' of UK financial institutions, he and Green saw 'a strong case for dismembering the large conglomerates into regional and local banks' that would serve local needs rather than the international money market. They wanted co-operative banks on the model of Mondragon in northern Spain, so that surplus value would not be creamed off. All this was very different from the economic policy of New Labour 15 years later. Finally, council staff should be 'committed to a new type of politics'.[28]

To all appearances, Blunkett was the most left-wing council leader that Sheffield had ever had and very different from the model established by Ernest George Rowlinson. Blunkett subsequently described himself as not 'hard left' but 'firm left' – 'durable and reliable, without being inflexible':

> We aimed to steer a different route from, on the one hand, the old Labour tradition of paternalistic 'do as I say' politics, in which everything was determined by the Town Hall and, on the other hand, Militant Tendency, which was rampant on Merseyside in the eighties. We endeavoured to create socialist policies which would be credible, viable alternatives to those of the Right of the Conservative Party as exemplified by Margaret Thatcher's monetarist deregulated market economics.[29]

All along, Blunkett hankered after Westminster politics, sensing that that was where the real power lay. In 1974, he stood for what was then the staunchly Conservative Hallam seat. In 1978, his failure to win the Penistone candidacy was a blessing in disguise, for he learned far more as council leader than he would have done at this time as a backbench MP. His national profile was enhanced by TV appearances on *Question Time*. In 1983, he was elected to the Labour Party's National Executive Committee (NEC) – the first non-MP in the constituency section since Harold Laski in the 1940s. He quickly became a pivotal member, between the left and the leadership.

## Rate Capping

Blunkett's biggest battle as council leader was over the Government's rate-capping policy, which he claimed 'removed powers of local government which had existed since 1601'.[30] He became leader not only of Sheffield's campaign but also of the national campaign of Labour local authorities.[31] It was a thankless role, since the Government threatened recalcitrant councillors with disqualification and individual surcharge. But, despite the failure of the campaign, Blunkett's national reputation was enhanced by it.

The background was a massive squeeze on local government expenditure. Sheffield suffered both from a big fall in business rates caused by the collapse of the steel industry and from a reduction in rate support grant by the Government from 53 per cent of council income in 1980-1 to only 24 per cent in 1986-7.[32] Blunkett and his colleagues wanted to preserve services and could only do so by pushing up the rates. But the Government wanted to lighten the burden of taxation and so capped rates. The crunch came in the spring of 1985.

An inner group within the council leadership – Blunkett, Clive Betts and Alan Billings – was convinced that a balanced budget and rate had to be set. But Blunkett played a dangerous game in deferring this in the hope that the Government would back down and he could retain national leadership of the non-setting campaign, thus heading off extremists like Derek Hatton of Liverpool. Alan Billings, as chair of the budget sub-committee of the council, even met the district auditor secretly (not even Blunkett knew) in a café in town. The DA said he would give a little more time to win colleagues over but then would have to act.[33] The council and the unions' big campaign in support of council services and expenditure culminated in a massive demonstration on 6 March 1985 – ominously, the very day when the miners returned to work after their lengthy strike. On the next day, councillors deferred setting a rate. However, Blunkett and his colleagues had to set a rate by 7 May or else they might suffer the penalties of surcharge and disqualification that had been inflicted on Clay Cross councillors in 1974. Blunkett and his inner team favoured setting a rate, while planning a deficit budget. But they were overruled by a vote of 81 to

48 at the district Labour Party, which at this time was dominated by the left. Alan Billings recalls that 'when he left the DLP that night, Blunkett's face was ashen.'[34]

The council meeting of 7 May 1985 was one of the most dramatic in the council's history. According to the *Sheffield Star*, Blunkett made an Agincourt speech and then 'spent most of the rest of the meeting patrolling the Labour ranks like an over-keen prefect'. Despite this, the Labour Party split and 20 Labour councillors, led by Dr Peter Jones, joined with 17 Conservatives and 9 Liberals to set a legal rate. The *Sheffield Star* commented: 'A three way split in the seemingly impregnable ranks that have controlled the City Council almost without interruption for the past 50 years has left the Party's pride and unity in tatters.'[35]

Blunkett called it 'the worst night of my life'.[36] But the Labour rebels, who were very unpopular in left-wing circles, had saved his career. Without them, he would have faced surcharge and disqualification. He still risked penalties for borrowing money to pay staff in the gap between the start of the financial year and the setting of the rate, but the district auditor decided that he and his colleagues had not acted 'wilfully'.[37] Blunkett had sailed very near the wind. His defeat gave him and the Labour Group as a whole the opportunity to rethink tactics towards the rising tide of Thatcherism. There was a disorderly retreat among the local authorities, which, under Blunkett's leadership, had earlier appeared ready to defy the Government. After this defeat, Blunkett, together with Tom Sawyer and Michael Meacher on the NEC, broke with Benn's idea of extra-parliamentary resistance to Thatcherism. Instead, Blunkett was prepared to take on what the right-wing press called the 'loony left' – the Liverpool militants.[38]

Thus in October 1985 at the Labour Party Conference, Blunkett made the extraordinary challenge to the Liverpool militant, Derek Hatton, described in Tony Benn's diary at the beginning of this chapter. On the previous day, Neil Kinnock, who was struggling to consolidate his leadership of the Labour Party, had vehemently attacked the Liverpool militants. Derek Hatton, leader of the Militant Tendency in Liverpool, had been a community worker in Sheffield in the 1970s, but had had no impact on local politics.[39] Blunkett was replying on behalf of the National Executive to a Liverpool motion calling for support for Liverpool councillors. He dramatically challenged Hatton to drop the motion and open the books of his council to the National Executive. Hatton's agreement thrilled the delegates. Kinnock was less happy and said to Blunkett, 'You're bloody good at skating on thin ice.' Blunkett replied: 'I didn't realise how thin it was.'[40] In reality, Blunkett's device was crucial in exposing the financial mismanagement of Militant Tendency and enabling Kinnock to ban them from the Labour Party.

## *The Employment Department*

As in the 1920s, Sheffield's specialisation in iron and steel made it vulnerable to global economic trends. The steel industry, already in decline earlier in the 1970s, began to collapse in 1979, owing to world over-production of steel and the Government's deflation of the economy. Between 1981 and 1984, over 50,000 jobs were lost in Sheffield steel, engineering and associated industries. Unemployment in Sheffield, which for years had been below the national average, now was consistently well above it, rising to 27,400 (9.3 per cent) in 1981 and peaking at 47,500 (16.3 per cent) in 1987. In stark contrast to all previous Sheffield history, the service industries overtook manufacturing as the main source of employment.

Blunkett was shocked by the Thatcher Government's repudiation of responsibility for full employment. He and colleagues like Bill Michie, who chaired the new employment

**94**   Industrial dereliction in 1980s Sheffield. These are the remains of Firth's Norfolk Works in September 1985 – one of many abandoned steelworks in the lower Don Valley at this time. The stones in the foreground are the masonry of the works entrance. Firth had been one of the greatest names in Sheffield.

committee, wanted the council to address the loss of jobs. Local authorities had no specific powers to intervene in economic matters but they could spend the equivalent of a two-penny rate on economic development.

They set up a Department of Employment and Economic Development within the council, led by John Benington, a radical socialist economist, with a staff of radical socialists.[41] They refused the Government's offer of an 'employment zone', since they believed that this would just shunt jobs between one area and another. They provided research assistance to the steel unions fighting to maintain production in Sheffield, encouraged workers' co-operatives and established training workshops for redundant workers. They agreed a carefully costed deal with Arthur Scargill to move the HQ of the National Union of

**95**   The People's March for Jobs passes under the Wicker Arch in May 1983.

Mineworkers to Sheffield, with local authority grants of £520,000.[42] They sponsored a jobs audit to show how beneficial council expenditure was to the city's economy.

Later on, Blunkett wrote: 'in the end we had to face the fact that even our investment in public services could not compensate for what was happening to our industrial base … The enormity of the market forces unleashed by global economics was underestimated by most industrialists, entrepreneurs and politicians alike.'[43] The council's regeneration strategy in the early 1980s was flawed, being over-dependent on radical socialist input and with no contribution from local business leaders.

Local business leaders were deeply unhappy both with Blunkett's Labour council and with the Thatcher Government. Thus, the Cutlers' Company's invitation to Mrs Thatcher to their annual feast in April 1983 was probably intended more as an opportunity for imparting home truths to her than as a gesture of support. There was a demonstration of 4,000 to 6,000 people on the cathedral side of Church Street: 'The scene had a whiff of 1789 or 1917 about it, with shrieking, chanting demonstrators on one side of the road and buses arriving with 'toffs' in evening dress looking down on them from their seats in the coaches.'[44] Mrs Thatcher was smuggled in quickly before the crowd realised she was there. Blunkett was outside, telling the demonstrators that 'Our people – those in work and those without – are paying for the meal that the people in the Cutlers' Feast are enjoying.'[45]

Inside the Cutlers' Hall, Mrs Thatcher spoke well and received a standing ovation, though some remained seated. But she was 'harangued by almost all the speakers about Government policy and the disastrous effect it was having on the Sheffield steel industry … she never came back again'.[46] The *Sheffield Star* wisely noted that there must be something wrong with the Lady's public image if she needed 1,000 police to protect her in a provincial city. Sheffield's once-powerful Conservative Party began to lose support so that in the 1990s the Liberals became the main rival to Labour in Sheffield.

**96**   Poster urging people to join the protest when Mrs Thatcher came to speak at the Cutlers' Feast in April 1983.

## The New Realism

By the mid-1980s, Blunkett saw that many of Labour's policies in Sheffield and in South Yorkshire were unsustainable under relentless pressure from central Government. The crucial turning point was the council's decision in May 1985 to set a legal rate, even if in the short term they used creative accounting devices to maintain services.[47] Alan Billings recalls: 'we were very creative, though the Government gradually got wise to this and attempted to head us off. But we borrowed from foreign banks; we sold off property and leased it back; we created companies to hold funds for us etc.'[48]

In 1986, the South Yorkshire County Council was abolished, having used up its reserves on cheap fares. Cheap fares came to an end when the Government imposed a cap on the new transport authority's spending and deregulated bus services.

Sheffield Labour became 'new realist' in industrial policy, realising the need to work with, rather than against, business leaders. Business leaders had been appalled by Labour's gesture politics, such as talking up the 'Socialist Republic of South Yorkshire', which would deter inward investment (see the opening quotation in this chapter). In 1986, council officers, influenced by a changing mood among leading councillors, proposed a new 'collaborative exercise between public and private sector agencies' to diversify the city's economic base. Under Blunkett's successor, Clive Betts, slanging matches between the council and the business community were replaced by public–private collaboration, leading ultimately to the creation of the Sheffield First Partnership.[49]

For Blunkett, his period as council leader was an extraordinary learning experience. He moved from being troublemaking leader of the Sheffield left to become a reconciling force in the national Labour Party. By the time he became MP for Brightside in 1987, Blunkett was already a 'new realist', though in 1988 he and Bernard Crick declared as their 'ultimate aim': 'a classless egalitarian society in a community of nations that can work together to abolish poverty and fear of war'.[50]

Now a national politician, he shared the impatience of his parliamentary colleagues at successive electoral defeats. Later, he would shift further as he became one of Tony Blair's closest allies in Government. He became an impatient reformer of schools, a critic

**97**   David Blunkett and his successor as leader of Sheffield City Council, Clive Betts, at a poll tax protest meeting in Longley in 1989.

of teaching unions, a scourge of judges, the architect of a harsh asylum regime and the advocate of identity cards to curb terrorism. Baroness Helena Kennedy, a well-known left-wing lawyer, complained of his 'shameless authoritarianism'.[51] His public profile today is very different from that of his socialist youth. Is there an analogy with Roebuck, who began as a radical reformer and ended up as an ardent British nationalist and conservative?

Left/right stereotypes can be too simplistic. An analysis[52] in 1996, just before New Labour came to power, argued that the young Blunkett was leftist mainly on the economy and defence; indeed, as late as 1996, he remained a closet unilateralist. But in other areas he did not follow the standard leftist line. He was always impatient of political correctness and 'trendy left' obsessions with positive discrimination. He always expected working-class people to work hard to better themselves, rather than relying on hand-outs. He has retained an interest in social mobility.[53] Indeed, a tough-minded advocacy of old-fashioned values, derived from his Methodist background and his own hard experience, can be seen throughout his career. Blair showed some skill in deploying his talents in education, law and order and social security, thus avoiding a conflict between the New Labour line and Blunkett's core beliefs.

Blunkett would see himself as a consistent radical reformer who shares the aspirations – and one might add the prejudices – of working-class people in constituencies like Brightside.

*Chapter 14*

# Epilogue

> One of the most puzzling things we have to deal with, and in a sense one of the most unfair things, is that those who disturb an existing situation are inevitably labelled in the public mind as the troublemakers; whereas the maintenance of an unjust status quo may be the real trouble.
>
> United States Senator Paul Douglas, 1953

For much of the last 200 years Sheffield has been a radical city, with troublemakers playing an influential role. It is not easy to generalise about complex movements spread over this time but we conclude by considering some questions about Sheffield's radicalism:

- What happened to the troublemakers?
- What are the characteristics of Sheffield radicalism?
- How far has Sheffield had a revolutionary tradition?
- How important has Sheffield's radicalism been in British history?
- What is the future of Sheffield radicalism?

## *What happened to the Troublemakers?*

As Senator Douglas's remarks at the opening of this chapter indicate, troublemakers often suffer for their beliefs. Thomas Paine and Karl Marx were much maligned in their lifetimes and died in obscurity with few mourners at their burials. Similarly, many of our Sheffield troublemakers suffered. Gales fled to the USA. Montgomery suffered two spells in prison. Johnny Blackwell had a 30-month prison sentence and eventually died in a poorhouse. Samuel Holberry died in prison. Ommanney was placed under discipline for many years by his bishops. Carpenter's private life was attacked in the press. J.T. Murphy received a gaol sentence at the Old Bailey in 1925. Alan Ecclestone suffered much obloquy in the press and from clerical colleagues.

In general, working-class troublemakers fared worst. Middle-class troublemakers like T.A. Ward, H.J. Wilson, Ethel Haythornthwaite and Arnold Freeman could use their powerful social networks to avoid victimisation. Others like Ernest George Rowlinson were successful enough to make themselves virtually impregnable.

Roebuck and Blunkett, having apparently been ardent radicals in their youth, appeared less radical in later life. Whether they were inconsistent is arguable. In both cases, signs of their later positions were evident from the start. Others, like Montgomery and J.T. Murphy in later life consciously repudiated their earlier beliefs.

*What are the Characteristics of Sheffield Radicalism?*

Sidney Pollard identified 'independence of spirit' and 'rebelliousness' as defining characteristics of South Yorkshire. Others might call it 'cussedness' or 'bloody-mindedness'. These are of course familiar Yorkshire characteristics, but in Sheffield they seem unusually strong. In the 1790s, the 1830s (over the new Poor Law) and the 1980s, Sheffield took a very different view from the national Government and fought unsuccessfully to be able to strike out on its own independent path.

External movements – intellectual, religious, social, political or even revolutionary –have affected Sheffield's troublemakers. Intellectual influences included Thomas Paine, Ebenezer Elliott, Robert Owen, Ruskin and Carpenter. Marx wrote for the *Sheffield Free Press* but his articles were so dense that they can have had little influence. It was not until the 1880s, when Marx's ideas were available in popular form, that Marxism began to have an impact in Sheffield. Even so, it was never as important as Methodism.

In the early days, the main religious influence was dissent, which was a dominant force among the middle classes. By the 1790s, 'rational dissenters', particularly the Unitarians at Upper Chapel, took up democratic ideas and provided radical leadership for several decades. By the late Victorian period, the Congregationalists had taken their place. Many Methodists too became fervent radicals, despite the Toryism of their founder. Roman Catholics were not a major force for radicalism, perhaps because numbers were not great and the Duke of Norfolk's influence was generally anti-radical. Sheffield's low church Anglicanism was mainly conservative, in both religion and politics, until a new wave of clergy appeared in the mid-20th century – Bishop Hunter, Wickham, Ecclestone, Billings and others. The present Dean of Sheffield, the Very Rev. Peter Bradley, reflecting on the assault on Vicar Wilkinson's Broomhall home in 1791, has declared: 'I am on the side of the mob.'[1]

The special character of the cutlery trade was crucial in fostering working–class radicalism. This trade's small workshops and little mesters created a more individualistic ethos than that of a great textile town like Manchester, with its large factories. In the early 19th century, Sheffield avoided a sharp division between the middle and working classes, though there were serious tensions about whether parliamentary reform should extend to the working classes. The cutlers' relative independence made them more self-confident and freer to engage in agitation than factory employees. Their economic insecurity led them to organise themselves both in political agitation and in developing trade unions. The influence of the cutlery trades began to wane as huge steel factories developed after 1850 and some traditional unions were discredited by the trade union outrages in the late 1860s. Trade unionism took on a different form, leading to separate political representation for Labour and to the formidable shop stewards' movement of the First World War.

Another influence was the voluntary organisation. Ever since the 18th century, Sheffield has had numerous voluntary organisations. Early examples were the anti-slavery movements – both male and female – the early trades unions, the Sheffield Society for Constitutional Information of the 1790s and the Sheffield Political Union of 1830-2. Later examples included the Sheffield Ladies Association, set up by Charlotte Wilson to combat the Contagious Diseases Act, the settlements, the women's suffrage bodies and the Clarion Ramblers. Sheffield has long been a centre for spreading radical propaganda into the surrounding area and sometimes to the whole nation. The voluntary organisation has also been a powerful means through which people with a privileged background, like Mary Anne Rawson, Father Ommanney, Edward Carpenter and Arnold Freeman, have dedicated their lives to working with and for people less fortunate than themselves.

Sheffield's radicalism has ebbed and flowed, with a lull in the mid-1850s and 1860s, followed by a period when Conservatives were more powerful than the divided Liberal Party and Labour was beginning to emerge as a significant force. Politicians like Mundella and Leng saw the need for the traditional parties to reach out to the working classes. Their successors instead coalesced in the Citizens' Party to resist Labour but could not prevent Labour coming to power in 1926.

Thereafter, apart from a few intermissions, Labour ran Sheffield and developed its own establishment, reinforced by its links with the trades unions and with Sheffield's extensive council estates. In this situation, Labour risked losing its radical edge but there were periodic challenges from dissidents within the party, from the Conservative Party and from a small but able Communist Party that skilfully campaigned on unemployment in the inter-war years and 'peace' during the Cold War. This book could not cover all the twists and turns of Labour history and instead focused on the left-wing radical movement of the 1970s and Blunkett's leadership of the council from 1980 to 1987.

### How Far has Sheffield had a Revolutionary Tradition?

Sheffield radicals have consistently been interested in foreign revolutions. It was the French Revolution that first set Gales and his colleagues on their radical path. In 1830, Roebuck rushed off to revolutionary Paris with J.S. Mill. In 1848, Ironside was so moved by the French Revolution that, following a meeting in Paradise Square, he took a communistic address to Paris for the French to adopt. In 1871, Carpenter visited Paris just after the left-wing commune had been crushed. In 1920 and 1921, Murphy visited revolutionary Moscow and conferred with Lenin.

In the late 18th and early 19th centuries, repression by the authorities helped to generate underground movements that plotted genuine revolutionary violence. Revolutionary artisan leaders, like John Blackwell, James Wostenholme and Samuel Holberry, appeared out of obscurity at times of crisis and, when the authorities were clamping down on them, held meetings on Sky Edge or other hills surrounding the town. Some younger radicals of the 1820s reappeared in the Chartist period. There were revolutionary plots in 1802, 1817, 1820 and 1839-40, but none since then.

In the 1880s and 1890s, Carpenter and his circle talked and wrote about the 'Socialist Revolution' or the 'SR', but it had the unreal and dreamlike quality of Morris's book *News from Nowhere*. It was a religious and millennial way of thinking, as was Arnold Freeman's objective for his educational settlement: 'To establish in the City of Sheffield the Kingdom of God.' The communist J.T. Murphy in his old age repudiated the party's rhetoric about the 'revolution': 'we British Marxists who witnessed the 1917 Revolution had more religion than reason in our mode of thinking.'[2]

Within the Sheffield labour movement, revolutionary ideas were largely superseded by the Fabian notion of the inevitability of gradualness. However, as David Blunkett said in 1988: 'There is nothing inevitable about gradualness and it can easily collapse into mere timeserving and office holding.'[3]

There was a revival of militancy just before the First World War as the militant suffragettes set fire to pillar boxes. During the war, J.T. Murphy's shop stewards' movement had revolutionary syndicalist overtones. In 1926 Sheffield labour gave unequivocal support to the General Strike without reflecting on its constitutional implications. But after Labour took over the council in 1926, only the communists still thought in terms of revolution.

Sheffield has a tradition of holding great protest meetings, most commonly in Paradise Square. These meetings can carry a risk of violence. One thousand police were mobilised to protect Mrs Thatcher when she attended the Cutlers' Feast in 1983 (chapter 13). It was not only Mrs Thatcher who was unpopular in Sheffield. On 19 December 1994, I was at a civil service meeting in Rockingham House, West Street, waiting to meet Michael Portillo, Secretary of State for Employment, who was hated by the left for his role in the poll tax. There was a large crowd with banners outside and rioters using mountaineering equipment climbed into our building. The police were called and our meeting with Portillo was held elsewhere.

Sheffield's strong trade union tradition can also spill over into violence, as in the trade union outrages (chapter 5) and the 'Battle of Orgreave' on 29 May 1984 on the outskirts of Sheffield in the miners' strike, though in the latter case there were accusations of police provocation.

Sheffield's serious revolutionary tradition largely disappeared with the demise of Chartism in the mid-19th century, but there have remained groups ready to use illegal methods and to seize opportunities, whether political or industrial, to push for revolutionary change.

### How Important has Sheffield's Radicalism been in British History?

Sheffield has contributed to virtually all the national radical movements of the last 200 years and at times has been national leader, though often unable to follow through its initiatives. In the 1790s, the first working-men's political association was established in Sheffield and

Gales generated propaganda right across the North of England. In 1851, the first women's suffrage movement appeared in Sheffield but it soon faded away. In 1852, Ironside seemed poised for a Chartist or Democrat takeover of the town council, but his party disintegrated. Murphy's formidable shop stewards' movement could not sustain its momentum after the First World War. The greatest radical success was Labour's takeover of the council in 1926, the first in a major city and a model to the struggling Labour Party elsewhere. In the 1980s, Blunkett's team led Labour councils across the country in their struggle against the Thatcher Government, but then had to back off.

At other times, the baton of radical leadership has moved elsewhere. It was in Birmingham at the time of parliamentary reform in the 1830s, in Manchester at the times of Peterloo, the anti-Corn Law campaign and the women's suffrage campaign, in Leeds in the Chartist movement of the 1840s and in Bradford

**98** The fine statue of Ebenezer Elliott in Weston Park – one of the few memorials to Sheffield's radicals.

in the establishment of the Independent Labour Party in 1893. And of course the capital has played an important part in many radical movements. But Sheffield has a formidable record as a centre of radical agitation.

## What is the Future of Sheffield Radicalism?

Sheffield's radical tradition is not now greatly evident in the city. It is true that Weston Park has a fine statue of Ebenezer Elliott and a bust of Holberry in its museum, and there are the Holberry cascades in the Peace Gardens. But compared, say, with Manchester, reminders are few. Paradise Square is no longer the scene of great political meetings but instead is a car park for solicitors and accountants. The Edward Carpenter Fellowship no longer holds an annual service at Millthorpe. The Holberry Society is quiescent. There is no longer a school named after Rowlinson. Sheffield does little to celebrate its great radicals.

In recent years, there has been an astonishing change in the whole character of Sheffield. What was once 'the largest purely manufacturing town in the country'[4] has now become more dependent on services, universities and Government departments than on manufacturing, though there is still a lively manufacturing sector with 30,000 employees. Structural change has left an uncomfortable legacy of poverty in parts of the city. The city is more cosmopolitan, with ethnic minorities comprising 13 per cent of the population and nearly 30 per cent of births.

The main sources of the city's radicalism – nonconformity, the cutlery trades and the trades unionism of the great steelworks – no longer carry great influence. Politics is shifting. The Labour Party remains relatively strong and is now linked to public sector unions and New Labour consumerism. The Liberal Party, having virtually died out in the 1920s, has revived as the Liberal Democrat Party, and took power in the 2008 local elections. The once-proud Sheffield Conservative Party was virtually destroyed in the aftermath of the bitter Thatcherite period.

Sheffield now aspires to be 'a successful, distinctive city of European significance'. However, now that it has lost much of its steel and cutlery industries, where will its distinctiveness lie? In part, it should lie in its radical tradition, which still exists, even if it is slumbering. Sidney Pollard defined this tradition as 'the defence of the weak against the strong, the poor against the rich, the under-privileged against those who have usurped power, pelf and privilege'. The council's policy of 'closing the gap' between rich and poor and their acceptance of the title 'City of Sanctuary' for asylum seekers give some hope that the idealism sought by Pollard is still alive.

# Notes

**Introduction**

1. Armitage, H., *Chantrey Land* (1910), p.131.
2. Odom, W. *Hallamshire Worthies* (1926).
3. Mather, H., *Steel City Scholars: The Centenary History of the University of Sheffield* (2005), p.203.
4. Pollard, S., and Holmes, C. (eds), *Essays in the Social and Economic History of South York shire* (1976), pp.5-6.
5. Taylor, A.J.P., *The Trouble Makers: Dissent over Foreign Policy 1792-1939* (1957), p.13.
6. Pollard, S., *A History of Labour in Sheffield* (1959).
7. Wickham, E.R., *Church and People in an Industrial City* (1957).

**Chapter 1: Sheffield at the Time of the French Revolution**

1. Williams, G.A., *Artisans and Sans-Culottes: Popular Movements in France and Britain during the French Revolution* (1968).
2. Brown, P.A., *The French Revolution in British History* (1918), p.145.
3. Hey, D., *A History of Sheffield* (1998), p.91.
4. Hey, D., *Historic Hallamshire*, p.9. This is coterminous with the present city council area, except that areas like Handsworth, Woodhouse, Norton and Dore have been added.
5. Leader, R.E., *Sheffield in the Eighteenth Century* (1905), p.99
6. Leader, R.E., *Sheffield in the Eighteenth Century* (1905), p.100.
7. Leader, R.E., *Sheffield in the Eighteenth Century* (1905), pp.84-5.
8. Leader, R.E., *Sheffield in the Eighteenth Century* (1905), p.2.
9. Hunter, J., and Gatty, A., *History of Hallamshire* (1875), p.158.
10. Stevenson, J., *Artisans and Democrats: Sheffield and the French Revolution 1789-97* (1989), p.16.
11. Walton, M., *Sheffield: Its Story and its Achievements* (1948), pp.87-8.
12. Manning, J.E., *History of the Upper Chapel* (1900), pp.82-3. The author is indebted to Rev. Geoff Usher for pointing out the book by Locke in the portrait of Rev. Evans.
13. *Sheffield Independent*, 16 November 1828.
14. Charlton Black, E., *The Association: Britain's Extra Parliamentary Political Organisation 1769-1793* (1963), pp.61-2.
15. Charlton Black, E., *The Association: Britain's Extra Parliamentary Political Organisation 1769-1793* (1963), p.208.
16. Hunter, J., and Gatty, A., *History of Hallamshire* (1875), p.271.
17. Gatty, A., *Past and Present*, p.20.
18. Stevenson, J., *Artisans and Democrats: Sheffield and the French Revolution 1789-97* (1989), p.11.
19. Lunn, D., *Chapters towards a History of the Cathedral and Parish Church of St Peter and St Paul, Sheffield* (1987), p.53.
20. Leader, R.E., *Sheffield in the Eighteenth Century* (1905), p.246.
21. Hunter, J., and Gatty, A., *History of Hallamshire* (1875), p.263.
22. Quoted in Hey, D., *A History of Sheffield* (1998), p.89.
23. Wesley's Journal, see Wickham, E.R., *Church*

and People in an Industrial City* (1957), p.54.
24. Leader, R.E., *Reminiscences of Old Sheffield* (1876), p.265. Wickham, E., op. cit., quotes the *Local Register* as saying that in 1736 there were 246 Roman Catholics (57 families).
25. Personal comment by Julie Macdonald. Also Winifred Gales' *Recollections* (see chapter 2) says that the *Sheffield Register* was widely read in workshops.
26. Binfield, C., and Hey, D., *Mesters to Masters: A History of the Company of Cutlers in Hallamshire* (1997), p.37.
27. Quoted in Aspinall, A., *The Early English Trade Unions* (1949), p.4.
28. Roberts, S., *Autobiography* (1849), p.37.
29. Macdonald, J., 'The Freedom of Election: The Company of Cutlers and the Growth of Radicalism in Sheffield 1784-1792,' PhD thesis, University of Sheffield (2005).
30. Macdonald, J., vol. II, pp.282-3.
31. *The Songs of Joseph Mather*, with introduction and notes by John Wilson (1862).
32. Stevenson, J., *Artisans and Democrats: Sheffield and the French Revolution 1789-97* (1989), p.8.
33. Crawshaw, H.N., 'Movements for Political and Social Reform in Sheffield 1792-1832,' MA dissertation, University of Sheffield (1954), p.4.

**Chapter 2: The Newspaper Editors and the French Revolution**

1. Roberts, S., *Autobiography* (1849), p.44.
2. Aspinall, A., *The Early English Trade Unions* (1949), p.4.
3. Macdonald, J., 'The Freedom of Election: The Company of Cutlers and the Growth of Radicalism in Sheffield 1784-1792,' PhD thesis, University of Sheffield (2005) and Armytage, W.H.G., 'The Editorial Experience of Joseph Gales 1786-94', *North Carolina Historical Review*, 28 (1951) pp.332-61. *Recollections* of Joseph and Winifred Gales in North Carolina University Archive.
4. Mrs Gales claimed that it was read by at least 10,000 workers through workshop subscriptions. *Recollections*, p.32.
5. *Recollections*, p.31.
6. Montgomery and Gales' sisters denied any contact between Gales and Paine (Holland, J., and Everett, J., *Memoirs of Montgomery*, vol. 1, p.156). But this may reflect Paine's notoriety.
7. Leader, R.E., *Sheffield in the Eighteenth Century* (1905), p.294.
8. *Recollections*, p.35.
9. *Sheffield Register*, 1 August 1789.
10. *Sheffield Register*, 4 December 1789.
11. Williams, G.A., *Artisans and Sans-Culottes: Popular Movements in France and Britain during the French Revolution* (1968), p.66.
12. *Sheffield Register*, 29 April 1791.
13. Armytage, W.H.G., 'The Editorial Experience of Joseph Gales 1786-94', *North Carolina Historical Review*, 28 (1951) p.338.
14. Paulus, C., *Some Forgotten Facts in the History of Sheffield and District* (1907), p.75ff.
15. Leader, R.E., *Sheffield in the Eighteenth Century* (1905), p.24.
16. Charlton Black, E., *The Association: Britain's*

Extra Parliamentary Political Organisation 1769-1793* (1963), p.248.
17. Armytage and other historians state that Gales helped to form the SSCI but Julie Macdonald points out that there is no evidence of this in the Gales' *Recollections*, which however state that he helped the freemen in their dispute with the Cutlers' Company (Macdonald, J., 'The Freedom of Election: The Company of Cutlers and the Growth of Radicalism in Sheffield 1784-1792,' PhD thesis, University of Sheffield (2005), p.92 and p.307). Evidence in the trial of SSCI leaders confirmed Gales's role as a writer for SSCI (Howell, *State Trials*, XXV col. 1119-21). Gales's farewell message confirmed that he belonged to SSCI.
18. Macdonald, J., 'The Freedom of Election: The Company of Cutlers and the Growth of Radicalism in Sheffield 1784-1792,' PhD thesis, University of Sheffield (2005), p.313.
19. Thompson, E.P., *The Making of the English Working Class* (1991), p.212.
20. Goodwin, A., *The Friends of Liberty* (1979).
21. Williams, G.A., *Artisans and Sans-Culottes: Popular Movements in France and Britain during the French Revolution* (1968), p.58.
22. Williams, G.A., *Artisans and Sans-Culottes: Popular Movements in France and Britain during the French Revolution* (1968), p.59.
23. Stevenson, J., *Artisans and Democrats: Sheffield and the French Revolution 1789-97* (1989), p.17.
24. Macdonald, J., 'The Freedom of Election: The Company of Cutlers and the Growth of Radicalism in Sheffield 1784-1792,' PhD thesis, University of Sheffield (2005), p.310.
25. Charlton Black, E., *The Association: Britain's Extra Parliamentary Political Organisation 1769-1793* (1963), pp.223-4.
26. *Sheffield Register*, 1 June 1792.
27. *Sheffield Register*, 8 June 1792.
28. *Sheffield Register*, 15 June 1792 and Mrs Gales's more vivid account in *Recollections*, pp.37-9. In the *Sheffield Register*, Gales may have played down the threat of mob violence.
29. See chapter 1 and opening quote to chapter 2.
30. *Sheffield Register*, 9 November 1792.
31. *Sheffield Register*, 19 October and 30 November 1792.
32. Macdonald, J., 'The Freedom of Election: The Company of Cutlers and the Growth of Radicalism in Sheffield 1784-1792,' PhD thesis, University of Sheffield (2005), p.322. Jones, B.P., 'The Political Reform Movement in Sheffield', *Transactions of the Hunter Archaeological Society* (*THAS*) vol. 4 (1937), p.61.
33. *Sheffield Register*, 14 and 28 December 1792 and 4 January 1793.
34. *Recollections*, p.40.
35. *Sheffield Register*, 8 February 1793.
36. *Sheffield Register*, 15 and 22 February 1793.
37. Armytage, W.H.G., 'The Editorial Experience of Joseph Gales 1786-94', *North Carolina Historical Review*, 28 (1951) p.347.
38. Quoted in Armytage, W.H.G., 'The Editorial Experience of Joseph Gales 1786-94', *North Carolina Historical Review*, 28 (1951) p.350.

39. *Recollections*, p.49.
40. *Recollections*. p.53.
41. *Sheffield Register*, 1 and 15 May 1794.
42. *The Memoirs of Montgomery*, vol. 1, p.171, claim that Gales was in Derby chasing after Henry Yorke, who had become intimate with his sister Sarah and had left Sheffield 'in an unsatisfactory manner, so far as his intentions towards the lady were concerned'. However, the affectionate tone in which Winifred Gales writes of Yorke in the *Recollections* make it unlikely that this was the explanation.
43. It is not known whether he was any relation to Thomas Paine (Armytage, W.H.G., 'The Editorial Experience of Joseph Gales 1786-94', *North Carolina Historical Review*, 28 (1951) p.360).
44. Beutner, H.F., 'With Fraternal Feelings Fired: the Life and Works of James Montgomery', PhD thesis, North West University (1967), p.47.
45. *Sheffield Register*, 26 June 1794.
46. *Recollections*, p.63.
47. Based on Winifred Gales's *Recollections*, pp.60-87.
48. In July 1795, Naylor pulled out of this partnership, making Montgomery sole owner. Naylor was marrying a lady of position and means on condition he pulled out of the *Iris* (Beutner, H.F., 'With Fraternal Feelings Fired: the Life and Works of James Montgomery', PhD thesis, North West University (1967)).
49. *Sheffield Iris*, 31 December 1795.
50. *Sheffield Iris*, 31 July 1794.
51. *Sheffield Iris*, 18 September 1794.
52. Macdonald, J., 'The Freedom of Election: The Company of Cutlers and the Growth of Radicalism in Sheffield 1784-1792,' PhD thesis, University of Sheffield (2005), p.331.
53. Stevenson, J., *Artisans and Democrats: Sheffield and the French Revolution 1789-97* (1989), p.22. Leader, R.E., *Sheffield in the Eighteenth Century* (1905), pp.296-9.
54. Baxter, J., 'Murder in Norfolk Street – The Story of Sheffield's Peterloo', *Holberry Society Bulletin*, 5 Autumn 1980, pp.13-14.
55. Donnelly, F., 'Gales, Joseph (1761–1841)', *Oxford Dictionary of National Biography* (2004).
56. Elizabeth died in 1821, Anne in 1838 and Sarah in 1857. Leader, *Reminiscences*, p.15.
57. Leader, R.E., *Sheffield in the Eighteenth Century* (1905), p.295. There is a mystery about Montgomery's celibacy. He himself said 'the secret is within myself and it is on the way to the grave …' (Odom, *Hallamshire Worthies*). Apparently, his closest attachment was to Hannah Turner of Swathe Hall near Barnsley, whose decision to marry another prompted the poet to write the melancholy poem *Hannah* in 1801 (See Beutner, H.F., 'With Fraternal Feelings Fired: the Life and Works of James Montgomery', PhD thesis, North West University (1967), p.73). But in a letter of 23 July 1796 to John Pye Smith, Montgomery revealed the 'secret' that he was already married. Schmoller, T., 'Letters from a Newspaperman in Prison', *History of the Book Trade in the North*, PH85 January 2002, p.28.
58. Holland, J., and Everett, J., *Memoirs of Montgomery*, vol. 1 (1854-6), pp.142-3.
59. *Sheffield Iris*, 28 April 1803.
60. Holland, J., and Everett, J., *Memoirs of Montgomery*, vol. 1 (1854-6), p.384.
61. Armytage, W.H.G., 'The Editorial Experience of Joseph Gales 1786-94', *North Carolina Historical Review*, 28 (1951) p.361.
62. *Sheffield Iris*, 14 August, 5 November and 19 November 1795. Stevenson, J., *Artisans and Democrats: Sheffield and the French Revolution 1789-97* (1989), p.33.

**Chapter 3: The Struggle for Parliamentary Reform 1801-32**

1. Grosvenor, C., and Beilby, C., *The First Lady Wharncliffe and her Family 1779-1856*, vol. 1 (1927), p.70.
2. *Sheffield Independent*, 29 January 1831.
3. *Sheffield Independent*, 1 December 1828.

4. Hunter, J., and Gatty, A., *History of Hallamshire* (1875), p.161, p.450.
5. The population of the central township grew from 31,314 in 1801 to 59,692 in 1831.
6. Flavell, N., 'The Economic Development of Sheffield and the Growth of the Town *c*. 1740-1820,' unpublished PhD thesis, University of Sheffield (1996), p.410.
7. Porter, W.S., *Sheffield Literary and Philosophical Society: A Centenary Retrospect 1822-1922* (1922), pp.2-9.
8. Walton, M., *Sheffield: Its Story and Achievements*, p.159.
9. 'English Bards and Scottish Reviewers', quoted in Pybus, S., *A Damned Bad Place, Sheffield* (1994), p.84.
10. Harman, R., and Minnis, J., *Sheffield* (2004), p.251.
11. Bell, A.B. (ed.), *Peeps into the Past* (1909), pp.206-7.
12. Wickham, E.R., *Church and People in an Industrial City* (1957), pp.67-8 and pp.131-4.
13. In a conversation with the author.
14. Halevy, E., *A History of the English People in 1815*, vol. 3 (1938), pp.219.
15. Leader, R.E., *Reminiscences of Old Sheffield*, p.232.
16. Leader, R.E., *Reminiscences of Old Sheffield*, p.56, p.232, p.229. Donnelly, F.K. and Baxter, J,K, 'Sheffield and the English Revolutionary Tradition 1791-1820' in Pollard, S., and Holmes, C. (eds), *Essays in the Economic and Social History of South Yorkshire* (1976), pp.107-8. Bell, A.B. (ed.), *Peeps into the Past* (1909), p.255.
17. Bell, A.B. (ed.), *Peeps into the Past* (1909), p.155.
18. Bell, A.B. (ed.), *Peeps into the Past* (1909), pp.162-3.
19. Crawshaw, H.N., 'Movements for Political and Social Reform in Sheffield 1792-1832', unpublished MA thesis, University of Sheffield (1954), pp.57-79.
20. Donnelly, F.K. and Baxter, J.K., 'Sheffield and the English Revolutionary Tradition 1791-1820' in Pollard, S., and Holmes, C. (eds), *Essays in the Social and Economic History of South Yorkshire* (1976), p.95.
21. Thompson, E.P., *The Making of the English Working Class* (1991) p.515.
22. Donnelly, F.K. and Baxter, J.K., 'Sheffield and the English Revolutionary Tradition 1791-1820' in Pollard, S., and Holmes, C. (eds), *Essays in the Social and Economic History of South Yorkshire* (1976).
23. Baxter, J.L., 'James Wostenholme's Second Coming', Paper for Society for Study of Labour History, Chartism day, conference June 2005, Newcastle University.
24. Halevy, E., *A History of the English People in 1815*, book two (1937), p.100.
25. Pollard, S., *A History of Labour in Sheffield* (1959), pp.50-77.
26. Pollard, S., *A History of Labour in Sheffield* (1959), p.66.
27. Jennett, G.D., 'TA Ward', unpublished MA thesis, University of Sheffield (1954), p.65.
28. Pollard, S., *A History of Labour in Sheffield* (1959), pp.68-71.
29. Donnelly, F.K. and Baxter, J.K., 'Sheffield and the English Revolutionary Tradition 1791-1820' in Pollard, S., and Holmes, C. (eds), *Essays in the Social and Economic History of South Yorkshire* (1976), p.97. Wells, R., *Insurrection: The British Experience 1795-1803* (1986), p.194, p.222.
30. Donnelly, F.K. and Baxter, J.K., 'Sheffield and the English Revolutionary Tradition 1791-1820' in Pollard, S., and Holmes, C. (eds), *Essays in the Social and Economic History of South Yorkshire* (1976), p.?? Wells, R., *Insurrection: The British Experience 1795-1803* (1986), pp.238-48. , E.P., *The Making of the English Working Class* (1991) p.521.
31. Donnelly, F.K. and Baxter, J.K., 'Sheffield and the English Revolutionary Tradition 1791-1820' in Pollard, S., and Holmes, C. (eds), *Essays in the Social and Economic History of South Yorkshire* (1976), p.102, quoting *from Life of Montgomery*.
32. Donnelly, F.K. and Baxter, J.K., 'Sheffield and the English Revolutionary Tradition

1791-1820' in Pollard, S., and Holmes, C. (eds), *Essays in the Social and Economic History of South Yorkshire* (1976), p.104.
33. Donnelly, F.K. and Baxter, J.K., 'Sheffield and the English Revolutionary Tradition 1791-1820' in Pollard, S., and Holmes, C. (eds), *Essays in the Social and Economic History of South Yorkshire* (1976), p.104.
34. Bell, A.B. (ed.), *Peeps into the Past* (1909), p.191.
35. Bell, A.B. (ed.), *Peeps into the Past* (1909), p.192.
36. Bell, A.B. (ed.), *Peeps into the Past* (1909), p.196. Donnelly, F.K. and Baxter, J.K., 'Sheffield and the English Revolutionary Tradition 1791-1820' in Pollard, S., and Holmes, C. (eds), *Essays in the Social and Economic History of South Yorkshire* (1976), p.105.
37. Hunter, J., and Gatty, A., *History of Hallamshire* (1875), p.176. Bell, A.B. (ed.), *Peeps into the Past* (1909), p.242.
38. Bell, A.B. (ed.), *Peeps into the Past* (1909), pp.241-2.
39. Donnelly, F.K. and Baxter, J.K., 'Sheffield and the English Revolutionary Tradition 1791-1820' in Pollard, S., and Holmes, C. (eds), *Essays in the Social and Economic History of South Yorkshire* (1976), p.107.
40. Bell, A.B. (ed.), *Peeps into the Past* (1909), p.245.
41. Donnelly, F.K. and Baxter, J.K., 'Sheffield and the English Revolutionary Tradition 1791-1820' in Pollard, S., and Holmes, C. (eds), *Essays in the Social and Economic History of South Yorkshire* (1976), p.108.
42. Bell, A.B. (ed.), *Peeps into the Past* (1909), p.261.
43. Still identifiable from Brocco Street and Brocco Lane.
44. *Sheffield Iris*, 26 October 1819. Leader, R.E., *Reminiscences of Old Sheffield*, p.209. Leader claims that Fitzwilliam spoke at the Sheffield gathering, but there is no evidence for this in either the *Iris* or the *Mercury*.
45. Bell, A.B. (ed.), *Peeps into the Past* (1909), pp.262-3.
46. Donnelly, F.K. and Baxter, J.K., 'Sheffield and the English Revolutionary Tradition 1791-1820' in Pollard, S., and Holmes, C. (eds), *Essays in the Social and Economic History of South Yorkshire* (1976), p.109.
47. Read, D., *Press and People 1790-1850: Opinion in Three English Cities* (1961). Bell, A.B. (ed.), *Peeps into the Past* (1909), p.269.
48. Read, D., *Press and People 1790-1850: Opinion in Three English Cities* (1961), pp.169-70.
49. Wickham, E.R., *Church and People in an Industrial City* (1957), pp.71-2.
50. Crawshaw, H.N., 'Movements for Political and Social Reform in Sheffield 1792-1832', unpublished MA thesis, University of Sheffield (1954), pp.89-95.
51. Crawshaw, H.N., 'Movements for Political and Social Reform in Sheffield 1792-1832', unpublished MA thesis, University of Sheffield (1954), pp.96-123.
52. *Sheffield Independent*, 29 January 1831.
53. LoPatin, N.D., *Political Unions, Popular Politics and the Great Reform Act of 1832* (1999), pp.56-7. Reproduced by permission of Palgrave Macmillan.
54. Crawshaw, H.N., 'Movements for Political and Social Reform in Sheffield 1792-1832', unpublished MA thesis, University of Sheffield (1954), p.120.
55. Crawshaw, H.N., 'Movements for Political and Social Reform in Sheffield 1792-1832', unpublished MA thesis, University of Sheffield (1954), p.123.
56. *Sheffield Independent*, 12 May, 19 May and 2 June 1832.
57. *Sheffield Independent*, 21 July 1832.
58. Wickham, E.R., *Church and People in an Industrial City* (1957), p.97.
59. *Sheffield Independent*, 19 May 1832.
60. Hunter, J., and Gatty, A., *History of Hallamshire* (1875), p.179. *Sheffield Independent*, 8, 15 and 22 December 1832.
61. *Sheffield Independent*, 7 July 1832.
62. Ibid p.299.
63. Leader, R.E., *Reminiscences of Old Sheffield*, pp.136-7.
64. Hunter, J., and Gatty, A., *History of Hallamshire* (1875), p.178.
65. *Sheffield Independent*, 15 December 1832.

## Chapter 4: The Age of the Chartists

1. Hunter, J., and Gatty, A., *History of Hallamshire* (1875), p.199.
2. Holland, G.C., *Vital Statistics of Sheffield* (1843), p.10, p.11, p.15, p.45, p.109, pp.111–114, p.123, pp.139-49.
3. Holland, G.C., *Vital Statistics of Sheffield* (1843), p.10.
4. Jennett, G.D., 'TA Ward', unpublished MA thesis, University of Sheffield (1954), pp.14-15.
5. *Sheffield Independent*, 29 April and 20 May 1837.
6. *Sheffield Independent*, 15 July 1837.
7. Holland, G.C., *Vital Statistics of Sheffield* (1843), p.44.
8. Elliott's evidence to Children's Employment Commission 1843, quoted in Smith, D., *Conflict and Compromise: Class Formation in English Society 1830-1914* (1982), p.55.
9. Smith, D., *Conflict and Compromise: Class Formation in English Society 1830-1914* (1982), p.55 notes that the 1851 census reported 359 beer-shop keepers in Sheffield.
10. Smith, D., *Conflict and Compromise: Class Formation in English Society 1830-1914* (1982), p.55.
11. Morris, K., and Herne, R., *Ebenezer Elliott: Corn Law Rhymer and Poet of the Poor* (2002).
12. The six points were: universal male suffrage, no property qualification for MPs, annual Parliaments, equal electoral districts, payment of MPs and a secret ballot.
13. Baxter, J.L., 'Early Chartism and Labour Class Struggle 1837-1840', in Pollard, S., and Holmes, C. (eds), *Essays in the Social and Economic History of South Yorkshire* (1976). Baxter, J.L.'James Wolstenholme's "Second Coming"'. Paper given at Society for Study of Labour History, Chartism day conference, June 2005, Newcastle University.
14. Baxter, J.L., 'Early Chartism and Labour Class Struggle 1837-1840', in Pollard, S., and Holmes, C. (eds), *Essays in the Social and Economic History of South Yorkshire* (1976), p.139.
15. Wickham, E.R., *Church and People in an Industrial City* (1957), p.99.
16. Quoted by Baxter, J., in Pollard, S., and Holmes, C. (eds), *Essays in the Social and Economic History of South Yorkshire* (1976), p.137.
17. Pollard, S., and Holmes, C. (eds), *Essays in the Social and Economic History of South Yorkshire* (1976), p.137.
18. Baxter, J.L.'James Wolstenholme's "Second Coming"'. Paper given at Society for Study of Labour History, Chartism day conference, June 2005, Newcastle University.
19. Wickham, E.R., *Church and People in an Industrial City* (1957), pp.99-101.
20. Baxter's essay in Pollard, S., and Holmes, C. (eds), *Essays in the Social and Economic History of South Yorkshire* (1976). Baxter, J., essay in *Samuel Holberry 1814-42: Sheffield's Revolutionary Democrat*, Holberrry Society (1978) and Leader, R.E., *Reminiscences of Old Sheffield* 2nd edition (1876), pp.272-9.
21. Baxter, J., in Pollard, S., and Holmes, C. (eds), *Essays in the Social and Economic History of South Yorkshire* (1976), p.146, and Baxter, J., 'The Origins of the Social War in South Yorkshire 1750-1855', PhD thesis, University of Sheffield, vol. 2 (1976), footnote 273, p.629. Blanqui led an unsuccessful French rising in May 1839.
22. Baxter, J., 'The Origins of the Social War in South Yorkshire 1750-1855', PhD thesis, University of Sheffield, vol. 2 (1976), pp.464-556.
23. Mathias, P., *The First Industrial Nation* (1969), p.236.
24. Salt, J., 'Isaac Ironside and Education in the Sheffield Region in the First Half of the 19th Century', unpublished MA thesis, University of Sheffield (1960). Barber, B., 'Sheffield Borough Council 1843-93', in Binfield et al, *History of the City of Sheffield 1843-1993: Volume I: Politics* (1993), pp.29-37.
25. It was between 201 and 217 Rockingham Street.
26. Holyoake, G.J., *Sixty Years of an Agitator's Life* (1892), pp.135-6.
27. Moore Smith, G.C., *The Story of the People's College, Sheffield. 1842-78*, p.41.

28. *Sheffield Independent*. 24 January 1852.
29. Walton, M., *Sheffield: Its Story and its Achievements* (1848), pp.184-5.
30. Armytage, W.H.M., 'Sheffield and the Crimean War', *History Today* (1955), p.475. Meroon, A., 'Sheffield Free Press 1851-66', *Local Pamphlets*, vol. 50 no. 8.

## Chapter 5: The Age of John Roebuck

1. Briggs, A., *Victorian People* (1970), p.64.
2. Baxter, J., 'The Origins of the Social War in South Yorkshire 1750-1855', PhD thesis, University of Sheffield, vol. 2 (1976), p.556.
3. Pollard, S., *History of Labour in Sheffield* (1959), p.119.
4. London. George Allen and Unwin. 1964.
5. Read, D., *Press and People 1790-1850* (1961), pp.176-7.
6. Pollard, S., *History of Labour in Sheffield* (1959), pp.122-4. Reid, C., 'Middle Class Values and Working Class Culture in 19th Century Sheffield – The Pursuit of Respectability', in Pollard, S., and Holmes, C. (eds), *Essays in the Social and Economic History of South Yorkshire* (1976), pp.275-91.
7. Tweedale, G., in Binfield, C., and Hey, D., *From Mesters to Masters* (1997), pp.71-2 says that 'there were few examples of rags to riches'.
8. Binfield et al, *History of the City of Sheffield*, vol. 1 (1993), p.36.
9. Binfield et al, *History of the City of Sheffield*, vol. 1 (1993), p.95.
10. This account draws on Leader, R.E., *Life and Letters of JA Roebuck* (1897) and on Wilks, S., 'An Independent in Politics: J.A. Roebuck 1802-79', unpublished DPhil thesis, Oxford University (1979).
11. Mill, J.S., *Autobiography*, pp.126-9.
12. Wilks, S., 'An Independent in Politics: J.A. Roebuck 1802-79', unpublished DPhil thesis, Oxford University (1979), p.188.
13. Briggs, A., *Victorian People* (1970), pp.66-7.
14. Speech to the Administrative Reform Association. *Times* 23 June 1856.
15. *Sheffield Star*, 11 October 2005. Report on an exhibition at the University of Sheffield Library on Florence Nightingale's early life.
16. Fletcher, D.E., 'Aspects of Liberalism in Sheffield 1849-86', PhD thesis, University of Sheffield (1972).
17. March, K.G., 'Life and career of WC Leng', MA dissertation, University of Sheffield (1966), p.131.
18. Alderman Gainsford, quoted Mathers, H., 'Sheffield Municipal Politics 1893-1926,' PhD thesis. University of Sheffield (1979), p.92.
19. Stainton, J.H., *The Making of Sheffield 1865-1914* (1924), p.265.
20. This account is based on 'The Trades Union Commission: Sheffield Outrages Inquiry', 1867. Pollard, S., 'The Ethics of the Sheffield Outrages', *Transactions of the Hunter Archaeological Society* (THAS), vol. 7, pp.118-139.
21. Pollard, S., 'The Ethics of the Sheffield Outrages' (THAS), vol. 7, p.127.
22. Stainton, J.H., *The Making of Sheffield 1865-1914* (1924), p.40.
23. *Sheffield Independent*, 29 June 1867.
24. Motion at a mass meeting on 30 September 1867, quoted in Pollard, S., 'The Ethics of the Sheffield Outrages' (THAS), vol. 7, p.131.
25. Letter to Thomas Hughes quoted in Pollard, S., *History of Labour in Sheffield* (1959), p.153.
26. Pollard, S., 'The Ethics of the Sheffield Outrages' (THAS), vol. 7.
27. Pollard, S., 'The Ethics of the Sheffield Outrages' (THAS), vol. 7, p.129.
28. Pollard, S., *History of Labour in Sheffield* (1959), p.158.
29. Masters, D., *The Plimsoll Mark* (1955). Fletcher, D.E., 'Aspects of Liberalism in Sheffield 1849-86', PhD thesis, University of Sheffield (1972), p.68. Unpublished essay by Valerie Bayliss.
30. Fletcher, D.E., 'Aspects of Liberalism in Sheffield 1849-86', PhD thesis, University of Sheffield (1972), p.75.
31. Fletcher, D.E., 'Aspects of Liberalism in Sheffield 1849-86', PhD thesis, University of Sheffield (1972), p.83.

32. Pollard, S., *History of Labour in Sheffield* (1959), pp.157-8.
33. Fowler, W.S., *A Study in Radicalism and Dissent: The Life and Times of HJ Wilson* (1961)
34. Leader, R.E., *Life and Letters of JA Roebuck* (1897), p.1.
35. Quoted in Wilks, S., 'An Independent in Politics: JA Roebuck 1802-79', unpublished DPhil thesis, Oxford University (1979), p.318.
36. Fletcher, D.E., 'Aspects of Liberalism in Sheffield 1849-86', PhD thesis, University of Sheffield (1972), p.118.
37. Quoted in Mathers, H., 'Sheffield Municipal Politics 1893-1926,' PhD thesis. University of Sheffield (1979), p.11.

## Chapter 6: Ruskin, Carpenter and Early Sheffield Socialism

1. Carpenter, E., *My Days and Dreams* (1916), p.92.
2. Carpenter, E., *My Days and Dreams* (1916), pp.139-40.
3. Armytage, W.H.M., *Heavens Below: Utopian Experiments in England 1560-1960* (1961), pp.294-6. Also Rowbotham, S., 'Our Party is the People' in Rule, J., and Malcolmson, R., *Protest and Survival* (1993).
4. This account draws on Hilton, T., *John Ruskin* (2002), Hewison, R., 'Art and Society: Ruskin in Sheffield, 1876', Guild of St George Lecture, 1979 (1981), Barnes, J., *Ruskin in Sheffield* (1985).
5. *Fors Clavigera* 27.116, quoted in Hewison, R., 'Art and Society: Ruskin in Sheffield, 1876', Guild of St George Lecture, 1979 (1981), p.13.
6. *Fors Clavigera*, July 1877.
7. Hewison, R., 'Art and Society: Ruskin in Sheffield, 1876', Guild of St George Lecture, 1979 (1981), p.11.
8. *Sheffield Daily Telegraph*, 14 April 1890 quoted in Hewison, R., 'Art and Society: Ruskin in Sheffield, 1876', Guild of St George Leture, 1979 (1981), p.18.
9. Vickers, J.E., *A Popular History of Sheffield* (1978), p.223, p.234.
10. Malloy, W.H., in *Commonweal*, 25 May 1889, quoted in Rowbotham, S., 'Our Party is the People' in Rule, J., and Malcolmson, R., *Protest and Survival* (1993), p.263.
11. Ruskin, J., Master's Report, 1885, Works, vol. XXX, p.93.
12. See Armytage, W.H.M., *Heavens Below: Utopian Experiments in England 1560-1960* (1961), pp.289-304. Also Hewison, R., 'Art and Society: Ruskin in Sheffield, 1876', Guild of St George Lecture, 1979 (1981).
13. *Sheffield Daily Telegraph*, 28 April 1876.
14. Collingwood, W.G., quoted in Hilton, T., *John Ruskin* (2002), p. 635.
15. Carpenter, E., *Sketches from Life* (1907), p.207.
16. *Fors Clavigera*, letter 76, April 1877. Works, vol. XXIX, p.98.
17. Armytage, W.H.M., *Heavens Below: Utopian Experiments in England 1560-1960* (1961), p.293.
18. Tsuzuki, C., *Edward Carpenter 1844-1929* (1980), p.41.
19. Malloy, W.H., quoted in Armytage, W.H.M., *Heavens Below: Utopian Experiments in England 1560-1960* (1961), pp.297-8.
20. Armytage, W.H.M., *Heavens Below: Utopian Experiments in England 1560-1960* (1961), p.300.
21. Rowbotham, S., 'Our Party is the People' in Rule, J., and Malcolmson, R., *Protest and Survival* (1993), p.269.
22. Hewison, R., 'Art and Society: Ruskin in Sheffield, 1876', Guild of St George Lecture, 1979 (1981), p.18.
23. 1888 letter from William Graham to Riley, quoted in Rowbotham, S., 'Our Party is the People' in Rule, J., and Malcolmson, R., *Protest and Survival* (1993), p.273.
24. Armytage, W.H.M., *Heavens Below: Utopian Experiments in England 1560-1960* (1961), p.299. Barnes, J., *Ruskin in Sheffield* (1985), p.24.
25. Carpenter, E., *Sketches from Life* (1907), p.35.
26. Carpenter, E., *Sketches from Life* (1907), p.64.
27. Carpenter, E., *Sketches from Life* (1907), p.321.

28. Carpenter, E., *Sketches from Life* (1907), p.77.
29. Quoted in Barnes, J., *Ruskin in Sheffield* (1985), p.7.
30. Carpenter, E., *My Days and Dreams* (1916), p.101.
31. Carpenter, E., *My Days and Dreams* (1916), p.137.
32. MacCarthy, F., *William Morris* (1994), p.456.
33. Carpenter, E., *My Days and Dreams* (1916), pp.159-60.
34. Tsuzuki, C., *Edward Carpenter 1844-1929* (1980), p.187.
35 Pelling, H., *The Origins of the Labour Party*, 2nd edition (1965), p.24.
36. Carpenter, E., *My Days and Dreams* (1916), p.115.
37. Carpenter, E., *Towards Democracy*, p.5.
38. Carpenter, E., *My Days and Dreams* (1916), p 126.
39. Tsuzuki, C., *Edward Carpenter 1844-1929* (1980), p.63.
40. Carpenter, E., *My Days and Dreams* (1916), p.133.
41. *Sheffield Local Register*, 25 November 1885.
42. Carpenter, E., *My Days and Dreams* (1916), pp.128-9.
43. Tsuzuki, C., *Edward Carpenter 1844-1929* (1980), p.66.
44. *Sheffield Weekly Echo*, 26 February 1887, quoted in Rowbotham, S., 'Our Party is the People' in Rule, J., and Malcolmson, R., *Protest and Survival* (1993), pp.277-8.
45. Carpenter, E., *My Days and Dreams* (1916), pp.135-6.
46. Tsuzuki, C., *Edward Carpenter 1844-1929* (1980), pp.83-4.
47. This section draws on Tsuzuki, C., *Edward Carpenter 1844-1929* (1980), chapter 8, Carpenter, E., *My Days and Dreams* (1916), p.132, and Rowbotham, S., 'Anarchism in Sheffield in the 1890s', in Pollard and Holmes Pollard, S., and Holmes, C. (eds), *Essays in the Social and Economic History of South Yorkshire* (1976), and Baruah, D.K., 'Carpenter and the early Sheffield Socialists' (*THAS*), 10 (1971), pp.54-62.
48. Carpenter, E., *My Days and Dreams* (1916), p.127.
49. This is based on Carpenter, E., *My Days and Dreams* (1916), Tsuzuki, C., *Edward Carpenter 1844-1929* (1980) and Rowbotham, S., and Weeks, J., *Socialism and the New Life* (1977).
50. Nield, K., 'The uses of Utopia', in Brown, T. (ed.), *EC and Late Victorian Radicalism*. (1990), p.20.
51. Nield, K., in *Dictionary of Labour Biography*, 2, p.90.
52. Based on Rowbotham, S., and Weeks, J., *Socialism and the New Life* (1977), pp.88-91.
53. Pelling, H., *The Origins of the Labour Party*, 2nd edition (1965), pp.142-3.
54. Quoted in Brown, T. (ed.), *EC and Late Victorian Radicalism*. (1990), p.1.
55. Booklet on Edward Carpenter Memorial Service 6 July 1947, Sheffield Local Studies Library.
56. 5 January 1905, quoted in Baruah , D.K., 'Carpenter and the early Sheffield Socialists' (*THAS*), 10 (1971), p.5.
57. Mathers, H., 'Sheffield Municipal Politics 1893-1926,' PhD thesis. University of Sheffield (1979), p.163.
58. Mathers, H., 'Sheffield Municipal Politics 1893-1926,' PhD thesis. University of Sheffield (1979), p.157.
59. Mathers, H., 'Sheffield Municipal Politics 1893-1926,' PhD thesis. University of Sheffield (1979), p.160.
60. Mathers, H., 'Sheffield Municipal Politics 1893-1926,' PhD thesis. University of Sheffield (1979), p.160 and p.169.
61. Pollard, S. in Binfield et al, *History of the City of Sheffield*, vol, 2, p.270.

**Chapter 7: Turbulent Priest: Father Ommanney**

1. Belton, F.G. (ed.), *Ommanney of Sheffield: Memoirs of George Campbell Ommanney 1882-1936* (1936), p.34.
2. Wickham, E.R., *Church and People in an Industrial City* (1957), p.80.

3. Wickham, E.R., *Church and People in an Industrial City* (1957), pp.107-65.
4. Canon Odom, *Memorials of Sheffield: Its Cathedral and Parish Churches, Northend, Sheffield* (1922), pp.19-20.
5. Wickham, E.R., *Church and People in an Industrial City* (1957), p.82.
6. Odom, W., *Fifty Years of Sheffield Church Life 1866-1916* (1917), pp. 14-17.
7. Belton, F.G. (ed.), *Ommanney of Sheffield: Memoirs of George Campbell Ommanney 1882-1936* (1936).
8. Kirk-Smith, H., 'Some aspects of the career of William Thomson as Archbishop of York 1863-1890', thesis, University of Sheffield (1953), p.141.
9. Information from the Confraternity's website.
10. Belton, F.G. (ed.), *Ommanney of Sheffield: Memoirs of George Campbell Ommanney 1882-1936* (1936), p.54-5.
11. Belton, F.G. (ed.), *Ommanney of Sheffield: Memoirs of George Campbell Ommanney 1882-1936* (1936), p.31.
12. Kirk-Smith, H., 'Some aspects of the career of William Thomson as Archbishop of York 1863-1890', thesis, University of Sheffield (1953), p.121.
13. Belton, F.G. (ed.), *Ommanney of Sheffield: Memoirs of George Campbell Ommanney 1882-1936* (1936), p.148.
14. Belton, F.G. (ed.), *Ommanney of Sheffield: Memoirs of George Campbell Ommanney 1882-1936* (1936), p.67.
15. *Sheffield Daily Telegraph*, 27 and 29 April 1882.
16. *Sheffield Daily Telegraph*, 16 June 1882.
17. Belton, F.G. (ed.), *Ommanney of Sheffield: Memoirs of George Campbell Ommanney 1882-1936* (1936), pp.79-80. Kirk-Smith, H., 'Some aspects of the career of William Thomson as Archbishop of York 1863-1890', thesis, University of Sheffield (1953), p.153.
18. *Sheffield Daily Telegraph*, 18 June 1883.
19. *Sheffield Daily Telegraph*, 28 June 1883.
20. Belton, F.G. (ed.), *Ommanney of Sheffield: Memoirs of George Campbell Ommanney 1882-1936* (1936), pp.83-6.
21. Kirk-Smith, H., 'Some aspects of the career of William Thomson as Archbishop of York 1863-1890', thesis, University of Sheffield (1953), p.162.
22. Belton, F.G. (ed.), *Ommanney of Sheffield: Memoirs of George Campbell Ommanney 1882-1936* (1936), p.118.
23. Belton, F.G. (ed.), *Ommanney of Sheffield: Memoirs of George Campbell Ommanney 1882-1936* (1936), p.117.
24. Belton, F.G. (ed.), *Ommanney of Sheffield: Memoirs of George Campbell Ommanney 1882-1936* (1936), p.121-4 and p.154.
25. Kirk-Smith, H., 'Some aspects of the career of William Thomson as Archbishop of York 1863-1890', thesis, University of Sheffield (1953), chapter IX.
26. Belton, F.G. (ed.), *Ommanney of Sheffield: Memoirs of George Campbell Ommanney 1882-1936* (1936), p.57.
27. Gould, P., and Memmott, R., *Ommanney Remembered* (1982).
28. Belton, F.G. (ed.), *Ommanney of Sheffield: Memoirs of George Campbell Ommanney 1882-1936* (1936), p.134.
29. Belton, F.G. (ed.), *Ommanney of Sheffield: Memoirs of George Campbell Ommanney 1882-1936* (1936), p.148.

**Chapter 8: The Settlement Movement**

1. Roach, J., and Pitchfork, J.R., *Croft House Settlement 1902-2002: A Centenary History*, p.3.
2. Fletcher, D.E., 'Aspects of Liberalism in Sheffield 1849-86', PhD thesis, University of Sheffield (1972), p.92.
3. Stainton, J.H., *The Making of Sheffield. 1865-1914* (1924), p.286.
4. Inglis, K.S., *The Churches and the Working Classes in Victorian England* (1963), p.155.
5. Roberts, J., 'The Sheffield Educational Settlement 1918-55', dissertation, Institute of Education, University of Sheffield (1961).

Also Gilchrist, R., and Jeffs, T., *Settlements, Social Change and Community Action* (2001) p.59.
6. *Sheffield and Rotherham Independent*, 19 March 1897.
7. Coit, S., *Neighbourhood Guilds: An Instrument of Social Reform* (1892).
8. *Jubilee: 50 Years of History, Progress and Activities at the Helen Wilson Settlement 1906-56*.
9. Fowler, W.S., *A Study in Radicalism and Dissent: The Life and Times of H.J. Wilson* (1961), chapter 6. Also Hall, L.A., 'Wilson, Helen Mary (1864–1951)', *Oxford Dictionary of National Biography* (2004).
10. Fowler, W.S., *A Study in Radicalism and Dissent: The Life and Times of H.J. Wilson* (1961), p.27.
11. Roach, J., and Pitchfork, J.R., *Croft House Settlement 1902-2002: A Centenary History*.
12. John Derry of the *Sheffield Independent* in 1920, quoted in Mathers, H., 'Sheffield Municipal Politics 1893-1926', PhD thesis, University of Sheffield (1979).
13. in Mathers, H., 'Sheffield Municipal Politics 1893-1926', PhD thesis, University of Sheffield (1979), p.123.
14. Roach, J., and Pitchfork, J.R., *Croft House Settlement 1902-2002: A Centenary History*, p.4.
15. Roberts, J., 'The Sheffield Educational Settlement 1918-55', dissertation, Institute of Education, University of Sheffield (1961), p.17.
16. This account draws on Roberts, J., 'The Sheffield Educational Settlement 1918-55', dissertation, Institute of Education, University of Sheffield (1961), Albaya, W., *Through the Green Door: An Account of the Sheffield Educational Settlement 1918-55* (1977), Hoy, G., *Inwardly Limitless: Education by Magic at the Sheffield Educational Settlement under Arnold Freeman* (1989)?.
17. Albaya, W., *Through the Green Door: An Account of the Sheffield Educational Settlement 1918-55* (1977), p.21.
18. *Chambers 21st Century Dictionary*.
19. *A Yorkshire Boyhood* (1983), p.157.
20. Albaya, W., *Through the Green Door: An Account of the Sheffield Educational Settlement 1918-55* (1977), p.87.
21. It remains an outward bound centre for young people run by the Lindley Educational Trust.
22. Roberts, J., 'The Sheffield Educational Settlement 1918-55', dissertation, Institute of Education, University of Sheffield (1961), p.199.
23. Albaya, W., *Through the Green Door: An Account of the Sheffield Educational Settlement 1918-55* (1977).
24. Albaya, W., *Through the Green Door: An Account of the Sheffield Educational Settlement 1918-55* (1977), p.66.
25. Albaya, W., *Through the Green Door: An Account of the Sheffield Educational Settlement 1918-55* (1977), p.102.
26. Roberts, J., 'The Sheffield Educational Settlement 1918-55', dissertation, Institute of Education, University of Sheffield (1961), p.258

**Chapter 9: The Women's Struggle**

1. Fulford, R., *Votes for Women* (1957), p.39.
2. Carpenter, E., *Love's coming of age* (1923), p.67.
3. This section owes much to Suzanne Bingham's 'Off the Shelf' talk on 1 November 2007. See also Twells, A., 'Missionary Domesticity, Global Reform and "Women's Sphere" in Early 19th Century England', *Gender and History*, vol. 18, no. 2, August 2006, pp.266-84.
4. Mackerness, D., 'Mary Anne Rawson and the Memorials of James Montgomery' (*THAS*), vol. 8. pp.218-28. Wilson, R., '200 Precious Metal Years – A History of the Sheffield Smelting Company 1760-1960' (1960).
5. Mackerness, D., 'Mary Anne Rawson and the Memorials of James Montgomery' (*THAS*), vol. 8. p.223.
6. Mackerness, D., 'Mary Anne Rawson and the Memorials of James Montgomery' (*THAS*), vol. 8. p.222.
7. Twells, A. 'Missionary Domesticity, Global

Reform and "Women's Sphere" in Early 19th Century England', *Gender and History*, vol. 18, no. 2, August 2006, p. 266.

8.  Sources include Copley, J.H., 'The Women's Suffrage Movement in South Yorkshire', dissertation for Sheffield City College of Education (1965-8). Also Rover, C., *Women's Suffrage and Party Politics in Britain 1866-1914* (1967). Also Rendall, J., *The Origins of Modern Feminism 1780-1860* (1985), p.308.

9.  Milligan E.H., 'Knight, Anne (1786-1862)', *Oxford Dictionary of National Biography* (2004).

10.  *Sheffield Free Press* and *Barnsley Advertiser*, 1 March 1851. The association was known by a variety of names.

11.  Fowler, W.S., *A Study in Radicalism and Dissent: The life and Times of HJ Wilson* (1961), pp.30-1.

12.  Mathers, H., *Steel City Scholars* (2005), p.3.

13.  Liddington, J., *Rebel Girls: Their Fight for the Vote* (2006), pp.220-2.

14.  *Sheffield Daily Telegraph*, 28 February 1907. Copley states that Mrs Witworth, Mrs Higgins and Mrs Lockwood from Sheffield were imprisoned. But this issue of the *Telegraph* reports the release of Mrs Whitworth (*sic*) and Mrs Yates.

15.  This account draws on Liddington, J., *Rebel Girls: Their Fight for the Vote* (2006), Copley, J.H., 'The Women's Suffrage Movement in South Yorkshire', dissertation for Sheffield City College of Education (1965-8) and a talk by Alice Collins in Sheffield Libraries' 'Off the Shelf' Series in 2006.

16.  Liddington, J., *Rebel Girls: Their Fight for the Vote* (2006), p.307.

17.  Liddington, J., *Rebel Girls: Their Fight for the Vote* (2006), p. 27.

18.  Information from Eva Wilkinson.

19.  Pankhurst, S., *The Suffragette Movement* (1977), p.361.

20.  This account draws on Molly Murphy's autobiography, *Suffragette and Socialist* (1998), Liddington, J., *Rebel Girls: Their Fight for the Vote* (2006), and Copley, J.H., 'The Women's Suffrage Movement in South Yorkshire', dissertation for Sheffield City College of Education (1965-8).

21.  Murphy, M., *Suffragette and Socialist* (1998), p.24.

22.  Darlington, R., *The Political Trajectory of JT Murphy* (1998).

**Chapter 10: The Triumph of Labour 1893-1926**

1.  This chapter draws on Helen Mathers' University of Sheffield thesis 'Sheffield Municipal Politics 1893-1926: Parties, Personalities and the Rise of Labour' (1979), also her essay 'The City of Sheffield 1893-1926', in Binfield, C., et al, *History of the City of Sheffield vol. II*. This quote is from Sheffield Local Studies Library Local Pamphlets, vol. 175.

2.  This contrasts with G.C. Holland's picture of Sheffield in 1843 (chapter 4) but is borne out in Mathers' thesis (p.2) by Board of Trade occupational statistics for major cities in 1908.

3.  In 1921, Sheffield's boundaries were extended to include Handsworth and Woodhouse.

4.  Binfield, C., et al *History of the City of Sheffield vol. I: Politics*, p.79.

5.  Fletcher, D.E., 'Aspects of Liberalism in Sheffield 1849-86', PhD thesis, University of Sheffield, p.92.

6.  Mathers, H., 'Sheffield Municipal Politics 1893-1926', PhD thesis, University of Sheffield (1979), p.128.

7.  Brown, J., 'How one local Liberal Party failed to meet the challenge of Labour', *Journal of British Studies*, XIV (1975), p.4.

8.  Mathers, H., 'Sheffield Municipal Politics 1893-1926', PhD thesis, University of Sheffield (1979), p.163.

9.  Binfield, C., et al, *History of the City of Sheffield vol. I Politics*, p.79.

10.  *Sheffield Guardian*. 8 October 1909.

11.  Darlington, R., *The Political Trajectory of JT Murphy* (1998).

12.  Mathers, H., 'Sheffield Municipal Politics 1893-1926', PhD thesis, University of Sheffield (1979), pp.192-3.

13.  Mathers, H., 'Sheffield Municipal Politics 1893-1926', PhD thesis, University of Sheffield (1979), p.186.

14.  *Sheffield Independent*, 28 July 1920.

15.  Styring, R., *My Life Story* (1940).

16.  *Sheffield Daily Telegraph*. 28 October 1920.

17.  Hill, H., *Secret Ingredient: The Story of Fletchers' Seven Bakeries* (1978).

18.  Mathers, H., 'Sheffield Municipal Politics 1893-1926', PhD thesis, University of Sheffield (1979), pp.196-8.

19.  Fred Marshall at Edward Carpenter Memorial Service, 1947. See note 1 above.

20.  Fred Marshall at Edward Carpenter Memorial Service, 1947.

21.  Bean, J.P., *The Sheffield Gang Wars* (1981). The author informs me that they were not known as the 'gang wars' at the time.

22.  Bean, J.P., *The Sheffield Gang Wars* (1981), p.39.

23.  Bean, J.P., *The Sheffield Gang Wars* (1981), p.42. Recollections of an 80-year-old interviewed by J.P. Bean in 1978.

24.  Bean, J.P., *The Sheffield Gang Wars* (1981), pp.117-18.

25.  *Cloak without Dagger* (1955).

26.  Based on Mathers, H., 'Sheffield Municipal Politics 1893-1926', PhD thesis, University of Sheffield (1979), and on Moore, B, *General Strike in Sheffield: Documents of the Strike* (1981).

27.  Ibid. p.220.

28.  Andrew Thorpe's essay in Binfield, C. et al, *History of the City of Sheffield vol. I: Politics*, p.88.

29.  *Sheffield Star*, 14 March 1977.

30.  Keeble Hawson, H., *Sheffield: The Growth of a City 1893-1926* (1986), p.325.

31.  Thorpe, A., in Binfield, C. et al, *History of the City of Sheffield vol. I: Politics*, pp.117-18.

**Chapter 11: The Struggle for the Countryside**

1.  Jones, M., *Protecting the Beautiful Frame: A History of the Sheffield, Peak District and South Yorkshire Branch of the Council for the Protection of Rural England* (2000), p.4.

2.  Sissons, D., *The Best of the Sheffield Clarion Ramblers' Handbooks* (2002), p.5.

3.  This account draws on Jones, M., *Protecting the Beautiful Frame: A History of the Sheffield, Peak District and South Yorkshire Branch of the Council for the Protection of Rural England* (2000).

4.  A slide lecture of 1945, quoted in Jones, M., *Protecting the Beautiful Frame: A History of the Sheffield, Peak District and South Yorkshire Branch of the Council for the Protection of Rural England* (2000), p.9.

5.  Information from Dave Sissons, who was told this by Gerald Haythornthwaite in 1991.

6.  Jones, M., *Protecting the Beautiful Frame: A History of the Sheffield, Peak District and South Yorkshire Branch of the Council for the Protection of Rural England* (2000), p.37.

7.  Jones, M., *Protecting the Beautiful Frame: A History of the Sheffield, Peak District and South Yorkshire Branch of the Council for the Protection of Rural England* (2000), p.4.

8.  The council's plans were 'interim' and only became firm in the 1970s.

9.  Jones, M., *Protecting the Beautiful Frame: A History of the Sheffield, Peak District and South Yorkshire Branch of the Council for the Protection of Rural England* (2000), p.75.

10.  Sissons, D., *The Best of the Sheffield Clarion Ramblers' Handbooks* (2002), pp.11-20.

11.  Essay by Martin Wright in *Edward Carpenter and Late Victorian Radicalism* (1990), p.74.

12.  Initially called *Walks near Sheffield* (1904).

13.  *Across the Derbyshire Moors* (1904), p.115.

14.  Sissons, D., *The Best of the Sheffield Clarion Ramblers' Handbooks* (2002), pp.7-9. Hill, H., *Freedom to Roam* (1980), pp.30-1.

15.  Hill, H., *Freedom to Roam* (1980), pp.31-2.

16.  1921-2 Handbook quoted in Hill, H., *Freedom to Roam* (1980), p.34.

17.  The Love Feast was a revival of an ancient 'Feast of Charity' in which the rich paid for food for the poor – see Hill, H., *Freedom to Roam* (1980), p.31.

18.  Paulus, C., *Some Forgotten Facts in the History of Sheffield* (1907).

19.  *Clarion Ramblers Handbook 1941-2*, pp.70-1 and p.75.

20.  Hill, H., *Freedom to Roam* (1980), pp.43-8.

21.  Hill, H., *Freedom to Roam* (1980), pp.51-2.

22.  Hill, H., *Freedom to Roam* (1980), pp.62-73.

23.  Estimates range between 200 and 800.

24.  Stephenson, T., *Forbidden Land* (1989), p.157.

25.  Howard Hill's account. But see also Smith, R. (ed.), *Right to Roam: A Celebration of the Sheffield Campaign for Access to Moorland* (2005), p.71, which refers to two gamekeepers and a cyclist at Bar Dike.

26.  Hill's account. Sissons, D., *The Best of the Sheffield Clarion Ramblers' Handbooks* (2002), p.71 says 40 gamekeepers.

27.  Howard Hill was a trainee electrician aged 19 at the time. In the 1930s, he was first in the ILP and then the Communists. He was councillor for Brightside from 1938-46 and invalided out of the RAF in 1943. He was full-time secretary of the Sheffield Communist Party from then until 1975. He stood unsuccessfully for Parliament seven times. His book, *Freedom to Roam*, was published in 1980.

28.  Hill, H., *Freedom to Roam* (1980), p.82.

29.  See Sissons and Smith, R. (ed.), *Right to Roam: A Celebration of the Sheffield Campaign for Access to Moorland* (2005).

30.  The SWP itself was not involved.

31.  Smith, R. (ed.), *Right to Roam: A Celebration of the Sheffield Campaign for Access to Moorland* (2005), p.7.

32.  BBC News website, 27 April 2002.

**Chapter 12: Provocative Parsons: Alan Ecclestone and Ted Wickham**

1.  The opening words of Wickham, E.R., *Church and People in an Industrial City* (1969).

2.  Gorringe, T., *Alan Ecclestone: Priest as Revolutionary* (1994), p.102.

3.  Hastings, A., *A History of English Christianity 1920-2000* (2001), p.388.

4.  Hewitt, G. (ed.), *Strategist for the Spirit – Leslie Hunter, Bishop of Sheffield 1939-62* (1985).

5.  This draws on Gorringe, T., *Alan Ecclestone: Priest as Revolutionary* (1994).

6.  Gorringe, T., *Alan Ecclestone: Priest as Revolutionary* (1994), p.28.

7.  Information from Michael Jarratt.

8.  Information from Michael Jarratt.

9.  Information from Michael Jarratt.

10.  *Sheffield Star*, 13 November 1950.

11.  Gorringe, T., *Alan Ecclestone: Priest as Revolutionary* (1994), p.93.

12.  Information from Noreen Smith.

13.  Recollection by Alan Billings.

14.  Shevchenko, A.N., *Breaking with Moscow* (1985), p.225.

15.  Gorringe, T., *Alan Ecclestone: Priest as Revolutionary* (1994), p.xiv.

16.  Hastings, A., *A History of English Christianity. 1920-2000* (2001), p.432.

17.  Based on Wickham papers at Sheffield City Archives, with Jenny Wickham's permission. Also Bagshaw, P. 'The Church beyond the Church: Sheffield Industrial Mission 1944-94' (*IMSY*) (1944). Bloy, P., *The Call to Mission Answered: Ted Wickham and the Sheffield Industrial Mission 1944-59* (2000).

18.  Letter of 2 April 1949 from Hunter to Wickham, Wickham papers

19.  Preece, J.D., 'LS Hunter 1890-1983', MPhil thesis, University of Sheffield (1986), p.164.

20.  Bloy, P., *The Call to Mission Answered: Ted Wickham and the Sheffield Industrial Mission 1944-59* (2000), p.22.

21.  Letter of 1 March 1957 from Tillich to Wickham, Wickham papers.

22.  Lutterworth (1957).

23.  Morris, J., 'Church and People 35 years on: A Historical Critique', *Theology*, XCIV, March/April 1991, p.92. Gill, R., 'The Myth of the Empty Church' (*SPCK*) (1993), pp.30-2.

24.  See Bagshaw, P. 'The Church beyond the Church: Sheffield Industrial Mission 1944-94' (*IMSY*) (1944). Also information from Michael Atkinson.

25.  *Guardian*, 15 March 1966.

26.  Walton, W., *A History of the Diocese of Sheffield 1914-79* (1981), p.133.

27. Hewitt, G. (ed.), *Strategist for the Spirit – Leslie Hunter, Bishop of Sheffield 1939-62* (1985), p.138.
28. Letter of 4 December 1979 from Wickham to Lurkins. Lurkins, E.H., 'The origins, content and ideology of Industrial Mission', PhD thesis, LSE.
29. *Theology*. vol. LXIX, no. 558, December 1966, p.539.
30. Price, D., 'Ted Wickham: A Reappraisal', *Crucible*, April-June 2004, pp.9-13.
31. *Mission-Shaped Church* (2004) states on p.xi: 'the existing parochial system alone is no longer able fully to deliver its underlying mission purpose ... A mixed economy of parish churches and network churches will be necessary.'

**Chapter 13: Blunkett and the Socialist Republic of South Yorkshire**

1. Cornwell, J.C., *The Tomb of the Unknown Alderman* (2006), p.47.
2. Winstone, R. (abr.), *The Benn Diaries* (1996), p.580.
3. Blunkett, D., *The Blunkett Tapes* (2006), p.415.
4. Blunkett, D., *On a Clear Day* (1995).
5. Blunkett, D., *On a Clear Day* (1995), p.19.
6. Blunkett, D., *On a Clear Day* (1995), p.22.
7. Blunkett, D., *On a Clear Day* (1995), pp.49-50.
8. Blunkett, D., *On a Clear Day* (1995), p. 62.
9. Blunkett, D., *On a Clear Day* (1995), p.193.
10. Blunkett, D., *On a Clear Day* (1995). Seyd, P., essay in Binfield, C., et al, *History of the City of Sheffield*, vol. I (1993), pp.151-85.
11. Hattersley, R., *A Yorkshire Boyhood* (1978), pp.183-4.
12. Seyd, P., essay in Binfield, C., et al, *History of the City of Sheffield*, vol. I (1993), p.157.
13. Seyd, P., essay in Binfield, C., et al, *History of the City of Sheffield*, vol. I (1993), p.158.
14. Seyd, P., essay in Binfield, C., et al, *History of the City of Sheffield*, vol. I (1993), p.158.
15. John Cornwell's recollections helped here.
16. Blunkett, D., *On a Clear Day* (1995), pp.146-50. Recollections of Alan Billings.

17. Blunkett, D., and Jackson, K., *Democracy in Crisis: The Town Halls Respond* (1987), pp.75-9.
18. Blunkett, D., and Jackson, K., *Democracy in Crisis: The Town Halls Respond* (1987), p.73.
19. Blunkett, D., and Green, G., *Building from the Bottom: the Sheffield Experience*, Fabian Tract 491 (1983).
20. Blunkett, D., *On a Clear Day* (1995), p.155.
21. Seyd, P., essay in Binfield, C., et al, *History of the City of Sheffield*, vol. I (1993), p.158.
22. Cornwell, J.C., *The Tomb of the Unknown Alderman* (2006), p.25.
23. Comment by Alan Billings.
24. Within the AMA, Blunkett was chair of the social services committee, Clive Betts was chair of the housing committee and Howard Knight was chair of the public services committee. Moreover, from South Yorkshire County Council, Roy Thwaites was AMA vice-chair and John Cornwell chaired the arts and recreation committee.
25. Following a resolution from Netherthorpe Labour Party.
26. Blunkett, D., and Crick, B., 'The Labour Party: Aims and Values. An Unofficial Statement', Spokesman Pamphlet no. 87, February 1988.
27. Comment by Alan Billings.
28. Blunkett, D., and Green, G., *Building from the Bottom: the Sheffield Experience*, Fabian Tract 491 (1983), pp.11-12 and p.26.
29. Blunkett, D., *On a Clear Day* (1995), p.170.
30. Blunkett, D., and Jackson, K., *Democracy in Crisis: The Town Halls Respond* (1987), p.158.
31. He was chair both of the Labour Party National Executive's Local Government Committee and the Local Government Campaign Unit.
32. Seyd, P., essay in Binfield, C., et al, *History of the City of Sheffield*, vol. I (1993), p.166.
33. Information from Alan Billings.
34. Information from Alan Billings.
35. *Sheffield Star*, 8 May 1985.
36. *Sheffield Star*, 8 May 1985.
37. Information from Alan Billings.

38. McSmith, A., *Faces of Labour* (1996), p.170.
39. Pollard, S., *David Blunkett*, p.157.
40. McSmith, A., *Faces of Labour* (1996), pp.171-2.
41. Seyd, P., essay in Binfield, C., et al, *History of the City of Sheffield*, vol. I (1993), pp.160-1.
42. McSmith, A., *Faces of Labour* (1996), p.155.
43. Blunkett, D., *On a Clear Day* (1995), p.173.
44. Cornwell, J.C., *The Tomb of the Unknown Alderman* (2006), p.69.
45. *Sheffield Star*, 29 April 1983.
46. Cornwell, J.C., *The Tomb of the Unknown Alderman* (2006), p.69.
47. Blunkett, D., and Jackson, K., *Democracy in Crisis: The Town Halls Respond* (1987), pp.189-90.
48. Information provided to author.
49. Seyd, P., essay in Binfield, C., et al, *History of the City of Sheffield*, vol. I (1993), pp.170-1.
50. Blunkett, D., and Crick, B., 'The Labour Party: Aims and Values. An Unofficial Statement', Spokesman Pamphlet no. 87, February 1988, p.14.
51. *Guardian*, 3 February 2004. Baroness Kennedy wrote a book, *Just Law*, attacking what she saw as the erosion of civil liberties by New Labour.
52. McSmith, A., *Faces of Labour* (1996), pp.156-8, pp.182-3.
53. In January 2008, he produced a pamphlet entitled 'The Inclusive Society? Social Mobility in 21st Century Britain' published by Progress.

**Chapter 14: Epilogue**

1. 'Strategies for Preaching God's Judgement', www.francisans.org.uk, May 2004.
2. Darlington, R., *The Political Trajectory of JT Murphy*, p.259.
3. Blunkett, D., and Crick, B., 'The Labour Party: Aims and Values. An Unofficial Statement', Spokesman Pamphlet no. 87, February 1988.
4. Professor Abercrombie, Sheffield: A Civic Survey (1924), p.6

# Select Bibliography

*Books*

Armytage, W.H.M., *AJ Mundella, the Liberal Background to the Labour Movement* (1951)

Armytage, W.H.M., *Heavens Below: Utopian Experiments in England 1560-1960* (1961)

Bagshaw, Paul, *The Church Beyond the Church: Sheffield Industrial Mission 1944-94* (1994)

Bean, J.P., *The Sheffield Gang Wars* (1981)

Belton, F.G. (ed.), *Memoirs of George Campbell Ommanney, Vicar of St Matthew's, Carver Street 1882-1936* (1936)

Binfield, C., Childs, R., Harper, R., Hey, D., Martin, D., Tweedale, G., *History of the City of Sheffield 1843-1993,* 3 volumes (1993)

Black, E.G., *The Association: Britain's Extra Parliamentary Political Organisation 1769-1793* (1963)

Blunkett, D., *On a Clear Day* (1995)

Briggs, Asa, *Victorian People* (1955)

Carpenter, Edward, *My Days and Dreams* (1916)

Cornwell, J., *The Tomb of the Unknown Alderman* (2006)

Darlington, Ralph, *The Political Trajectory of JT Murphy* (1998)

Fowler, W.S., *A Study in Radicalism and Dissent: Life and Times of Henry Joseph Wilson 1833-1914* (1961)

Gatty, A., *Sheffield Past and Present* (1873)

Gorringe, T.M., *Alan Ecclestone: Priest and Revolutionary* (1994)

Hawson, H. Keeble, *Sheffield: The Growth of a City 1893-1926* (1968)

Hey, David, *A History of Sheffield* (1998)

Hey, David, *Historic Hallamshire* (2002)

Hill, Howard, *Freedom to Roam* (1980)

Holland, G.C., *The Vital Statistics of Sheffield* (1843)

Holland, J., and Everett, J., *Memoirs of James Montgomery*, 7 volumes (1854–6)

Hunter, J., Gatty, J., (ed.), *History of Hallamshire* (1875 edn)

Jones, Melvyn, *The Making of Sheffield* (2004)

Jones, Melvyn, *Protecting the Beautiful Frame* (2001)

Jones, Melvyn, (ed.), *Aspects of Sheffield: Discovering Local History*, Vols 1 and 2 (1997, 1999)

Leader, Robert, (ed.), *Reminiscences of Old Sheffield* (1876)

Leader, Robert, *Sheffield in the 18th Century*, 2nd edn, (1905)

Leader, R., and Bell, A.B., (eds), *Peeps into the Past: The Diaries of Thomas Asline Ward* (1909)

Liddington, Jill, *Rebel Girls: Their Fight to Vote* (2006)

LoPatin, N.D., *Political Unions, Popular Politics and the Great Reform Act of 1832* (1999)

Manning, J.E., *History of Upper Chapel* (1900)

Mathers, Helen, *Steel City Scholars: The Centenary History of the University of Sheffield* (2005)

Pollard, Sidney, *A History of Labour in Sheffield* (1959)

Pollard, Sidney and Holmes, Colin, (ed.), *Essays in the Economic and Social History of South Yorkshire* (1976)

Pybus, Sylvia, *Damned Bad Place, Sheffield* (1994)

Read, Donald, *Press and People 1790-1850 Opinion in three English cities* (1961)

Roberts, Samuel, *Autobiography* (1849)

Sissons, D., (ed.), *The Best of the Clarion Ramblers Handbooks* (2002)

Smith, Dennis, *Conflict and Compromise: Class Formation in British Society 1830-1914 A Comparative Study of Birmingham and Sheffield* (1982)

Smith, E.A., *Whig Principles and Party Politics: Earl Fitzwilliam and the Whig Party 1748-1833* (1975)

Stainton, J.H., *The Making of Sheffield 1865-1914* (1924)

Tsuzuki, Chushichi, *Edward Carpenter 1844-1929* (1980)
Walton, Mary, *Sheffield: Its story and its achievements* (1948)
Wickham. E., *Church and People in an Industrial City* (1957)
Williams, Gwyn, *Artisans and Sans-Culottes: Popular Movements in France and Britain during the French Revolution'* (1968)

*Articles and Pamphlets*

Albaya, Winifred, 'Through the Green Door: An Account of the Sheffield Educational Settlement 1918-55',
     University of Sheffield (1977)
Armytage, W.H.G., 'The Editorial Experience of Joseph Gales 1786-94', *North Carolina Historical Review* 28 (1951).
Barnes, Janet, 'Ruskin in Sheffield', Sheffield Arts Department (1985)
Baxter, J., 'Murder in Norfolk Street – The Story of Sheffield's Peterloo', *Holberry Society Bulletin*, 5, Autumn (1980)
Blunkett, David, and Green, Geoff 'Building from the Bottom: The Sheffield Experience', *Fabian Tract 491* (1983)
Gales, Joseph and Winifred, 'Recollections', *North Carolina Historical Archive*
Hewison, Robert, 'Art and Society: Ruskin in Sheffield 1876' Guild of St George (1979)
Hoy, Grace, 'Inwardly Limitless ... Education by Magic at the Sheffield Educational Settlement under Arnold Free
     man', (1989?)
Martin, David, 'Arnold Freeman and the Sheffield Educational Settlement', *Transactions of the Hunter Archaeological Society*,
     20, pp 71-9
Morris, Keith, and Hearne, Ray, *Ebenezer Elliott: Corn Law Rhymer and Poet of the Poor* (2002)
Pollard, Sidney 'The Ethics of the Sheffield Outrages', *Transactions of the Hunter Archaeological Society (THAS)*, Vol.7,
     pp. 118-139
Price, David, 'Ted Wickham: A Reappraisal', *Crucible*, April- June 2004, pp. 5-14
Roach, J., 'The Sheffield Community and Public Work 1790-1914', *Yorkshire Archaeological Journal*, Vol 77, 205,
     pp. 225-40
Roach, J., and Pitchfork, J.R., 'Croft House Settlement 1902-2002: A Centenary History'
Sissons, Dave, and Smith, Roly, 'Right to Roam: A Celebration of the Sheffield Campaign for Access to Moorland',
     *SCAM* (2005)
Stevenson, John, 'Artisans and Democrats: Sheffield in the French Revolution 1789-97', *Historical Association* (1989)

*Theses and Dissertations*

Baxter, John, 'The Origins of the Social War in South Yorkshire ... 1750-1855', PhD Thesis, University of Sheffield (1976)
Beutner, H.F., 'With Fraternal Feelings Fired. The Life and Works of James Montgomery', PhD Thesis, North Western
     University (1967)
Copley, John H., 'The Women's Suffrage Movement in South Yorkshire', Dissertation for Sheffield City College of
     Education (1965-8)
Crawshaw, H.N., 'Movements for Political and Social Reform 1792-1832', MA thesis, University of Sheffield (1954)
Flavell, Neville, 'The Economic Development of Sheffield and the Growth of the Town *c*.1740-1820', PhD Thesis,
     University of Sheffield (1996)
Fletcher, D.E., 'Aspects of Liberalism in Sheffield 1849-86', PhD Thesis, University of Sheffield (1972)
Jennett, G.D., 'TA Ward', MA Thesis, University of Sheffield, (1954)
Macdonald, Julie, 'The Freedom of Election: The Company of Cutlers and the Growth of Radicalism in Sheffield
     1784-1792', PhD Thesis, University of Sheffield (2005)
Mathers, Helen, 'Sheffield Municipal Politics 1893-1926. Parties, Personalities and the Rise of Labour', PhD thesis,
     University of Sheffield (1979).
Preece, J.D., 'LS Hunter 1890-1983', M Phil thesis, University of Sheffield (1986)
Roberts, John, 'The Sheffield Educational Settlement 1918-55', Dissertation, Institute of Education, University of
     Sheffield (1961)
Salt, John, 'Isaac Ironside and Education in the Sheffield Region in the first Half of the 19th Century', MA Thesis,
     University of Sheffield (1960)
Smith, H. Kirk, 'Some aspects of the career of William Thomson as Archbishop of York 1863-1890', Thesis,
     University of Sheffield (1953)
Wilks, Sarah, 'An Independent in Politics: JA Roebuck 1802-79', D Phil thesis, Oxford University (1979)

# Index

Numbers in **bold** refer to illustration page numbers.